Rethinking Human Rights for the New Millennium

RETHINKING HUMAN RIGHTS FOR THE NEW MILLENNIUM

A. Belden Fields

First published 2003 by
PALGRAVE MACMILLAN™
175 Fifth Avenue, New York, N.Y. 10010 and
Houndmills, Basingstoke, Hampshire, England RG21 6XS
Companies and representatives throughout the world

PALGRAVE MACMILLAN is the global academic imprint of the Palgrave Macmillan division of St. Martin's Press, LLC and of Palgrave Macmillan Ltd. Macmillan® is a registered trademark in the United States, United Kingdom and other countries. Palgrave is a registered trademark in the European Union and other countries.

1–4039–6061–5 hardback
1–4039–6062–3 paperback

Library of Congress Cataloging-in-Publication Data Available from the Library of Congress

A catalogue record for this book is available from the British Library.

Design by Newgen Imaging Systems (P) Ltd., Chennai, India.

First Palgrave Macmillan edition: January, 2003
10 9 8 7 6 5 4 3 2 1

Printed in the United States of America.

To the memories of Daniel Singer and Paul Wellstone, who never lost the ability to imagine and work toward a more humane rights-respecting new millennium; to the Staley workers in Decatur, Illinois, who understood their human rights as workers and fought valiantly for them; and to the people in my community who have nurtured me in our struggles together for human rights whether in Central America, Decatur, or our own community.

CONTENTS

ACKNOWLEDGMENTS

I would like to acknowledge the following people for reading and critiquing this manuscript: George Kent, Wolf-Dieter Narr, Neil Stammers, Walter Feinberg, and Joy James. George Kent is the most thorough and critically helpful reader that any author could hope for. Wolf-Dieter Narr was responsible for my becoming interested in human rights as an object of study. I would also like to acknowledge the excellent work of Phyllis Koerner who formatted the manuscript before it was submitted to Palgrave Macmillan, of Laura Lawrie who copyedited it, of Sonia Wilson who, as my production editor at Palgrave Macmillan, shepherded the manuscript through the process, and of Martin L. White who did the index. On a more personal note, I want to thank my wife, Jane Ellen Mohraz, for her love and support while I was working on this and other projects throughout our many years together.

INTRODUCTION

As was the case during the Cold War in the final century of the last millennium, the words "human rights" are still constantly presented to us by politicians, the media, and activists claiming to work for the advancement of these rights. Human rights rank along with democracy and free markets in the normative language of our age. Human rights are often used as the ultimate normative reference point. Several years ago, I attended a conference on nationalism and ethics. There was a great deal of difficulty in coming to grips with the negative aspect of nationalism, but a wish to capture the positive, self-determining aspects of it. One participant offered that nationalism was acceptable so long as human rights were respected. Everyone at the conference seemed to agree that a solution to the conundrum had been found, as though the meaning of human rights was crystal clear while the meaning of nationalism was murky.

Human rights can all too easily be used as the ultimate resolution of ambiguous or complex problems, so long, that is, as human rights themselves are taken as simple and self-evident. But are human rights so simple and self-evident? Is there just one correct interpretation of what we mean by "human rights"? If there are differing interpretations, is there one that's right while the others are in error, just as two plus two makes four, not five? And what do we make of the fact that the concept of human rights is a relatively new one in human history? Simone Weil tells us: "The Greeks had no conceptions of rights. They had no words to express it. They were content with the name of justice."[1]

Martha Nussbaum, a contemporary scholar more invested in the classical Greek tradition than Weil, tells us that while the Greek Stoics are an important part of the tradition leading up to the concept of human rights, "neither Greek nor Roman society contained any developed notion of basic human rights." Their commitment to human equality, for example, did not lead them to a critical view of slavery.[2]

Why did the Greeks, who reflected so deeply on problems of politics, not have a concept of human rights? Why did the Romans have a concept of rights attached to Roman citizenship but not of people just because they were human beings? And what about this conception of justice to which Weil refers? Is it possible that part of what the Greeks meant by justice is what we mean by rights, by human rights?

These are very perplexing questions, especially because human rights are presented as universals that inhere in the very nature of human beings. Are we "naturally" so different from the Greeks, perhaps as different from them as the Greeks thought they were from the barbarians of Europe or the "nonrational" people of Asia,[3] that we inherently have this quality of rights-bearing creatures while the Greeks did not? Is it the case that it is not just that the Greeks did not recognize what was there, but that it was not there to be recognized?

If the people of Greece and Rome did not talk about human rights, when did this kind of "rights talk" begin? Where did it begin? Who began it? Why, or what was it supposed to do for the people who used it? And how did it and does it mesh with other normative concepts used by people engaged in rights talk, as well as by people who did not engage in rights talk? Here we have to be sensitive to both time and space. For example, might we find analogues to human rights in other concepts used by people before the beginning of rights talk (such as "justice"), or does the concept of human rights represent something that the earlier people did not have in their heads at all? In parallel fashion, might we find at any given time human rights talk used in one culture but not in another, but there might be analogous concepts? What might answers to these questions tell us about the universality or the relativity of the concept of human rights?

Alas, these are complex questions and issues. But they are not abstract. There is a relationship between conceptualization and practice. One of the themes of this book is that human rights practices in the twentieth century left much to be desired. And this deficiency crossed the political and ideological configurations of the Cold War. Indeed, it will be argued, the rhetoric of human rights was all too often used as an attempt to legitimize human rights violating practices on both sides of the "Iron Curtain" as well as in what we used to call the Third World. The attempt of this book is to rethink the concept of human rights in light of these practical distortions, to see if we cannot come up with a conception of human rights that is both intellectually sound and that will serve as a legitimizing force to end human domination and the suffering it causes.

We will proceed in the first portion of the book by examining the interplay between concrete material struggles, the words of theorists, and the words of actors on the stage of history as represented in the great human rights documents at the end of the eighteenth century. Chapter 1 begins with the demands of the seventeenth-century Digger Gerrard Winstanley, arguing for everyone's right to the necessities of life, and then examines the work of four great theorists in the Western tradition—Hobbes, Locke, Rousseau, and Kant—insofar as their work contributes to our modern thinking about human rights. We then move to a consideration of the seminal statements on human rights drafted by revolutionary actors at the end of the eighteenth century, the U.S. Declaration of Independence, the U.S. Constitution and its first ten amendments (the Bill of Rights), and the French Declaration of the Rights of Man and Citizen. These theoretical and declaratory documents did not meet with universal acceptance. The chapter concludes with an examination of the eighteenth- and nineteenth-century rejections of the idea of human rights by Burke, Bentham, and Marx as well as the implicit undermining of a conception of human rights based on reason in the thought of Hume.

In Chapter 2, we move to the twentieth century. Here we discuss phenomena of that century that were distinctively unfriendly to the idea and practice of human rights: the rise of totalitarianism, genocide on an unprecedented scale, and world war. We then examine the post-World War II response to this in the form of international documents that were agreed to by representatives of nation-states. We examine differences that emerged over the content of these documents in the mid-1960s. We then critically examine a variety of the grounds for accepting the concept of human rights offered in the second half of the twentieth century. These include the grounds of faith and belief, theoretical but nonrationalist grounds, and rationalist grounds.

In Chapter 3, I offer a different way of thinking about human rights from those discussed in Chapter Two, one that rejects making a single value or concept the foundation of human rights. This is what I call a "holistic" way. The argument takes the form of eleven propositions and elaboration on them. The key concepts, in the order in which they are developed, are human potentialities, co- and self-determination, material and cultural contextualization, domination, struggle, and social recognition. The chapter ends with a table and brief discussion of the variety of possible human rights violators and victims based on the preceding conceptual propositions and arguments.[4]

Chapter 4 explores more deeply the issue of the holders and violators of human rights that was raised schematically at the end of the last chapter. It makes the argument that it is an error to restrict rights-holders to individuals as is often argued, especially in the West. It looks at the kinds of groups or collectivities that can make valid human rights claims. It is also argued that entities other than the state can violate human rights. The point is made that one should look at the effects and victims first, a "bottom-up" approach, and then make the determination as to who or what is the violator.

Chapter 5 focuses on the concept of social recognition as it applies to the areas of economics and labor, which, it is argued, ultimately cannot be separated from the political. The first kind of recognition is distributional in nature, entailing the recognition of the right to a standard of living commensurate with human dignity. The second kind of recognition is participatory in nature. This kind of recognition entails workers or other economically excluded or exploited people with economic and social rights claims having a say in how their rights are implemented. Here our concept of co- and self-determination becomes important, but it becomes even more important in the final form that is not just participatory but entails actual worker ownership and control over the process within which they are working. I argue that this form of social recognition is the most consistent with the declaration of the International Labor Organization that "labor is not a commodity." I offer some thoughts on the institutional forms that this kind of recognition might take.

Chapter 6 looks at the modern state and human rights. Even if there can be and are nonstate violators of human rights, the fact is that the major human rights violations during the last century have either been because of the use of state power or a refusal by states to use their power to prevent human rights abuses within or outside their borders. I argue that the modern state occupies a contradictory position vis-à-vis human rights. Human rights and the modern state were born together, especially in the creation of the United States and the French Republics. States have subscribed to human rights through U.N. declarations and international covenants, and inscribed them in their own constitutions. Yet, states are major violators, and this includes even the liberal constitutional states. This chapter looks at some of the processes in which modern states engage—aggregation and differentiation of people, constitutionalization, and, above all, violence and coercion—to get a clearer understanding of this dual and contradictory nature of the modern state.

Chapter 7 offers a more empirical examination of the violent and coercive practices of the state. I raise the question of whether Michel Foucault was right when he argued that the modern state has substituted observation and normalization for violence over the bodies of its citizens. Looking principally but not exclusively at concrete practices in the United States, which proclaims itself to be the world leader in the struggle for human rights and assumes the responsibility for systematically judging the performance of other states, we find that there are severe human rights abuses directed disproportionately against the bodies of specific categories of people, thus entailing violations of both individual and collective or group human rights. In the United States, the trope of "war"—war against communism, crime, drugs, and most recently, terrorism—has been used by political elites to justify such rights violations.

The Conclusion sums up the arguments of the preceding chapters, reiterating particularly the importance of three things: recognizing the equal status of liberty, equality, and solidarity as essential normative underpinnings of the indivisible span of human rights; self-critical dialogue and action across cultural boundaries concerning how to implement these values in practice; and commitment to political/ economic democracy as a guide to the development of institutional forms that are consistent with the holistic conception of human rights. All three will be required if the new millennium, which has not gotten off with an auspicious beginning, is to offer us a substantially more human rights-respecting existence than the millennium we have just left behind.

The Conclusion is followed by two appendixes. The first one tells the story of how workers in Decatur, Illinois, struggled for their rights against a transnational corporation that imposed drastic changes in the conditions under which they worked. The workers lost, the community divided, and some of the workers' lives were devastated in this demonstration of power by the transnational.

The second appendix is an article that I wrote for the *Publici*, an independent monthly newspaper produced by the Independent Media Center in Urbana-Champaign, Illinois examining the implications of September 11, 2001 from my holistic human rights perspective. It was written approximately a week and a half after the terrorist attack, well before the U.S. government retaliated in Afghanistan.

CHAPTER 1

THE BIRTH OF THE HUMAN RIGHTS
IDEA AND ITS DETRACTORS

INTRODUCTION

It would defeat the purpose of both this chapter and the entire book to à priori define human rights here. But there is something about the subject that pulls most of us to it, even if we can't or don't want to analyze it. Of all political concepts, it seems to be the one that most touches our concern for human suffering and the domination of some people by others with superior power. As Micheline Ishay shows us in her historical narrative of human rights texts, such concern goes back at least as far as the Old Testament (especially Exodus 22: 20–27: "Thou shalt neither vex a stranger, nor oppress him; for you were strangers in the land of Egypt" and Leviticus 19:13–19: "neither shalt thou stand aside when mischief befalls they neighbor") and Mahayana Buddhism's description of the compassionate Bodhisattva ("I take upon myself the burden of all suffering... all beings I must set free").[1]

Lacqueur and Rubin, by contrast, begin their historical narrative with a later secular document (although it demanded rights for the English church), the Magna Charta of 1215.[2] Several things are interesting about this document. The first is its location. It is a Western document; more specifically, an English document. Second, it was written long before the modern nation-state system was instituted in Europe and at a time when the British state was not yet developed. Third, it was written during a time of struggle between three sets of powers: the king, the church, and the barons (the aristocracy). Fourth, with few exceptions, it did not concern individuals *qua* human beings. It attempted to decenter power. The king lost certain powers because he was king, and others gained power or degrees of freedom because they were members of specific groupings with particular interests: the feudal aristocracy, the church, or freemen. Thus, while attempting to throw off what was regarded as an unjustifiable domination by the king that caused them great suffering, the clear universalistic prescriptions of the earlier religious texts are not there. This is not to say that people could not or did not draw general lessons about the undesirability of concentrated or absolute power. It is an extremely important document for just that reason; absolute power is inconsistent with human rights. But the rights that this document claims are specific to either the church or people of specific social standings. And this continued through the medieval period in Europe. To the extent that rights were at all an issue, they were rights that almost always attached to roles and power positions within institutional frameworks. This did not prevent those who claimed and exercised such rights from attempting to justify them as "natural," and even attributing a kind of contractual "freedom" to the dominated, as Carole Pateman has so clearly analyzed in the cases of slavery, serfdom, and marriage.[3]

HUMAN RIGHTS STRUGGLES AND THE EUROPEAN CONTRACT THEORISTS

The medieval mold was broken in the seventeenth century, when the idea that human beings have rights claims *qua* human beings was explicitly articulated. England of the 1640s is best known to us for its wars between adherents of different religions and political constitutions. But it also was characterized by widespread misery because of high food prices, rents, taxes, unemployment, and landlessness. With the demise of feudalism, the property rights of the landed had become absolutized. The admonitions of Aristotle that property holders had an obligation to share their property with those in need, and of St. Thomas Aquinas that those who took from others because of a need to survive (provided that the others had enough to survive after the taking) were not guilty of the sin of theft, were as much a matter of past history as was the medieval lord's obligations to his serfs. The "masterless men" of the seventeenth century found themselves in a situation in which others were no longer recognizing them or their needs in a very nasty world.[4] Rights claims were at once an expression of suffering and agony and the reminder of the obligations that we have to each other to extend a certain kind of social recognition. If feudalism contained extreme inequalities, it also set limits and insisted on recognition of a differential set of rights claims that even the lowly serf could demand of his lord. With the breaking up of the feudal pattern of recognition, human beings increasingly were conceived of as individual monads. They were free, in the sense of being released from the bonds of obligation and recognition with a master. But since the former master continued to hold on to the property and wealth that had been built on the labor of the serfs, those freed serfs were as vulnerable as the slaves that were freed after the American Civil War.

Gerrard Winstanley, a spokesperson for the Diggers, who squatted on and planted the land of wealthy owners in the 1640s in order to merely survive, countered the absolutist property rights claims of the owners by invoking "the righteous Law of our Creation."[5] Winstanley wrote:

> Seeing and finding our selves poor, wanting Food to feed upon, while we labour the Earth, to cast in Seed and to wait tell the first Crop comes up; and wanting Ploughs, Carts, Corn and such materials to plant the Commons withal, we are willing to declare our condition to you, and to all, that have the Treasury of the Earth, locked up in your Bags, Chests, and Barns, and will offer up nothing to this publike Treasury; but will rather see your fellow-Creatures starve for want of Bread, that have an equal right to it with yourselves, by the Law of Creation.[6]

In the minds of Winstanley and the other Diggers, the "righteous law of our creation" gave the poor of England a *right* to use land because they needed it in order to survive and, notwithstanding rights claims by the aristocracy on the basis of natural superiority or free contractualism, the ownership was rooted in an act of violence that dominated and dispossessed other people, that is, the Norman Invasion. Three things are important in this challenge. First, rights are being claimed by people purely on the ground that that they are human beings. Second, a religious authority is invoked; we are God's creations, and thus the refusal to recognize our survival needs is an offense to God. Third, the claim is made within the context of a concrete, material struggle. The Diggers acted and claimed rights at the same time. Indeed, while secular arguments have challenged religious ones, the philosophical discourses over rights have never been dissociated from concrete materialities and struggles over them, even if philosophers have not been fully conscious of that fact.

Hobbes: The Beginning of the Western Philosophical Discourse on Human Rights

Although Winstanley was an articulate advocate of the Digger position, he was not a philosopher. The first philosopher to argue that human beings have rights claims *qua* human beings is Winstanley's contemporary, Thomas Hobbes. Hobbes, too, ties his conception of rights to physical survival, but Hobbes gives us a purely secular rational foundation for his conception. He is more interested in the nature of human beings themselves than in the claim that they are God's creations, although he is not above strategic use of biblical sources when they support his rationalist arguments.

Hobbes is an ironic source for the idea of human rights. While the Magna Charta was committed to the dispersion of power away from the king into what we would call today elements within civil society, and while in modern times we associate human rights with democracy, or at the very least with strictly circumscribed political power, Hobbes is committed to centralizing and absolutizing political power. While he would accept political power being centralized in a legislature, his preference is centralization in the hands of a king where, he felt, factionalism would not be the issue it is in a plural body. The crucial point for Hobbes is that the power be absolute.

How can it be that a philosopher who (1) felt that power had become too diffuse since the Magna Charta, (2) opposed the English Petition of Right, and (3) viewed with hostility the advocacy of democracy by elements within the antiroyalist army is the first to come up with a philosophical justification of the concept of universal rights that people have *qua* human beings?

The mid-seventeenth century was a period of intense political, economic, religious, and intellectual struggle. A variety of serious institutional and group interests were at stake. The monarchy had to contend with the parliamentary forces. The more conservative parliamentary forces under Cromwell had to contend with political and economic/class challenges among the antiroyalists.[7] The bourgeoisie was challenging the power of the monarchy and trying to protect itself from political and economic radicalism. Adherents of the Church of England were fighting with Catholics for control over the monarchy, and both were trying to stamp out the religious radicalism of the Quakers and other sects. There was enormous development in the mathematical and scientific world (Galileo, Kepler, Harvey, and Descartes) that influenced Hobbes in rejecting scholastic thought in favor of a more "realist" scientific theory of politics. Hobbes's rejection of Aristotelian/scholastic thought in favor of scientific realism threatened organized religion as well as both monarchist and parliamentary political elites. In a synthetic response to this dual threat, a committee of the House of Commons, suspecting atheism as the root of his dangerous thoughts, investigated Hobbes. While Galileo was forced to recant by papal authority, Hobbes was forced into silence on political matters by the identity of interest between institutionalized religion and institutionalized politics, the latter including both the royalist defenders of the divine right of kings and the advocates of parliamentary government.

In subsequent epochs, those who theorized and advocated human rights would do so against authority, particularly that of the state. But for Hobbes, the danger from individuals came not from some central, powerful authority but precisely from the lack thereof. He felt that human beings were prey to all of these conflicts between institutions and belief systems. It was obvious to him that these institutions were not working. The ultimate proof of that was the English civil wars. In his most famous phrase, in which he tries to describe what he calls the theoretical state of nature (but surely he was referring to the concrete environment in which he was living), life is "nasty, brutish, and short."[8]

Hobbes thus becomes the first peace theorist in Western philosophy and social science. His primary objective is to get out of this hellish state and into one in which the security of individuals could be guaranteed, or at least maximized. From the very nature of the individual as a sensate being who experiences pain and pleasure, Hobbes draws the lesson that the worst pain of the individual is the threat of the termination of that sensate experience we call life, and the greatest pleasure is its preservation. Moreover, most other human values such as culture and industry are dependent on that bottom-line value, security.

From this, Hobbes concludes that the one fundamental human right that everyone everywhere has, simply by virtue of his or her inherent nature, is the right to life. Hobbes thus becomes the advocate par excellence of the right of every human being to peace and security. But there is a contradiction. If we have this right, it also is true that there are impulses within us (diffidence, competitive urge, and the desire for glory) that lead us to be aggressive. Rejecting the Aristotelian concept of the naturally social and political man, Hobbes sees a human being quite prepared to aggress against the other. The problem is aggravated by the similarity of our desires and the scarcity of those things we designate as "goods" that are available to us in our environment. Thus, both the inside of our being (our ontological essence) and the outside of our existence leads us to aggression.

The only way out of this impasse is to create and maintain an enormously powerful center of political sovereignty, something that Hobbes, despite his dislike of metaphors, refers to as the Leviathan. Each of us as individuals, who are naturally antagonistic, must come together and agree to obey this sovereign center. Only if we subject ourselves to such a center can we be secure. A conditional clause is written into this contract that we make with each other, whereby if that sovereign power does not in fact protect us, our obligation to it ceases and we are back in the state of nature.

This is a crucial move. Hobbes has turned the traditional way of thinking about politics and citizenship on its head. Rather than accepting the traditional view that obligation takes precedence over rights (e.g., the Roman had rights because he was a dutiful Roman citizen), Hobbes makes obligation dependent on the recognition of an inalienable right of the individual. As Leo Strauss correctly pointed out, this opens the way for the claim of modern liberalism that the legitimacy of political systems is contingent on their respect for rights.[9] As we shall see further on, in the case of liberalism, traditionally it has been the rights of individuals only. In the case of human rights, it is contested as to whether the rights are exclusively individual. Hobbes, himself, talks only about the rights of the individual. He claims that if the sovereign threatens your life but not mine, regardless of the reason or justification, it is none of my business. This kind of radical atomization and alienation of individuals has not been without effects on modern liberalism and the classical and neoclassical economic thinking that has accompanied it.

Some have concluded from this that Hobbes is a theoretical precursor of that supreme nemesis of twentieth-century human rights, totalitarianism. I think that this is a serious misreading. Hobbes suggests that the wise sovereign would permit much economic freedom. Indeed, I read his comments on money and commerce as a kind of exchange, a grant of wide economic freedom at the price of political liberty. Hobbes is willing to let the naturally aggressive impulses work themselves out in the competitive economic domain. Rather than setting up a state-run or corporate economy, Hobbes advises the sovereign to make sure that monopolies do not develop because they are the antithesis of competition. Let the money flow and the goods be traded, in other words, laissez-faire up to the point of monopolization. Relatively free and competitive economic activity would thus constitute a safety valve through which competition and antagonism over conflicting interests could be released outside of the political arena. But economic freedoms, like other freedoms that might exist within civil society, do not constitute absolute natural rights like the right to life. They are prudential in the sense that the sovereign always reserves the right to step in if the sovereign judges these freedoms to be politically destabilizing. They are desirable in the sense that Hobbes seems to appreciate values other than biological life itself. Because these other values, whether they be economic, cultural, or spiritual, are dependent on the effective protection of life itself, they logically become secondary or contingent. Thus, there is no human right to anything cultural, spiritual, or economic in the way that there is to the life of the human body itself.

Locke: A Crucial Expansion of Human Rights at the Expense of State Power

Hobbes's follower in the chain of Western contract theorists, John Locke, wrote the *Second Treatise of Civil Government* the year after the Bloodless Revolution of 1689 severely weakened the monarchy and the political claims of Catholicism. Locke's work was a post facto justification of that revolution and the political (parliamentary), economic (propertied, commercial), and religious (Protestant) interests it represented. Locke retained from Hobbes two crucial things: (1) the ascription of rights to individuals *qua* individuals; and (2) the insistence that the individual's obligation to the state is contingent on the state's respect for, and protection of, the rights of the individual.

But Locke's theory of rights also differs from Hobbes's in two fundamental ways. First, Locke expanded the realm of rights. While the right of life is maintained in Locke, he adds the rights of liberty and of property. Second, Locke substituted limited constitutional government with a preference for parliamentary supremacy for Hobbes's absolutist, and preferably monarchical, centralized government.

Two other important issues are ambiguous in Locke's theory of rights. The first is the extent of political rights. The second is that of individualism and its economic implications. In Hobbes, the extent of political rights is clear. There are no political rights claims against the sovereign unless one's life is threatened. Then one is back in the state of nature where there is little point in talking about rights that others have an obligation to recognize. It becomes simply a contest of power. Because Locke advocated parliamentary supremacy, one might presume that a fundamental right would be the right to participate in the election of the legislature as voter or candidate. And it cannot be claimed that no one would have thought of such a thing in

Locke's time. The issue was raised by the Levellers in the Cromwellian army a half-century earlier.

Locke seems to have followed Aristotle in feeling that those who are preoccupied with manual labor or petty commerce are unfit for rights to participate in political life. That should be left to those engaged in economic stewardship and intellectual reflection. He writes in the little-known text, *The Reasonableness of Christianity,* that the likes of "day-labourers," "tradesmen," "dairy-maids," and "spinsters" (a slight categorical error perhaps!) are not reasonable. Since they cannot know, but can only believe, they must be led by others.[10] While Locke might have been tolerant of the rights of such people to express their political beliefs, it is very doubtful that he would have supported their right to participate in the selection of those who would govern them (indeed, they did not have that right in Great Britain until the nineteenth-century Reform Acts), much less the right to present themselves as candidates.

This relates to the priority that Locke assigns to property rights. Indeed, in one place in the *Second Treatise,* Locke tells us that when he uses the word property, he is to be understood to mean the rights to life and liberty as well as land, goods, and money.[11] (In fact, he uses the word property inconsistently.) The right to property is presumed to come from two legitimizing sources, labor and inheritance. If the franchise is extended to only those with substantial property, it is difficult to imagine that the legislature would do anything to infringe on property rights (understood as rights to land, goods, or money), since they have an immediate material interest in maintaining those rights. Thus, when Locke asks at the end of the *Second Treatise,* "Who shall be judge whether the prince or legislative act contrary to their trust?" and answers, "The people shall be judge," there is little reason to doubt that he is referring exclusively to the "rational," propertied people. This fundamental political right of judging legitimacy turns out not to be a human right but, rather, the right of a particular segment of the population. But by extending the concept of property to one's own body, Locke can argue that everyone is of necessity propertied. He can thus, in effect, join Hobbes in stripping the majority of the population of the rights of active political agents while claiming that their "property rights"—what Hobbes would call their rights to physical survival—are preserved.

This still leaves Locke with the problem of scarcity, because if human beings do not have the basic material necessities outside of their own bodies, they will die, that is, lose their property in their bodies. This is particularly interesting because of the implications for people outside of England. Locke argued that when all the common land to which everyone had access had been closed off placed in the hands of private parties, the most enterprising of the people left without land would go to claim their property rights elsewhere, where there was no scarcity. He writes: "God and his reason commanded him [man] to subdue the earth, i.e., improve it for the benefit of life, and therein lay out something upon it that was his own, his labor. He that in obedience to this command of God subdued, tilled, and sowed any part of it, thereby annexed to it something that was his property, which another had no title to, nor could without injury take from him."[12]

Locke encourages the landless of England to ensure their natural rights to their property in their bodies by going out and claiming the right to land elsewhere. He gives a justification, based on the labor theory of value and what we now call "trickle-down" economics, for those who are excluded from the possession of land in England taking the land occupied by indigenous people elsewhere. When he looks to America, he asks, "whether in the wild woods and uncultivated waste of America, left to nature, without any improvement, tillage, or husbandry, a thousand acres yield the needy and wretched inhabitants as many conveniences of life as ten acres equally fertile land in Devonshire, where they are well cultivated."[13] Scarcity then is not a problem for the enterprising of England or Europe. The right to property, both in terms of property in body (life) and property in land and goods, is open to those who will but seize the opportunities that the earth presents to follow God's commandment to subdue it. What had already been going on in the Americas, called imperialism in the nineteenth century, was crucial for Locke to overcome the scarcity problem in his theory of natural rights.

The second issue that is important for conceiving of human rights but remains cloudy in Locke is the degree of Locke's individualism. Is Locke as individualistic as Hobbes? Is it everyone for him- or herself in this endeavor to use one's rights to create wealth by exploiting the earth? If it is true that there is plenty out there to be exploited, and that the exploitation by the most industrious will create a greater supply of wealth that will trickle down ultimately for the benefit of everyone, why would we need a concept of rights other than a purely individualistic one? Is Locke then not a forerunner of economic theorists such as Frederick von Hayek and Milton Friedman, who argue that the laissez-faire, enrichessez-vous, private property/free market economic system is the most efficient allocator of resources, and that any attempt to meddle with it through some notion of rights (other than the absolute property rights that legitimize it) or distributive justice would only bring greater impoverishment and misery?

Jack Donnelly, in one of the most important theoretical books on human rights in recent years, makes the argument that Locke is not as individualistic as some, for example, C. B. Macpherson, portray him.[14] Donnelly argues that contemporary liberal advocates of social and economic human rights (inconsistent with unlimited individual accumulation of property) as well as political rights can refer back to Locke for support.

Donnelly contends that Locke places three important limitations on individual property rights. The first is that one cannot morally permit goods to spoil. The second is what Donnelly calls a "use-limit" (the right to take only what one will indeed use)—but is very close, if not precisely the same thing, as the injunction against spoilage. The third is that there must be enough left in common for others to enjoy. These three limits, which Donnelly refers to as "natural law limits," when combined with Locke's general injunction ("For, by the Fundamental Law of Nature, Man being to be preserved, as much as possible ... ") lead Donnelly to argue that there are severe limits to Locke's individualism. As in other places, Locke appears to be inconsistent. On the one hand, he argues for the defense of individual private property and even subsuming the right to life under that conception. On the other, he imposes some limits and a moral prescription that we ought to be concerned with the preservation of all our fellow human beings.

There is always ambiguity and even contradiction in theoretical texts. Without completely rejecting Donnelly's reading of Locke, it must be pointed out that there are at least two considerations that weaken Donnelly's argument that these "natural law limits" severely limit Locke's individualism. The first has already been mentioned. If Locke has solved the problem of scarcity by saying that those deprived in one country can just go elsewhere, he has simultaneously argued that there is enough left and it is up to individuals to seize the opportunity to take what is left *and* that these European individuals need not be concerned about the issue of rights accruing to indigenous people who may use this land for their own survival in ways that their cultures sanction (which most often did not include individual titles). Second, the prescription that Man should be preserved as much as possible is indeed a recognition that we do have obligations to others, but it does not tell us the nature of that obligation. While rights always involve obligations (to respect those rights), obligations do not always involve rights. The right to private property is clearly a rights claim that I, as a property holder, can make on others who do not hold title to that property. Presumably, my claim will be supported by law and effective state action if someone violates my property rights. But the injunction to preserve human beings as much as possible could be read as merely a moral injunction that might be satisfied, for example, by a voluntary commitment to charity. In that case, we cannot speak of those who are in need of aid to survive as having a right to it. They are completely dependent on the good will of the potential provider of the charity.

Because Locke does not tie the obligation to recognize and act on everyone's need to survive to the functions of the state the way he does with property rights, I think that Donnelly pushes the argument too far when he contends that Locke's *Second Treatise* provides liberals with a legitimization of economic or social rights beyond individual private property. I might add that I agree with Donnelly's position that there are valid economic and social human rights claims that require positive state action. I am just not as convinced as Donnelly that Locke's *Treatise* is the most fruitful place to look for theoretical or ideological justification of that.

Rousseau: Rights and the Community—and Kant's Alternative Vision

The third of the great contract theorists, Jean-Jacques Rousseau, is a much more likely source for such a justification. For, while Hobbes ties rights to individual physical security, and Locke ties them to both physical security and individual property rights claims, Rousseau ties rights to two conceptions that were to be given prominence during the French Revolution but are less evident or missing in Hobbes and Locke—equality and fraternity. Unlike Locke, who wrote the justificatory *Treatise* for the Bloodless Revolution after it had already occurred, Rousseau wrote his work before the French Revolution. The relevance of Rousseau's work penetrated much further down into the class hierarchy than did that of Locke. Reflections of it could be seen in the dynamics between the bourgeoisie and the artisans and peasants during the revolutionary process. The "General Will" was a phrase constantly invoked by revolutionary orators to justify their positions and actions.

It is particularly interesting to compare Rousseau's analysis of the relationship between property and rights with Locke's. Against Locke's position that there is property in nature, thus strengthening the individual's claim to property and the gravity of the offense of the state if it tries to interfere with that right, Rousseau argued that there is no property in nature. There is only possession. But possession is a physical fact. The strongest or the fastest might possess something because of these qualities. But these qualities are amoral and say nothing about the "right" of possessors to whatever is possessed. When we use the word "property," what we mean is that the person *legitimately* possesses something, that is, that he or she has a right to it, that the rest of us have an obligation to respect that right, and that the force of state and law will be brought to bear against us if we violate that right. Indeed, in Rousseau's thinking, one of the reasons that we enter into the social contract is so that we can have property rather than mere possessions, so that the state and its citizens will recognize and protect what we legitimately possess.

It is because Rousseau takes this position that Louis Althusser, the French Marxist philosopher, sees little difference between Rousseau and Locke. That is, he sees Rousseau as basically a bourgeois philosopher protecting bourgeois property rights.[15] But that is not a sufficient understanding of Rousseau. First, since property as opposed to possession is a social construction, it cannot be unlimited. It is a good, but a good that must be structured according to the welfare of the community through the General Will.[16] Rousseau tries to mediate between the right of the individual to property and the rights of other individuals and the claims of the collectivity itself:

> The peculiar fact about this ... is that the community, so far from despoiling them only ensures them legitimate possession, and changes usurpation into a true right and enjoyment into proprietorship. Thus the possessors, being regarded as depositories of the public good, and having their rights respected by all the members of the State and maintained against foreign aggression by all its forces, have, by a cession which benefits both the public and still more themselves, acquired, so to speak, all that they gave up.[17]

Rousseau thus tries to mediate between the collectivity and the individual—on the one hand, he is unequivocal that "every man has naturally a right to everything he needs for his subsistence."[18] On the other, he insists that rights to property as well as political rights are civil rights in that they both must be determined and protected by the collectivity taking into account the general interest. Unlike in Locke's work, in which it seems that only property holders would represent interest in the legislative body and the interests and rights of the propertied would be presumed to be in the general interest, in

Rousseau's all male citizens would be property holders and would participate directly in the making of the laws. This obviously would require a great dispersion of property, but not an absolute equality, which Rousseau thought was impractical.

Thus, for Rousseau there could be no liberty without a large measure of both political and economic equality. Hobbes renounced liberty in favor of the right to physical security guaranteed by an all-powerful sovereign. Locke saw liberty as intimately tied to the right of private property guaranteed by propertied legislative representatives who would ensure that the state did not intrude on those rights. Rousseau saw individuals possessing measured amounts of land and wealth entering into a contract with each other, a contract in which the physical act of possession is transformed into property ownership, but with the collectivity assuming the responsibility of assuring that all have at least what they need to survive, and with none becoming so wealthy that they could use economic power to usurp political control. The thinking here is communitarian rather than individualistic. Natural rights are exchanged for civil rights. Property ultimately belongs to the whole but stewardship is turned over to individuals who will not use it in ways detrimental to the general interest. All make a public commitment to the welfare of the community as a whole (*fraternité*) and all males fulfill both the right and the duty of directly participating in the political decision-making process. Freedom is then defined as abiding only by laws that one has participated in authoring.

Rousseau's thinking poses at least two problems for human rights. First, it is not clear how human rights could figure in the exchange of natural rights for civil rights. Civil rights are limited to a particular community. Human rights transcend the community. Hobbes talks about everyone anywhere having the right to life. Locke talks about everyone everywhere who owns property having an inviolable right to that property. In Rousseau, it is the General Will, determined by all male citizens, which will determine what the rights in that particular society will be. This appears to preclude human rights in the sense of people having specified rights merely by virtue of being human beings rather than by virtue of being a citizen in this or that political entity. Rousseau, as opposed to the Greeks, specifically builds in rights. But, like the Greeks, he does not transcend the polis. If "human" rights are to mean anything, they must transcend the polis.

The one transcendent principle in Rousseau is the right of every adult male to participate in the determination of the General Will in the first place. Without this, there can be no legitimate government in Rousseau's eyes. Mary Wollstonecraft was correct to point out that this limited the universalism of Rousseau's participatory principle on the basis of prejudice rather than reason.[19] However if he had not discriminated on the basis of gender, we would have something akin to a universal human rights principle, because Rousseau rejects the legitimacy of any system not so governed. But a second problem for human rights is opened up by Rousseau's commitment to the proposition that at any given point in time in any given community there will be a correct position, and those who do not accept it are objectively wrong and must admit to being so. They are required to grant that the reasoned will of the majority has indeed detected the truth of the matter. The role of the dissenter is thus an uncomfortable and possibly even dangerous one. Rousseau's attempt to minimize the chances of such disagreement and dissent, that is, insistence on a homogeneous population, poses further human rights problems. When equality and fraternity are based on enforced uniformity of thought or other variable human characteristics, human rights go by the wayside. The world saw this played out in the Terror during the French Revolution in which the General Will (*la Volunté Générale*) rhetorically justified many a death by guillotine.[20]

Immanuel Kant, the German moral philosopher and metaphysician, has an interesting relationship with Rousseau's thought. He was much influenced by Rousseau's concept of a rationally determined General Will and shared Rousseau's position that, in society, rights are derivative from law that incorporates collective reason. But Kant tried to mitigate the danger of Rousseau's collectivism. He insisted on the autonomy of the will and freedom of each rational human being who was an end in him- or herself. Thus, there was a corollary duty of each person to treat all (including the self) equally as an end and never just as a means. This intrinsic value of the person was what Kant called "dignity."[21] Kant also argued for a republican constitution (which he defined as a separation of legislative and executive power) rather than direct democracy as "the only one which does complete justice to the rights of man."[22] While Kant's implied critique of Rousseau is on target, his own view of the human being as the manifestation of reason, and hence freedom, autonomy, and dignity, lacks the concrete relational connections that Hobbes (conflict based on similar desires and scarcity and a collective search for security), Locke (relationships centering around property), and Rousseau (critique of existing inequalities and proposals of immediate discursive relationships in determining the General Will) attempt to establish. He is thus more abstract, as one would expect from a metaphysician, than the three political theorists. This has not prevented him from being influential in subsequent liberal thinking about human rights.

To sum up the discussion of the relationship between the three major contract theorists and the concept of human rights: (1) they were Western theorists writing within a particular time frame; (2) their thinking did not just come out of their heads in some abstract thought process but was stimulated by concrete struggles that were going on at the time of their writing; (3) the writing of their texts was a political as well as a speculative act—it became a part of that struggle over power and interests; (4) these Western theorists stressed different values that continue to be focused on as underlying human rights values (rights to life, to bodily security, to property and concern over its distribution, to limits on the reach of government, and to political participation).

It is both an intellectual mistake and an affront to those outside of the Western tradition to look back at any one of these thinkers as the historical point of authority for how we should think about human rights. We should, rather, look at them as illustrating how human rights can be seen from a variety of angles and the problems that arise when we approach the subject from each of these angles. And just as these theorists did not write in a social, political, or economic vacuum, so we, too, will bring to those texts certain orientations and interests coming out of our understanding of history and out of our own contemporary situations. We must account for the dramatic changes, for example, the development of the nation-state system, the growth of both public and private bureaucracies, the simultaneous concentration and globalization of economic power, the rights struggles of minorities and women, and the addition of non-Western voices to human rights discourse, which pose new problems for human rights, and even new human rights, since these early theorists began the philosophical discussion.

EUROPEAN AND AMERICAN HUMAN RIGHTS DOCUMENTS AT THE END OF THE EIGHTEENTH CENTURY

But the human rights heritage is not just a set of philosophical texts. We also have a set of documents, which are usually taken as seminal statements, drafted by political actors as to what constitutes human rights. There were early documents against monarchical absolutism. The Magna Charta of 1225 and the English Bill of Rights of 1689 were both of this nature. But, as indicated earlier, the major thrust of the Magna Charta was an attempt by the lords of the realm to gain some of the power that the king had been exercising. The 1689 document does have some more universalistic statements within it, such as the prohibition of cruel and unusual punishment and the right of petition (in this case to the king), which would make their way into later documents.

But the "grand documents" of human rights are the American and French documents drafted at the end of the eighteenth century. These are the U.S. Declaration of Independence (1776), the U.S. Constitution and its first ten amendments, which constitute the Bill of Rights (1789 and 1791), and the French Declaration of the Rights of Man and Citizen (1789).

The Declaration of Independence is the first document to declare that "all men are created equal; that they are endowed by their creator with certain inalienable rights; that among these are life, liberty, and the pursuit of happiness. That to secure these rights, governments are instituted among men, deriving their just powers from the consent of the governed; that whenever any form of government becomes destructive of these ends, it is the right of the people to alter or abolish it." The Declaration of Independence also attacks the British monarchy for undercutting the elected legislatures that had developed in the colonies. The Declaration is a very Lockean document. Locke, too, argued that we were all "equal and independent" in the state of nature.[23] This, however, did not translate into political equality in Locke's thinking or in the U.S. Constitution.

The Constitution permitted property qualifications for voting, the exclusion of women from the political process, and slavery. It even specified the weight of slaves in the representation of the states at the national level. But the Bill of Rights was remarkable in that for the first time it elaborated a set of rights that were not just restricted to the citizens of the country. With the exception of slaves, all people were considered by the Constitution to have rights such as habeas corpus, trial by jury, and freedoms of speech, association, and religion. While the U.S. government could only ensure those rights within the territorial boundaries of the United States, it is significant that it was not only citizens that enjoyed these fundamental rights. The spirit of the Constitution was thus consistent with the "all men" (women also were accorded most of the nonparticipatory rights, thus holding the status of political subjects with certain guarantees of legal rights, for instance, habeas corpus and trial by jury—but not by peers) terminology of the Declaration of Independence. As retrograde as this appears from our present historical vantage point, the application of basic rights to "all men" rather than just all citizens of the particular country was a large step forward in the struggle for human rights. The French Declaration of the Rights of Man and Citizen, issued in the same year, significantly specifies in its title that this is not just for French citizens, but for everyone. Thus, the French and the American documents, in contradistinction to the earlier British documents, seek to rise to the level of generality of the contract theorists, to speak to the world at large, at the same time that they guarantee rights to their own citizens. The opening paragraph of the French Declaration first addresses the world at large. It says, "The representatives of the French people, organized in National Assembly, considering that ignorance, forgetfulness, contempt of the rights of man are the sole causes of public misfortunes and of the corruption of governments, have resolved to set forth in a solemn declaration the natural, inalienable, and sacred rights of man, in order that such declaration, continually before all members of the social body, may be a perpetual reminder of their rights and duties."[24]

This document establishes basically the same rights as the U.S. Constitution, with two major exceptions. First, it is more Rousseauist in that it makes reference to a general will in which all have the right to concur: "Law is the expression of the general will; all citizens have the right to concur personally, or through their representatives, in its formation; it must be the same for all, whether it protects or punishes. All citizens, being equal before it, are equally admissible to all public offices, positions, and employment, according to their capacity, and without other distinction than that of virtues and talents."[25] Thus, it is a more democratic document than the U.S. Constitution, which is more Lockean. But, in practice, the Declaration did not open up rights of political participation for women. It thus manifested the same blind spot for which Wollstonecraft had criticized Rousseau. In fact, French women would not get the vote until after World War II.

The second distinction, which reflects the fact that contrary to the American Revolution there was a change in class control in the French Revolution, is that the French Declaration insists that taxes "be assessed equally on all citizens in proportion to their means."[26] The French Declaration thus raises a question of economic rights, or what some would call social justice, at the same time that it declares property to be "a sacred and inviolable right, [that] no one may by deprived thereof unless a legally established public necessity obviously requires it, and upon condition of a just and previous indemnity."[27]

Regardless of these two distinctions, the French and American documents have a great deal in common. They proclaim fundamental freedoms, the right to security, and rights to a trial with fair processes. And while they do this for their own citizens, they also proclaim that these are fundamental rights that everyone in the world ought to enjoy simply by virtue of being human beings. Thus, they were meant by their drafters to serve as beacons of light, calling on others to recognize the universal validity of these documents and to follow them. It seemed reasonable that this would happen in the Age of Reason. But, alas, there was not a universal acceptance of the invitation.

Rejection of Universal or Human Rights in the Eighteenth and Nineteenth Century

There were at least three important theoretical objections to the rationally grounded human rights position of the contract theorists in these two centuries. The first I shall call the antirationalist objection. It is manifested most strikingly in the writings and speeches of Edmund Burke, but is also contained at least by implication in the work of David Hume. The second objection is to be found in the historical/scientific materialism of Karl Marx. The third is in the utilitarianism of Jeremy Bentham.

The Antirationalist Response

Rousseau serves as a bridge of sorts to the antirationalist rejection of human rights by Burke and Hume. This is because while he, like Hobbes and Locke, posited universal natural rights, Rousseau insisted on an exchange of those natural rights for civil rights. These civil rights, above and beyond the rights of adult males to participate actively in determining the General Will, are contingent on that very will. There is no reason to believe that those determinations would be the same across societies. While in Rousseau's amoral state of nature, human beings were guided in their actions by instinctive concern for others of the same species (*pitié*) and by instinctive concern for their own welfare, in civil society their actions and their discourses and determinations regarding the General Will should be guided by reason. Reason, unperverted by egoism, should tell them what is best for the whole polity. Civil rights would then be rationally imbedded within this General Will.

Rousseau's work held great interest for Burke and Hume. For a while, there was constant contact between the three of them. When it became too threatening for Rousseau to remain on the continent of Europe, Hume offered him hospitality in London, where there were continual discussions among these three great thinkers.

Burke held an organic view of politics. Political institutions did not grow up according to some kind of rational design or plan or deliberation. They resulted rather from the living traditions and customs in the society. Those that stood the test of time proved their validity in just doing so. They become part of a permanent contract that requires no criteria, outside of the ongoing social practices themselves, by which to evaluate the moral validity of social practices or institutions. Those practices are self-justifying. It is difficult to discern any fact/value distinction in Burke. A noncritical posture toward tradition replaces it. Any change that is not incremental and thus incorporating much of the prior tradition is dangerous. It would lead either to tyranny or to chaos.

For Burke, the "rights of man" were an abstraction. That was enough to make them a wrong-headed idea. Politics ought not to be conceived through the lens of abstractions. Rather, it ought to be conceived of as a concrete and delicate process of evolution that is driven by dynamics within the bodies politic. From this perspective, Rousseau did not need natural rights at all. It sufficed that he had civil rights. That is all that we as human beings can claim, those civil rights that have evolved in our bodies politic and have withstood the test of time. That also meant that the civil rights and rights holders would differ from political system to political system.

Burke writes, "Government is not made in virtue of natural rights, which may and do exist in total independence of it, and exist in much greater clearness and in a much greater degree of abstract perfection; but their perfection is their practical defect . . . as the liberties and the restrictions vary with times and circumstances and admit to infinite modifications, they cannot be settled upon any abstract rule; and nothing is so foolish as to discuss them upon that principle."[28]

The rights of an Englishman are the rights only of an Englishman. People of other political communities may or may not have the same or similar rights. The question is settled by convention and prudence. To use a term much in currency with contemporary postmodernists, rights within any society are a social construction, but not necessarily a conscious and rational one. To attempt to change society on the basis of an abstract philosophical conception of rights would only result in breaking the solidifying bonds of the society itself and the loss of liberty for everyone. Again, the options are chaos and tyranny, and in the French Revolution Burke thought that he saw both occurring simultaneously. By contrast, he was favorably inclined toward the concrete demands of the American colonists, although not the recourse to the natural rights justifying language to be sure, because in his view they were not attempting to change the basic norms and social structure of the society.

Like Rousseau, Burke can be described as a communitarian. Unlike Rousseau, he is not an egalitarian communitarian. It is not at all necessary in Burke's mind that people must participate in the making of the decisions that affect their lives or that they would have anything like equal access to the resources of a society in order to be free. That is an unwarranted philosophical assumption. The fate of political and cultural traditions is much better off in the political hands of "gentlemen" than in those of a "swinish multitude."[29] Rather, prudence and what he calls "just prejudices," those that have seemed to produce good results, are a much better guide to society than reason and abstraction.

Burke's attack on universal rights itself drew immediate attacks from Thomas Paine and Mary Wollstonecraft. The latter also attacked Rousseau for the exclusion of women from virtually any rights. But Burke remains very influential today. There is a wing of contemporary conservatism that is influenced by his nonlibertarian and elitist communitarianism. Some postmodernists who insist on the validity of local knowledge, and their invulnerability to any kind of external, rational evaluation, bear a similarity to Burke despite their desire to remain egalitarian. Finally, Burke's argument that rights must be relative to the specific society could provide some comfort to the leaders of non-Western nations who reject the idea that they should be judged on the basis of an idea generated by Western philosophers and passed off as universal. One can imagine such a non-Western leader, called to account for human rights violations by the U.S. State Department's yearly human rights report, responding in great irony with the words of Burke:

> Thanks to our sullen resistance to innovation ... we still bear the stamp of our forefathers. ... We know that *we* have made no discoveries, and we think that no discoveries are to be made, in morality, nor many in the great principles of government, nor in the ideas of liberty, which were understood long before we were born. ... We have not yet been completely embowelled of our natural entrails; we still feel within us, and we cherish and cultivate, those inbred sentiments. We have not been drawn and trussed, in order that we may be filled, like stuffed birds in a museum, with chaff and rags and paltry blurred shreds of paper about the rights of men. We preserve the whole of our feelings still native and entire, unsophisticated by pedantry and infidelity.[30]

Indeed, the Burkean historian Daniel Boorstin, in his book *The Genius of American Politics,* argues on good Burkean grounds that we really have nothing to offer such people by way of our political norms and institutions.[31]

While David Hume did not engage in polemics against the idea of natural or universal rights the way Burke did, and indeed wrote much more about morals than about politics, his moral theory was one that undercut natural rights understood as a concept that could be rationally grounded. Hume's criticism of Rousseau is that Rousseau never should have let go of that feeling of compassion that he exchanged for reason when people entered the social contract.

Hume bears an important similarity to Hobbes. Like Hobbes, he thinks that the feelings that we have of pleasure and pain are the root of our morality. Hobbes builds a political theory around the propositions that what we call good and bad in the state of nature are what we feel to be pleasurable or painful. Since the most painful experience that a human being can endure is the threat of imminent death, in Hobbes's mind we ought to be willing to give up all other rights claims in order to minimize the possibility that we will face such a threat. Such security, and the economic and cultural benefits it makes possible, ought to maximize our pleasure. The theory is rational in the sense that we should know what we have to do in order to gain such security, that is, give up all other rights and institute an absolutist government, but the grounding of the theory is utilitarian. It is based on *feelings* of pleasure and pain or happiness and unhappiness.

For Hume, Rousseau's problem was that he did not understand that morality was felt, not reasoned. In Hume's words:

> the distinguishing impressions by which moral good or evil is known are nothing but *particular* pains or pleasures ... An action, or sentiment, or character, is virtuous or vicious; why? because its view causes a pleasure or uneasiness of a particular kind. ... The very *feeling* constitutes our praise or admiration. We go no further; nor do we inquire into the cause of the satisfaction. We do not infer a character to be virtuous because it pleases; but in feeling that it pleases after such a particular manner we in effect feel that it is virtuous. ... I have objected to the system which establishes eternal rational measures of right and wrong.[32]

Hume's objection would, of course, include rationally grounded human rights, particularly as they are manifested in Locke or Rousseau. Indeed, Hume would object to both the idea of a right in the state of nature, as well as to the very ideas of a state of nature and a contract. He shares the organicism of Burke, but he does so with stronger philosophical reasoning.

Hume also is concerned with the kind of solipsism or egoism that can be read into Hobbes. The quality that permits us to overcome these is sympathy. Sympathy, not reason, is the quality that makes humans social beings. When society determines that something is right, let us say something comparable to a specific determination within Rousseau's larger General Will structure, it must be considered "in general, without reference to our particular interest."[33] This leads to an ethic of social approval. Instead of saying that all come together and rationally deliberate on the General Will as Rousseau does, for Hume we look at social consensus on what gives the most pleasure to a society. As in the case of Burke, we are back to the fact/value problem. We can always say that certain social norms and practices exist *because* they give the society pleasure and that there can be no external criteria by which to evaluate these norms and practices. And since Hume is more of a moralist than a political thinker, he does not ask the question, *whose* pain or pleasure are we really talking about? The Burkean organic assumptions, which themselves are an abstraction (i.e., whole societies don't "like" anything), seem to cover over the fact that generality is not so easily attained. Hume might have learned that from Rousseau's not altogether successful grappling with a concept like the General Will.

Just as for Burke, morality is conventional, not natural. Hume will permit us to say that morality is natural in only two senses. One is that it is not miraculous. The second would be that it is ubiquitous. In the latter sense, he argues that there are three fundamental laws of nature: the stability of possession, the transference of possession by consent, and the performance of promises.[34] In Hume's view, any society will incorporate these laws of nature. They, in fact, imply Locke's property rights, property understood here to mean legitimate possession of land, goods, or money. It is presumed that these are *felt* by all societies to offer pleasure to the society at large. There is no room in this formulation for *rationally* grounded natural rights. But if in all societies people felt good about adhering to natural or universal rights, if the adherence to human rights were ubiquitous across societies, that would presumably be enough to establish their position as natural rights. This clearly was not the case in Hume's time. It may or may not be the case today. That is an empirical rather than a theoretical matter.

The Rational Utilitarian Response

The line of utilitarianism, the reliance on pleasure or happiness as the ultimate standard for moral and political good, runs from Hobbes, through Hume, to Jeremy Bentham. Bentham shares Hobbes's desire to turn politics away from a speculative enterprise and toward a "realistic" scientific one. Pleasure and pain relate to the very nature of the human as a sensate being. The reactions to pleasure and pain are much more immediate, much more potent in their impact, and much more determinable than are intellectual/rational constructs or religious revelations. They thus provide a much firmer foundation for building theories of politics and law than the latter.

If Hume laid the foundation for morality built on feelings of pleasure and pain, Bentham tried to lay the foundations for theories of politics and law. Bentham, too, employs the mechanism of sympathy as the social quality that enables us to overcome egoism and solipsism. But while Hume stops at the level of general moral and social theoretical propositions, Bentham is concerned with operationalizing the greatest happiness principle so that legislators can use it as a guide in determining the optimal social policy. In fact, perhaps unknown to many of the children, Bentham is the father of contemporary optimizing policy studies. He attempts to take into account the various dimensions of pleasures and pains (e.g., intensity, duration, propinquity). All of these dimensions are quantifiable. This is intended to give an element of precision to legislators or other policy makers that is missing in more subjective notions of politics and the political good.

Bentham differs from Hobbes and Hume in that he attempts to advance the cause of democracy. But unlike Rousseau, he advances the cause of representative and not direct democracy. While Rousseau declared that the British were free only once in every seven years, that is, during the campaign period when the parliament was NOT in session, Bentham was busy pushing for electoral reforms so that all of the classes (including Burke's "swinish multitude") could participate in the election of members of parliament. People needed to be able to vote for these members and express their pleasures and pains to them for Bentham's scientific politics to work. Unlike Rousseau, who saw the rationally and discursively determined General Will as being much more than the sum of the particular wills in the society, Bentham's standard was how the sum of the particular pleasures and pains of each individual would array themselves on the societal scale. Moreover, only quantitative and not qualitative dimensions would be permitted. One could not say, as did Plato and Bentham's heir apparent as leader of the utilitarian "movement," John Stuart Mill, that the intellectual and aesthetic pleasures were better than the sensual or material pleasures. That would be a purely subjective judgment, most likely of intellectuals and artists advancing their own interests.

Bentham thus tried to construct a scientific system of politics and jurisprudence that expunged subjectivity. There was no room for any conception of natural or human rights in this conception. If one used the pleasure/pain principle to pass laws, one did not need the concept of natural rights. The system itself contained elements that would do whatever natural rights were supposed to do. There were no criteria similar to pain and pleasure to make natural or human rights sufficiently precise and objective. Such rights claims would only add an element of arbitrariness and thus serve some interests unjustifiably. While differing on the criteria and the method that should be used to determine the general good, Bentham joins Rousseau in insisting that civil rights, that is, rights accorded by law, are the only rights we can talk about if we want to talk sense. Bentham put it succinctly:

> There are no other than legal rights—no natural rights—no rights of man, anterior or superior to those created by the laws. The assertion of such rights, absurd in logic, is pernicious in morals. A right without a law is an effect without a cause. We may feign a law, in order to speak of this fiction—in order to feign a right as having been created; but fiction is not truth. We may feign laws of nature—rights of nature, in order to show the nullity of real laws, as contrary to these imaginary rights; and it is with this view that recourse is had to this fiction—but the effect of these nullities can only be null.[35]

Utilitarianism thus became the one school of liberalism that rejected natural rights.

The Historical Materialist Response

There are three important similarities between Marx and Bentham. First, they both attempt to provide us with a rigorous science for obtaining a better understanding of the political world. Second, they both draw from their understanding lessons for political action. Bentham's prescriptive lessons are directed to political decision makers in order that there might be more enlightened legislation and jurisprudence. He conceives of political change as evolutionary, for example, a progressive expansion of the electorate. Marx's lessons are directed toward a particular class, the proletariat. He conceives of change as revolutionary. Third, they both reject any conception of natural rights or human rights.

While Marx makes reference to the issue in a number of his works, including *The Critique of the Gotha Program, The Holy Family,* and *The Civil War in France,* his most extensive critique of the concept of human rights comes in his 1843 critique of two studies of the social and political situation of Jews by another Young Hegelian, Bruno Bauer. He thus entitled this essay *On the Jewish Question*. The essay is a delicate one as some have read it as demonstrating an anti-Semitism on Marx's part, even though he came from Jewish ancestry.[36] Bauer had maintained that Jews could not emancipate themselves politically, could not claim the "universal rights of man," without renouncing Judaism. Bauer echoes an old characterization of Jews that they have set themselves apart from others. This is, of course, a reference to the claim to be the chosen people, to the Jewish refusal to proselytize, and to the communal bonds and shared cultural characteristics among Jews. Marx quotes Bauer:

> The idea of the rights of man was only discovered in the Christian world, in the last century. It is not an innate idea; on the contrary, it is acquired in a struggle against the historical traditions in which man has been educated up to the present time. The rights of man are not, there-fore, a gift of nature, nor a legacy from past history, but the reward of a struggle against the accident of birth and against the privileges which history has hitherto transmitted from generation to generation. These are the results of culture, and only he can possess them who has mer-ited and earned them.[37]

In Bauer's view, the Jew has not earned them because the Jew remains separated from this history by his particularism and his faith. Under these conditions, the Christians cannot simply confer such rights, which emanate from their cultural and religious tradition, on the Jews.

Rather than confronting Bauer directly on the issue of whether Jews can claim universal rights, Marx probes what those rights really are. He analyzes rights stipulated in some of the major rights docu-ments written at the end of the eighteenth century: the French Declaration of the Rights of Man and Citizen and constitutions of 1793 and 1795; the Constitution of the United States, and the con-stitutions of Pennsylvania and New Hampshire.

Of particular interest to Marx is that a distinction is made between the rights of man and the rights of a citizen. Marx argues that the rights of man, as opposed to the rights of a citizen, for example, the right to vote, is in reality the right of a member of civil society. That is to say that the distinction between state and society, first made analytically in the works of Hegel, is unconsciously made in these documents. In fact, these documents universalize what is in reality profoundly particularistic. The "rights of man," as opposed to the rights of citizen, are in reality the rights of the individualistic, self-interested monad. This is why he writes: "The practical application of the right of liberty is the right of private property."[38] And the right of private property is "the right to enjoy one's fortune and to dispose of it as one will; without regard for other men and independently of society. It is the right of self-interest. This individual liberty and its application, form the basis of civil society. It leads every man to see in other men not the *realization* but, rather, the *limitation,* of his own liberty. It declares above all the right 'to enjoy and to dispose *as one will,* one's goods and revenues, the fruits of one's work and industry.'"[39]

So much for "liberty." "Equality," Marx argues, is only the equal right to the liberty to dispose of one's goods and revenues. It thus also becomes a monadic concept, pertaining only to the individual in his or her self-interested particularity.

Equality thus becomes a Hobbesian conflictual or competitive relationship, cut off from the *fraternité* proclaimed by the French Revolution. Marx refers to the Constitution of 1795, in which it is related to law, which is the same for all. But, of course, people are in vastly different situations vis-à-vis the property, if any, under their control, that is, their "liberty."

"Security," defined in the Constitution of 1793 as "the protection afforded by society to each of its members for the preservation of his person, his rights, and his property," is seen by Marx as the "supreme concept of civil society, the concept of the police."[40] Law, such as the laws of the *ancien régime,* protected the property of a particular class constellation. There is little that leads Marx to believe that law under the new French and American regimes have done anything other than that. The class constellations might be different, but the function of law, which ideologically is supposed to protect universal rights, in fact is to protect particularistic rights of men in society. Since the French Revolution, it is more specifically bourgeois man's rights that are being protected under the guise of the legitimizing universalism of natural, universal rights. Whereas the old society preserved a political character-istic under the monarchy and feudal systems, that is, "the vital functions and conditions of civil society remained political ... the political revolution ... *abolished the political character of civil society.* It dissolved civil society into its basic elements, on the one hand *individuals,* and on the other the *material and cultural elements* which formed the life experience and the civil situation of these individuals."[41]

Particularistic and egoistic man in civil society now becomes the foundation of the political state, rather than the state giving civil society a political character that permitted civil society to overcome pure egoism. The "rights of man," that is, the rights of "bourgeois man," are rooted in his particularistic egoism and thus cannot possibly be universal. Natural man now appears to be this nonpoliticized man. Thus, Bauer's talk about Jews not being able to enjoy the rights of man because they are so attached to their own particularism is nonsensical. *On the Jewish Question* is one of Marx's earliest writings. He is still a Young Hegelian writing in Hegelian categories. But as his writing progresses, he develops a theory of historical materialism. He will no longer write at length about rights because they fit under a larger category that is the superstructure of society. This includes not only rights but also law, religion, and the state itself. The base, or the determining aspect of social and political life, is the relationship between humans and nature, that is, the processes by which humans mold nature to meet their needs (the technological forces of production) and the social relations that are generated by these processes. So long as there are classes created by these social relations, "rights" can never be universal. They can only protect those classes that are dominant in this process. Under these conditions, rights only appear to be emancipatory. They are in fact an ideological mystification, part and parcel of the system of domination. And in the absence of class, there would be a system of genuine equality in which people's basic needs would be met and in which people would be free to direct their lives in multiple and intrinsically rewarding directions. There would be no more need for the concept of rights than there was in Bentham's system. Just like Bentham, Marx saw the concept of universal or human rights as not merely meaningless in any rational sense but as an impediment to the achievement of a good and fulfilling life for most human beings.

It is not without irony that Bruno Bauer was using that very concept of rights to exclude Jews.

CONCLUSION

The idea of human rights, that is to say a right that every human being enjoyed simply by virtue of being human, was first elaborated in the West in the seventeenth and eighteenth centuries. It was advanced by the Diggers in their struggle to claim the very necessities of life. It was given its initial philosophical form by Hobbes, who claimed that every person did indeed enjoy a natural and inalienable right to life. But while the Diggers had an affinity with the Levellers, who were pushing for political democratization, Hobbes argued that, given the real nature of human beings, the right to life could best be ensured by political absolutism.

Locke expanded the notion of rights, giving priority to property rights and even subsuming the right to life under them. In his defense of the Bloodless Revolution, he also gave priority to rule by the legislature. But he gave no sign of opening up the political process across the class as the Levellers in Cromwell's army had been demanding a half-century earlier. Locke's rights were thus associated with constitutional government as opposed to Hobbes's absolute government, but not with the more democratic form demanded by the Levellers.

It is not until Rousseau that natural or human rights were associated with such strong democratic conceptions, but in Rousseau these rights were exchanged for civil rights. This exchange, coupled with Rousseau's absolutist and unitary conception of the General Will, risked a communitarianism that is not congenial to human rights. This ambiguity in Rousseau was picked up by two of his contemporaries in the philosophical world, Burke and Hume, whose theoretical frameworks are antithetical to the very idea of rationally grounded natural or human rights. These are writers who are very congenial to later conservative thinking in the West. But the liberal systematizer of moral, political, and jurisprudential thought, Jeremy Bentham, also took aim at the notion. Finally, Marx attempted to show that what went by the name "rights of man" in fact amounted to very particularistic and egoistic claims of one class in civil society to maintain its possessions against others. He felt that he had unmasked this rights discourse as an ideological legitimizing tool for class domination.

Thus, by the mid-nineteenth century, the attempts to rationally ground human rights had come under conservative, liberal (utilitarian), and Marxist attack. But that did not mark the end of the proclamation of human rights and of the assault on them.

CHAPTER 2

SOME TWENTIETH-CENTURY
REFLECTIONS ON HUMAN RIGHTS

AN UNFRIENDLY ENVIRONMENT

The one hundred years from the middle of the nineteenth century to the middle of the twentieth were characterized by much domination and deliberately inflicted human suffering. True, slavery had been abolished in the United States, but African Americans experienced severe discrimination and even death at the hands of lynch mobs and law enforcement officers. True, the franchise was expanded in most of the Western industrial countries in terms of both social class and gender. But African Americans were largely excluded in the United States, either through state laws incorporating grandfather clauses or literacy requirements, or just by physical intimidation. Imperialism and colonization characterized this period. So did extreme exploitation of working people. Unions were formed, but in many countries the struggle to organize was met with both physical and ideological repression. Few North Americans know that May Day commemorates not something that occurred in Russia but, rather, in Chicago, Illinois, in 1886. Few know that it was related to the struggle for the eight-hour day and that people who were not even there were hanged because police officers were killed when a bomb was thrown when they tried to break up the rally. Labor unions were formed, but in Europe there was repression of the organizers. In the United States the repression was particularly bloody. The formation of the National Guard in the United States has its roots in the suppression of the struggles of labor.[1]

Lest one get the impression that history has been linear in terms of human rights, the first half of the twentieth century left even more to be desired than the last half of the nineteenth in terms of suffering and domination. Not only did we continue to have imperialism and colonialism; in addition, we saw the rise of totalitarianism, genocide, and world wars that did not discriminate in terms of weapons or civilian/military distinctions.

Absolute monarchies and dictatorships have existed as long as human history. It is democracy within nation-states, as opposed to the small Greek polis, that is new. But totalitarians claimed to be acting in the name of the "people," the *volk,* or the proletariat. Totalitarians went well beyond Hobbes's Leviathan, which extracted absolute political obedience but left realms of other human activity relatively free of political intrusion. Hobbes wanted to *pacify* people politically. Totalitarians tried to *mobilize* them into very active political support roles. They left no realm of civil society free from state/party penetration and domination. All activity, from the family through economic and educational institutions, had to demonstrate fidelity to the political order in active ways. Modern technology was crucial for totalitarianism. It opened up the possibility of much more effective surveillance, repression, propagation of ideology, and effective elimination of opponents and scapegoats. It was not possible for all Germans to attend the spectacular mass rallies of the Nazi party. But it was possible for the mesmerizing voice of the Nazi propagandist Joseph Goebels to penetrate into every German home over the radio. Family, civil and economic organizations, party, and government all had one supreme purpose under totalitarian regimes. For the Nazis, there were no valid rights that could be claimed by German citizens against the German state. The very act of enunciating such a claim could place one in a concentration camp or into the hands of a torturer or executioner. In the Soviet Union, such enunciation could earn one entry into a mental hospital or a hard labor camp from which many never exited alive.[2]

It is interesting that while the Nazi state never used "rights talk," the Soviet state did. The various constitutions of the Soviet Union made reference to political and civil rights as well as to economic and social rights. But a careful reading of both the Constitution of 1936, written during the height of Stalin's reign, and the revised post-Stalinist Constitution of 1977 (as amended in 1988) indicates that the accordance of such rights was conditional on the uncritical acceptance of the supremacy of the party/state. After initially talking about "strengthening the system of people's control," the 1977/88 Constitution goes on to declare the Communist Party to be "the leading and guiding force of Soviet society and the nucleus of its political system, of all state organizations and public organizations."[3]

Soviet practice carried this party role so far that the party became indistinguishable from the state. Those who refused to remain uncritical and who used rights claims to challenge that party role were treated as subversives and counterrevolutionaries.

"Uncritical" is the key concept here, because in no system are political rights accorded unconditionally to those who disobey laws. For example, in the United States, convicted felons lose their rights to vote—forever, in many states—because they have been convicted of violating laws.[4] But in the Soviet Union, a demand to be able to vote for someone other than the party candidate, or an attempt to organize to be able to do so, was itself taken as a violation of law and of obligation to state and society, because the constitution gave the party control over both.

While Nazism cannot be differentiated from Hitler's thinking, we must not conflate Marx's thinking with the empirical situation in the totalitarian Soviet Union. Nowhere does Marx call for such a totalitarian state. Indeed, in *The Civil War in France*, Marx suggests just the opposite. There he is enthusiastic about the decentered, associationist forms of politics that he observed in the 1871 French Commune, and Engels points us to that work if we want to have an understanding of what Marx himself meant by the "dictatorship of the proletariat."[5] Moreover, Marxists were among the first critics of the early authoritarian manifestations of the Russian Revolution (e.g., Rosa Luxemburg and Karl Kautsky) and the full-blown totalitarianism of the Stalinist period (e.g., Leon Trotsky). In fact, the earliest use of the term "totalitarianism" that I can find is in Trotsky's *The Revolution Betrayed*, written in 1936.[6] Thus, the fact that Marx critiqued the conception of the "rights of man" as it was expressed in documents at the end of the eighteenth century did not mean that he or all subsequent Marxists supported totalitarianism.

The twentieth century brought us not only totalitarianism but also genocide on a grand scale. Indeed, there had been many historical precedents. The word genocide refers to the destruction of a culture as well as the physical elimination of a people.[7] Thus, the institution of slavery was genocidal as was the treatment of indigenous people in both North and South America. Prior to the eighteenth-century French Declaration of the Rights of Man and Citizen and U.S. documents, there were many acts of genocide in human history. One might have hoped for human improvement after that century, for the world to become more "civilized." It did not happen that way. Quite the contrary, the outside world seemed to care very little when the Turkish army slaughtered Armenians during World War I.

Hitler is quoted as responding, "Who remembers the Armenians?" when someone on his staff questioned whether or not the outside world would permit the Nazis to destroy the Jews. And it is precisely that slaughter, of Jews, Gypsies, gays, and political opponents, in sheer number and sophistication of organization and technology, which constituted the major genocidal event in history. This experience has had major effects on our general political psyches. The films and photographs of the piles of bodies, of the emaciated survivors of the concentration campus, of the ovens, as well as the Nuremberg trials and recognition of the state of Israel in 1948, have framed our contemporary politics in very profound ways. And new manifestations of it arise every day: the revisionist historians deny that it ever happened or minimize it; Nazi skinheads arise all over Western Europe and the United States; the French are forced to confront the active complicity of their own government and police in the deportations of French Jews to certain death; the Swiss banks are revealed to have accepted and kept wealth stolen by the Nazis from their Jewish victims; Madeleine Albright, when U.S. Secretary of State, is overwhelmed when presented with evidence that while raised as a Catholic she is really of Jewish background and that most of her family perished at the hands of the Nazis in Czechoslovakia.

On and on it goes. There is no comparable international event that has molded our psyches, and caused the international community to make formal proclamations about human rights, the way this destruction of millions of people has.

That is not to say that genocide has stopped. Sometimes it is widely known and the outside world responds, if belatedly; witness Bosnia and Rwanda. Sometimes the outside world knows, or pretends to know, relatively little. For a long time, that was the case with East Timor, where it is estimated that one-third of the population had been killed by the Indonesian military from 1975 to 1999, where there was torture and forced sterilization of women, and where the indigenous language was forbidden (a genocidal measure to destroy a people's culture and identity). In other cases, there is even active complicity of one or more Western democracies, as in the U.S. role in overthrowing the democratic government of Guatemala and installing a military government that has cost the lives of approximately two hundred thousand Guatemalans, mainly highland Indians.

While the Holocaust is indeed a unique event from the point of view of the sheer numbers of people killed, the attempt to wipe out both a culture and all the individuals that comprise it, and the technological and logistical efficiency of the operation, Douglas Porporo is quite correct that there is a danger in viewing it as too unique.[8] If we view it as too unique, we can fail to recognize that the same sort of things, "Holocaust-like" events, are happening in the here and now. Perhaps it is not happening to six million people. But it is still genocide and the sufferings of those affected are no less intense because the numbers are smaller.

The experience of world war also has changed our political universe and psyches. The weapons have been particularly nasty and destructive of life and environment. In World War I, it was poison gasses that inflicted horrible deaths and illness on masses of troops and submarines that spread terror on the high seas. We have already made reference to genocide against the Armenians during that war. In World War II, the terror was even more high-tech. Rockets hit the cities of England. The reciprocation was the firebombing of Dresden. The Japanese delivered untold misery on the people of China and Korea, including massacres of civilians (e.g., Nanjing), forced use of women for the sexual pleasure of their troops, and medical experiments on live and nonanesthetized civilians (the latter also practiced by the Nazis in their concentration camps). And the United States dropped the atomic bomb on two of Japan's most populous cities. In the United States, Japanese Americans lost their property and were herded into camps on the West Coast simply because of their ancestry. Much of Europe, Asia, and North Africa came to resemble Hobbes's state of nature where life was "nasty short, and brutish" during these enormously destructive wars. While sometimes war might have to be fought to stop an assault on human rights—I have no moral doubt that the Third Reich had to be defeated militarily—war itself always entails human rights violations.

HUMAN RIGHTS OFFICIALLY RESTATED

Thus, the combination of world war, totalitarianism, and genocide was an unprecedented assault on any conception of human rights. Obviously, something official had to be said and done about this after World War II was over and Nazism defeated.

Three things were done. First, some of the Nazi leadership was tried in Nuremberg by an ad hoc tribunal of judges from the victorious nations. The charge was "crimes against humanity." Since there was no body of international statutory law or agreed-on documents, the offense was one against a higher but unwritten moral code that should have been known by any reasonable human being. In effect, this was a reliance on the traditional Judeo-Christian concept of

Natural Law. Every person, except those born with mental deficiencies, was supposed to have sufficient reason to be able to grasp the fact that certain things are morally impermissible even if a body of positive law declares them to be permissible or if a contrary order is given by a superior.

Second, the United Nations was created to foster more cooperative and more peaceful international relations. Part of the U.N. structure was an International Court of Justice sitting at the Hague, which was empowered to handle cases of genocide. Third, the United Nations issued official statements on human rights. These were the first such statements to be issued since the French and American documents of the late eighteenth century. The difference is that these statements were issued in the name of a world body and governments had to agree or dissent from them.[9] They were thus intended to represent a consensus of international opinion. Given the experience of the Nazi genocide, reliance on everyone's understanding of general Natural Law/Natural Rights precepts were not enough. Human rights had to be spelled out and proclaimed in the form of written documents.

Since the publication of Karel Vasak's seminal article, "Pour une Troisième Génération des Droits de l'Homme," it has been common, especially in international law circles, to refer to "three generations" of rights articulated by these documents.[10] The first generation of rights are constituted by political and civil rights. These rights had been articulated by the eighteenth-century documents as well. The second generation is economic, social, and cultural rights. Economic and social rights go beyond the right to private property, and include rights such as that to a job with fair wages, to a decent living, to social security, to the right to paid vacation, and to an equitable distribution of world food supplies in relation to need. Of the eighteenth-century documents, only the French Declaration touches on economic and social rights when it proclaims that taxes should be levied on all citizens in proportion to their means. It is nowhere near as extensive as the 1966 International Covenant on Economic, Social, and Cultural Rights.[11] While the economic and social rights contained therein are extensive, the only cultural rights specified are the rights to education, and the "right of everyone to take part in cultural life."[12]

The third generation of rights, relatively recent in their conceptualization, is what Vasak called "solidarity rights." He enumerated these rights as the rights to development, peace, environment, communication, and common patrimony shared by all humanity (e.g., the oceans). There have already been two declarations of the United

Nations that fall into this category: the 1984 Declaration on the Right of Peoples to Peace and the 1986 Declaration on the Right to Development. For Vasak, the essential characteristic of such rights is that "they can only be realized by all of the actors in the social world: the individual, the state, public and private entities, and the international community. Their realization presupposes that there is a minimum of social consensus at national and international levels for an act of solidarity, indeed upon the recognition that we have such a solidaristic responsibility."[13]

There also are documents that prohibit violations of a single right, deemed especially important given present practices of rights violations. They detail specific dimensions of those violations. These are: the Convention on the Prevention and Punishment of the Crime of Genocide (1951), the Convention on the Elimination of All Forms of Racial Discrimination (1969), the Convention on the Suppression and Punishment of the Crime of Apartheid (1973), the Convention on the Elimination of All Forms of Discrimination Against Women (1979), the Declaration on the Elimination of All Forms of Intolerance and of Discrimination Based on Religion or Belief (1981), and the Convention Against Torture and Other Cruel, Inhuman, or Degrading Treatment or Punishment (1984).

Three of the documents are regarded as the most general and the most crucial. The first specific declaration on human rights (there are brief references in the United Nation's 1945 Charter) is the United Nations Universal Declaration of Human Rights (1948). It refers to political, economic, social, and cultural rights. The crucial concept that underlies it is that of human "dignity." The two others are the previously mentioned 1966 covenant dealing with economic, social, and cultural rights and another covenant of the same year dealing with civil and political rights. These three documents often are referred to as the "International Bill of Rights." Aside from these documents, another agency, the International Labor Office, has issued texts, which are called "conventions," which are important for human rights. Most of these conventions deal with quite specific labor rights, many having to do with work in maritime shipping. But one, the Indigenous Tribal Populations Convention No. 107 (1957 and amended in 1989), is the most thorough consideration of the rights of indigenous peoples.

Aside from the documents inviting the signatures and ratification of all states, there are a number of regional texts, such as those stipulating human rights understandings in Europe, in the Americas, and in Africa. In Europe and the Americas, there are courts that have been established specifically to handle instances of human rights violations that have occurred in those regions. In Africa, a special court composed of African jurists has been entrusted with handling of trials of those accused of participating in the Rwandan massacre.

Thus, it would appear that there is a world consensus on "human rights." It is true that virtually all governments in the world have signed and ratified one or more human rights agreement. They agree that there is something called human rights. And some of the agreements, such as the Convention on the Rights of the Child, have been ratified by almost all (191) nations. But there still persists disagreement on what should constitute those human rights. For example, some—most notably the British political philosopher Maurice Cranston—argued back in the 1960s that the list of rights should be as short as possible, because the more extended the list was, the more trivial it would appear and the less seriously it would be taken.[14] Cranston also wanted to keep the list confined to political and civil rights, claiming that the economic and social rights could not as easily be translated into law and that they often applied to partial segments of humanity, so were thus not universalistic as human rights must be. He treats with particular ridicule and disdain the claim that workers have a human right to periodic holidays with pay (which would be codified in Article VII, section d of the 1966 Covenant on Economic, Social, and Cultural Rights mentioned below) because it applies only to the "*employé* class," and would be impossible to apply in poorer, less industrialized countries.[15]

In fact, despite President Franklin Delano Roosevelt's championing of a "Second Bill of Rights" guaranteeing economic security in his 1944 State of the Union Address, and Eleanor Roosevelt's strong support for such rights when she represented the United States on the U.N.'s Commission of Human Rights during the Truman Administration, in the 1950s the Cold War had begun in earnest and the political climate within the United States had changed. As early as 1951, the unease of some Western governments with the social and economic rights articulated in the 1948 Declaration and disagreements with the Communist Bloc caused those trying to negotiate a more legally binding covenant to decide that it would be best to propose two covenants, separating the political/civil and economic/social/cultural texts. Thus, by 1966, Cranston was voicing the views of many political leaders in the West, the United States included.[16] When the drafts of the two separate covenants were ready for member governments to sign in that year, the United States resisted the signing of the Covenant on Economic, Social, and Cultural Rights.

Eleven years later, in 1977, President Carter did sign on. But it has been bottled up in the U.S. Senate, which must ratify it, ever since. Indeed, since the "Reagan Revolution" and the advent of neoliberalism, the sentiment in the United States to limit human rights to political and civil ones has grown ever stronger. The same hostility toward economic and social rights was exhibited by the Conservative British governments in their attitudes toward European human rights agreements, a point to which we shall return in Chapter 3.

The Soviet Union and the countries of Eastern Europe had already recognized many of the economic and social rights within their own constitutions and practices—certainly establishing a much better record on these than on political and civic rights—and the newly independent countries of the third world were particularly interested in the international distribution implications of the covenant. After so many years of colonial domination, they felt that they had that much coming.

Thus, while there at least seems to be broad agreement that there is something called human rights, there is not an agreement on what constitutes that thing. The disagreement is not only over the length of human rights lists, or whether they can be economic and social as well as political and civil, but also over who are the holders of these rights; that is, can collectivities as well as individuals claim human rights? We will be coming back to this issue.

But if there is broad popular and official agreement that there is something called human rights, there still persist denials that there can be any basis, or any rational basis, to it. The distinction is important. There are indeed still Burkean conservatives (e.g., Daniel Boorstin) who argue that such universalized concepts are meaningless because rights, like democracy, are contingent on culture and tradition. They are not an export product. Other conservatives argue that human rights are inconsistent with the principle of national sovereignty that they prize. Then there are still Marxists who argue that human rights are not only empty abstractions but also that they continue to form a vital part of the ideological superstructure of capitalist domination. They are not at all surprised that the U.S. government would accept the principle of civil and political rights, but reject those of economic and social rights, except for the right to private property for individuals and corporations. Then there are other schools such as postmodern deconstructionists and critical legal theorists (with the exception of Roberto Unger)[17] that present an objection similar to that of the more traditional Marxists but with deeper cultural and legal analyses than traditional Marxists offer.

There are, however, others who accept human rights, but do not offer, or indeed reject, rationalist arguments for them. The latter, those who actually reject rational arguments and offer other kinds of arguments for human rights, are usually referred to as "antifoundationalists." Indeed, human rights can be advanced on nonrationalist bases from a number of perspectives.

NONRATIONALIST GROUNDS FOR ACCEPTING HUMAN RIGHTS

I want to make clear here that when I use the expression "nonrationalist," I do not mean to imply that these grounds are "irrational" in the sense that they fly in the face of reason and thus should be dismissed. I only mean to say that reason, in terms of an elaborated secular argument based on absolutist notions of truth and a fixed discernible human nature, are not the basis of the commitment. Nor am I attempting to establish a Platonic hierarchy here where the rationalist automatically trumps the nonrationalist. There are in fact several possible bases for nonrationalist approaches that strike me as eminently "reasonable" without being "rationalist" as I am using the term. I will discuss these under two categorical headings, atheoretical (faith and belief) and theoretical (nonfoundationalist).

Atheoretical Grounds: Faith and Belief

One of these grounds is religious faith. In fact, this constitutes one of the oldest commitments to human rights. It will be recalled that both Winstanley and Locke made reference to humans being God's creation. In Winstanley, rights claims are made to the necessities of life and others are expected to honor those rights claims because the claimants are God's creatures and thus as deserving of survival as those who possess more than the necessities. For Locke, as has already been pointed out, there is an obligation to attempt to preserve all that can be preserved of God's creatures, but he stops short of agreeing with Winstanley that this obligation is the necessary flip side of natural rights. Locke finesses the issue by denying that there is any real scarcity and thus any possible claim on the property of others, regardless of how much they possess and how little others possess.

One of the strongest commitments to human rights today, in both word and deed, comes from segments of the organized religious community. At the theological level, Liberation Theology—especially as developed within the context of Latin America by both indigenous and European priests—offers us a good example of human rights being incorporated into a religious conception. Here, distributive justice is a key element of human rights. It is seen through the "preferential option for the poor," going back to Christ himself. At issue are both social and political rights, the abject poverty of the multitude and the riches of the few supported by civilian and military structures that repress any attempt to change the status quo. Faith in the message of Jesus Christ and many of his very early followers, and bearing witness to the misery that human beings experience in our own time, is enough to justify a commitment to human rights.[18]

While the Liberation Theologians write about the commitment to social justice and human rights, there are also Catholic Church-run human rights organizations in Central America. Because of direct contacts with specific communities through local churches, they often have been the most reliable sources of documentation of kidnappings, torture, and killings in El Salvador and Guatemala. Both in regard to the theological work of the Liberation Theologians and the practical work done by the human rights groups in the field, this faith-based human rights work has been challenged by a conservative turn in the Catholic Church under Pope John Paul II and by a right-wing Christian fundamentalism that preaches obedience to authority and salvation in the afterlife. These fundamentalists have been especially powerful in Guatemala. Some of the worst human rights violations took place under the presidency of General Rios Montt, a right-wing fundamentalist whose party is at present the most powerful one in Guatemala.

But not all non-Catholic Christians, and not even all fundamentalists, are so hostile to political as well as social and economic human rights. Witness for Peace, which sent people to stand between the U.S.-supported Contras and the Sandinistas in Nicaragua, and that still actively attempts to aid the poor in Central America, is made up of people adhering to a mixture of Christian persuasions, including some fundamentalists. The Sanctuary movement in the United States, which offered sanctuary to people who had fled Central America but whom the immigration service wanted to deport back to extremely dangerous situations, enjoyed the participation of people of a variety of religions. In San Francisco, a synagogue was involved in that movement. In the United States, churches and religious movements have been deeply involved in the domestic civil rights movement, in opposition to the U.S. government's role in oppression in Central America, and in opposition to apartheid in South Africa. This has made U.S. churches and religious movements among the most important centers of the struggles for human rights.

Of course, such activity is not confined to the United States. Even as the Dutch Reformed Church supported apartheid, many of the other South African churches struggled against it. Next to Nelson Mandela, perhaps the best-known South African fighter against apartheid has been a clergyman, Bishop Desmond Tutu. And Bishop Belo of East Timor won the 1996 Nobel Peace Prize for his work in trying to tell the world about the genocide being perpetrated against the East Timorese by the Indonesian army. The Bah'ai people have supported the rights of others even as they are persecuted in Iran. Some Islamic women in Malaysia and elsewhere challenge the interpretation of Islam by men as they fight for rights of women in their society and use Qur'anic interpretation in their cause.[19]

Human rights and religion are very closely interwoven in today's world, even if adherents of religions, of both Western and non-Western origin, are not always friends of human rights. Religious faith is one possible basis for adhering to the idea of human rights, and it has stimulated some very powerful movements acting out this commitment in practice.

But one does not have to be religious to believe in something. One can as easily be a humanist and believe that every person has certain rights just by virtue of being a human being. One need not add to that "God's creation" or any theological trapping. A number of years ago, I was on a panel dealing with human rights with a colleague from another department in my university who also works in the area of human rights. At one point in the discussion, he said, "You either believe in it [human rights] or you don't." Such belief can be the end of it. While theorists can start from a position of belief and try to give rational grounding and elaboration to the belief, it is perfectly valid to hold the belief and try to convert others to it without any such elaboration. Given a choice between theorizing but no action, and purely faith or belief-based action, I would much prefer the latter.[20]

But as valid and important as faith and belief-based commitments to human rights are, many people in the present era do not hold to them. In the West, at least, this is not a sacral age, and religions give very conflicting messages both internally and between different religions. Moreover, if we are seriously to take up the challenge of the often very good arguments posed by the theoretical critics of the concept of human rights, we must have some grounding beyond faith and belief. If we don't, the dialogue concerning human rights will just stop and it will become a matter of dogma. Our understanding of human rights will be impoverished. And, as those three great critics of human rights—Burke, Marx, and Bentham—have demonstrated in their own lives through parliamentary, revolutionary, and reformist action, respectively, theory no more precludes action than does faith or belief. It can convince us that we have good reasons as well as good intuitions and intentions to struggle for something we deem to be important for the good life. Since the aim of human rights struggles is to achieve human rights-driven policies at both national and international levels—the latter especially entailing agreements that cross cultural and religious lines—there is not only a theoretical interest here but also a very pragmatic political one in attempts to ground human rights in an adequate conceptual framework. We may never find the final grounding for all time. I don't think that we will. But the search and continuing dialogue are crucial.

Let us next turn to some secular attempts to ground human rights without using a rationalist foundation.

Theoretical Non-Foundationalist Grounds

Three nonfoundationalist theoretical approaches to grounding human rights are particularly interesting. I will refer to them as sentimental, consensus, and strategic.

Sentimental Theory (Richard Rorty)[21]

The philosopher Richard Rorty reaches back to that antagonist of the rationalist rights theorizing of the contract theorists, David Hume, to make an antirationalist argument. He accepts the label of "antirationalist" in the sense that he denies "the existence of morally relevant transcultural facts." But, he adds, one need not be irrationalist in the sense of ceasing to "make one's web of belief as coherent, and as perspicuously structured as possible."[22]

Rorty agrees with Hume that morality is more properly felt than reasoned. He rejects any notion of a fixed human nature, any descriptions of human beings that are transhistorical. He also rejects the idea that we have to search for some sort of transcendental truth in order to know how to behave morally, an assumption made and argued for by philosophers in the Western tradition from Plato to the Enlightenment. Rorty is a pragmatist. Thus, the issue for him is how to get a hold on human history so that one can produce the kind of humane utopia dreamed of by some of the Enlightenment thinkers. It seems to him that the only prominent thinker of that epoch who offers us a fruitful way to think about the rights issue is not one of the rationalists but David Hume.

Rorty does not deny that, at the time the Enlightenment rationalists wrote, theirs was perhaps the best way to think about issues such as equality, democracy, freedom, and rights. But two things have happened since then. First, we have seen that human beings are more malleable than the rationalists thought they were two hundred years ago. Second, humans have experienced the enormous amount of suffering referred to above.

The problem for this pragmatist philosopher is to identify why people behave differently and badly toward those who are not in their group or community (e.g., Nazis and Jews, Serbian Bosnians and Moslem Bosnians) and to appeal to them to behave well. For Rorty, the task is not one of looking for some Platonic or Kantian truth that can rationally be taught to others who will then respect other people. He argues (without telling us how he knows this to be true) that the difference between us and other animal species is not that we know things while they merely feel, but rather that "We can feel *for each other* to a much greater extent than they can."[23]

The quality that we must rely on is therefore moral sentiment. We must recognize that in Western history—and in much of the world still today—identity was bound up with who you were not. The moral community was thus constrained. It was constituted either by family, clan, or tribe. It was risky to extend oneself beyond this, for one's very identity was at stake.[24]

The task, and for the pragmatist a practical task is inseparable from conceptualization, is to appeal to people's sentiments rather than their rationality. Overcoming insecurities and building on sympathy for others is the key to establishing a world governed by human rights. Stories of human suffering, like that of the Holocaust, or slavery, or the genocide of Indians, or Bosnia or Rwanda or East Timor, are more likely to be effective in establishing a human rights respecting world than any naturalistic or rationalist argument for obligations that we have to each other.

In place of the old question of moral education, "Why should I be moral?," which would anticipate a response based on Platonic, Aristotelian, or Kantian rationality, Rorty proposes another question and another set of answers. The question he proposes is, "Why should I care about a stranger, a person who is no kin to me, a person whose habits I find disgusting?" He argues that the traditional answer, "Because kinship and custom are morally irrelevant, irrelevant to the obligations imposed by the membership in the same species," has never been convincing. This is because it begs the issue of whether being a member of the species is indeed equivalent to closer kinship, and it is vulnerable to Nietzsche's criticism that only the minds of slaves—and Rorty adds intellectuals or priests—who have a vested interest in such universalistic propositions would accept such an answer. He goes on, "A better sort of answer is the sort of long, sad, sentimental story which begins 'Because this is what it is like to be in her situation—to be far from home among strangers,' or 'Because she might become your daughter-in-law,' or 'Because her mother would grieve for her.' "[25] These words, appealing to the sentiment, have had more effect on inducing the powerful to be more tolerant and "even cherishing" of the powerless than any rational arguments. He sees in the modern world a rapid progress of sentiments that has led to the human rights phenomenon being " 'a fact of the world.' "[26]

But, alas, one may ask the pragmatist, who is as concerned with effectiveness as with conceptualization, if the appeal to either sentiment or to reason has deterred this century from becoming perhaps the cruelest in recorded history. How *does* one confer security to the insecure? How *does* one, by appealing to sentiment, get people victimized at one point in history to desist from inflicting the same cruelty on others at another point? The irony of Bosnia, which was very much in Rorty's mind when he gave his Oxford lecture, is just that the Bosnian Serbs delivered unto the Moslems what the Germans and the Croats had delivered unto the Serbs during World War II. Direct experience with suffering sometimes seems to have a hardening effect on the victims who are determined that it will never happen to them again, "Never Again!," and leads them to adopt uncompromising and often very cruel postures toward "others" who are seen as possible threats. Even daughters-in-law of a different ethnic background were not safe in Sarajevo.

There is something attractive about appealing to the heart as well as to the head, to feeling as well as reason. But if we give up totally on "the existence of morally relevant transcultural facts," we are hard-pressed to address those whose sentiments have in fact been channeled into very cruel directions, either through elements within their own cultures or through the manipulations of persecutory regimes such as that of the Nazis.

Consensus Theory (Jack Donnelly)

This approach is taken by Jack Donnelly, whose interpretation of Locke we have already discussed. Donnelly offers what he calls an "analytic or descriptive" theory of human rights. He writes that "this theory does not provide a comprehensive or philosophical account of human rights. It seeks principally to describe and explain the way human rights actually work in contemporary social relations."[27]

Thus, rather than offering any kind of view of human nature the way the contract theorists did, Donnelly offers us a theory based on social practices involving the concept of human rights. He argues, "Human rights specify a structure of social practices to achieve a particular realization of human potential."[28] Just as Burke looked at the rights that existed within any given society, Donnelly looks at the rights practices that already exist at the international level and accepts them—or at least those that he finds acceptable—without the application of any other criteria.

The rights exist above all because they are found in internationally agreed-upon documents. Those documents stipulate that human rights arise from "the inherent dignity of the human person." A denial of that dignity strips the human individual of that quality that is uniquely human and impedes the development of the person according to his or her choices. To repeat, human rights are not God-given, as Locke and Winstanley would have it.[29] They are imbedded in the concept of human dignity and what is required to live a life of dignity, and in social practices within culture, politics, and economies.

Donnelly refuses to give criteria for those practices, and argues that this "substantive 'emptiness'" of his theory is intentional.[30] Given this, some of the positions that he does take leave him open to the charge of arbitrariness. For example, he argues that human rights can only apply to individuals, not to groups. Why? Because they arise out of Western liberalism, beginning with Locke, which insisted on the individual as the unit of all rights. But this is a philosophical position on which there is no international or universal consensus on which Donnelly can rely. Indeed, there is much arguing for group as well as individual rights today both in the West and in the non-West.[31] The U.N. documents have not put an end to this disagreement.

Donnelly's whole point was to develop a theory that did not have to deal with these issues because it could remain at the descriptive level where a consensus was self-justifying. In other words, it could beg the issue of a rational, normative foundation by making reference to concrete practices. But when Donnelly argues against group or collective human rights, he does so on the authority of the Western tradition of human rights going back to Locke. There are two ironies in this. First, there is not a consensus on the issue, and for Donnelly to be consistent with his theory he has to argue from the position of consensus. Second, he valorizes the Western rights tradition going back to Locke, but his rejection of Lockean rationalistic naturalism has rendered the premises of that tradition useless to him. While much of his book is extremely interesting, theoretically he ends up with no grounding at all, a sort of internationalist Burkean who can at best make judgments on human rights on the basis of "just prejudices" gained from a Western liberal tradition that he has at least partially undercut.

Strategic Theory (Andrew Levine)

Andrew Levine argues that human rights are a product of contradictions within liberal democratic thought and the nature of liberal democratic institutions. The contradiction in liberal democratic thought is that on the one hand there is a commitment to "respect for persons, for human dignity as such,"[32] which would imply both certain political rights and minimal levels of material existence requisite for the real practice of citizenship, while on the other the underlying notions of freedom and interest in liberalism are those of monadic beings whose primary task in life is to maximize self-interest.

Here, although Levine does not refer to Locke himself, we are indeed back at the tension within Locke's thinking, the prescription that we must be concerned about the preservation of all God's human creatures, on the one hand, and the absolutist, individualist notion of individual property rights, on the other. The latter proved so strong in Locke's thinking that he refrained from arguing that individual property rights had to be limited by an obligation based on solidarity within the human species.

For Levine, exactly the same problem persists within liberal democracy today. While, on the one hand, modern liberalism asserts its commitment to the dignity of every human being, on the other, human beings are instrumentalized by an "atomic individualism."[33] Such instrumental atomization is inconsistent with any conception of human dignity.

Levine points to liberalism's attachment to "free markets" as an illustration of how liberal democracy is incapable of thinking about individuals in any way other than an instrumental one. Working people become no more than "a determinant exchange value." He writes:

> Historically committed to a view of human beings as acquisitive, rational egoists and therefore, at least tendentially, to atomic individualism, liberal democrats who rely on markets as institutional embodiments of liberal democratic ideals need the concept of (human) rights to save (free, self-interested) human beings from themselves, and thereby to maintain and promote human dignity. Without such rights, a free society of "rational economic agents" threatens to become a society of things, of instrumentalities; a collection of atomic individuals for whom everything and everyone are means only. Rights claims—that is, claims for inalienable (human) rights—counter this threat. Inalienable

rights *limit* markets. By definition, inalienable rights cannot be bought or sold. Neither are they, in general, subject to other market criteria.[34]

But the fact that liberals might "need" rights for this purpose does not make any more consistent a theory that holds to an atomic/ instrumental view of human beings, on the one hand, and a concept of inherent human dignity with the social and economic requisites of that dignity, on the other. Nor can any recourse to consensus, on the order of Donnelly's, solve the problem. There is an incoherence of rights claims within the framework of a basically individualistic view of human nature.

Nevertheless, given the present set of liberal economic and political institutions, Levine sees human rights as providing a reference point for criticism of institutional effects. And he sees no other device that can do this under present institutional and ideological conditions. Thus, for purely pragmatic reasons, it would not make any sense to scrap the idea of human rights. The consequences of that would be to give the negative effects of liberal institutions even less constrained play. As a democratic socialist, he does, however, look forward to a time when there would be a different set of institutions that would promote greater solidarity and call for a reconceptualization of human rights more congruent with the conception of human dignity and human solidarity.

Levine's book was published in 1981. That was the year that Ronald Reagan assumed the presidency of the United States. Since that time, the logic and exigencies of "the market" have been imposed on the world with greater intensity than at any time since the 1930s. One can always say that without the conception of human rights the situation would be even worse. But the fact is that the human rights in the international documents that are intended to advance the causes of solidarity and equality have proved to be a very weak bulwark indeed against the global onslaught of privatization, free markets, and the dismantling of public services. If this is the case, one must question whether or not it makes sense to hold on to a concept that one is convinced has no solid foundation anyway. From a purely strategic point of view, one might have to give up on human rights and agree with Marx and Bentham that the concept is ideologically more useful for purposes of domination than it is for purposes of emancipation.

Among the three nonfoundationalist formulations we have been discussing, only Rorty gives us criteria for human rights. The one constant about human beings is that they can suffer and empathize with others who suffer. This observation alone is sufficient to justify a concept such as human rights, the aim of which is to minimize suffering and cruelty by an appeal to feelings.

RATIONALIST GROUNDS FOR ACCEPTING HUMAN RIGHTS

Just as in the case of antifoundationalism, there are a variety of rationalist grounds that have been proposed for accepting human rights. There are theories that try to ground human rights in freedom and agency, in equality, in needs, and in discursive inclusiveness. Since there is much more literature on rights of this kind than of the antifoundationalist variety, and since there is considerable overlap in the above categories, the discussion of it will be admittedly selective, quite schematic, but hopefully insightful.

Freedom and Agency

Theories based on freedom and agency offer us an ontological view of the human being. This is to say that they try to give us a "thicker" description of what it means to be a human being. The contract theorists were the first in the Western tradition to build theories around freedom and agency. The act of contracting was itself a manifestation of this uniquely human quality of freedom and purposiveness. Kant built his rationalist moral theory around such freedom and purposiveness.

While Jack Donnelly claimed to offer only a nonfoundationalist and descriptive theory of human rights, in fact he relied heavily on the word "dignity," which appears repeatedly in the U.N. documents. But to the philosopher Alan Gewirth, "dignity" is far too vague a term to offer much theoretical purchase. Dignity does not precede action. Rather, "there is a direct route from the worth of the agent's ends to the worth or dignity of the agent himself."[35]

What Gewirth calls the "objects of human rights" are the conditions that are necessary for purposive or willed human action. This grounding in the objects of human rights gives human rights their justification and distinguishes them from other rights claims.

Gewirth offers five reasons for so grounding human rights. First, the conditions for purposive action are supremely important to human beings. Second, they are directly connected to morality; it would be difficult to conceive of morality without willed action, and willed action without its conditions. Third, they are more specific and less disputable than a concept like dignity. Fourth, this approach emphasizes that the very reason for rights is to ensure people of a moral status. Finally, it offers a proof that there are rights because every human agent *must* admit that there are necessary conditions to action.[36] Gewirth does not outright reject the concept of "dignity." It is simply too vague to stand by itself as a grounding for human rights. But conceived of as something that one brings on herself by her intentional acts, Gewirth argues that dignity becomes an active and important concept. It becomes connected to very concrete conditions without which a person cannot be said to have dignity.

But there are risks to approaching rights through freedom and agency. An ontology of freedom and agency can become extremely individuated and even solipsistic. This is the case in theories as divergent as the early existentialism of Jean-Paul Sartre, particularly in *Being and Nothingness,* or in the implicit ontologies of such radical individualists on the right wing of the political spectrum as Ayn Rand, Milton Friedman, or Friedrich von Hayek.

But such an ontological view could also be extended to *collective* self-determination. If it is, it runs into two problems for human rights. The first is the problem of communalism that we saw in Rousseau. The community's will might be very different from the will of one or more of its members. If it is, and if it prevails, does this constitute a violation of the freedom and agency of the dissenter? If the minority dissenter holds a veto power by virtue of her rights, does this violate the freedom and agency of the other members? Consensus appears to be a way out. Under this conception of decision making, we willfully enter into a relationship *in order to* reach an agreement that might not be exactly what we would have wanted when we started. Our freedom and agency gives priority to the relationship and to the process over a fixed prior willed position. Unlike Rousseau's General Will, it need not be the "best" policy in any other sense than that on which we can agree. It will have no more transcendental truth value than the ability to hold the community together in a way that is normatively acceptable to its members.

The other, but related, problem attached to viewing the human being through an ontology of freedom and agency is the representational system through which such freedom and agency is expressed in most contemporary democracies. Rousseau rejected such representation as inadequate to the task. Andrew Levine and a number of other contemporary critics make the same objection today that, rather than encouraging freedom and agency, contemporary representative institutions, while better than dictatorships, nevertheless pacify, reify, or, in Sartre's term, "serialize" people. In other words, while offering the illusion of freedom and agency, they in fact discourage them. Freedom and agency then become depoliticized self-interested activity, the kind Hobbes's sovereign could have easily tolerated. Politically, we only want the government to leave us alone in our personal freedom and agency (Isaiah Berlin's "negative liberties")[37] and the right to vote periodically in elections. At the extreme, we come back full circle to the optimistic individualism that sees the right to exercise freedom and agency over private property and the choice of commodities, and to be protected in that exercise, as the key human right.

My attempt here is not to discredit the ontological view of human beings as free agents. It is merely to indicate that there are pitfalls and that one can go in a variety of directions with it. It is, however, probably more philosophically challenging than "human dignity." But it also may be politically much more problematic.

Equality

In his book *Taking Rights Seriously*, the legal philosopher Ronald Dworkin contends that anyone who does take rights seriously must do so on the basis of either equality, or dignity, or both. He writes:

> The institution of rights against the Government is not a gift of God, or an ancient ritual, or a national sport. It is a complex and trouble-some practice that makes the Government's job of securing the general benefit more difficult and more expensive, and it would be a frivolous and wrongful practice unless it served some point. Anyone who professes to take rights seriously, and who praises our Government for respecting them, must have a sense of what that point is. He must accept, at the minimum, one or both of two important ideas. The first is the vague but powerful idea of human dignity. This idea, associated with Kant, but defended by philosophers of different schools, supposes that there are ways of treating a man that are inconsistent with recognizing him as a full member of the human community, and holds that such treatment is profoundly unjust.
>
> The second is the more familiar idea of political equality. This supposes that the weaker members of a political community are entitled to the same concern and respect of their government as the more powerful members have secured for themselves, so that if some men have freedom of decision whatever the effect on the general good, then all men must have the same freedom.[38]

In this segment of his work, Dworkin begs off from elaborating on these two concepts. When the elaboration does come, however, it is not devoted to that "vague but powerful idea of human dignity" but, rather, to equality. Equality, Dworkin tells us, has to do with the distribution of goods, opportunities, and liberties. He distinguishes between two different rights that might be understood by the liberal principle that says that each person has an equal right to concern and respect when it comes to such distribution. The first is what he calls the "right to equal treatment," by which he means equality of result in the form each person having the same goods and opportunities. This, he points out, has been accepted by the courts in the United States when it comes to voting power—one person, one vote.[39] Of course, it has not been accepted when it comes to distribution of goods.

The second understanding is what he calls "the right to treatment as an equal." This he defines as "the right to equal concern and respect in the political decision about how these goods and opportunities are to be distributed."[40] This means that everyone's interest must be taken into account, for example, that if people are injured by a proposed policy, that injury must be entered into the calculation. This latter understanding, within which Dworkin *may* feel that he has subsumed "dignity," is the right that he holds must be taken as fundamental under the liberal conception of equality. The former conception of equality, that of equal treatment, is one of the special cases that must be justified by a more fundamental principle, such as equal political representation in a democracy.

An interesting aspect to Dworkin's writing is his explicit rejection of Benthamite utilitarianism on the basis that it does not really protect political equality, that only a theory that accepts a concept of rights can protect equality. As will be recalled from our discussion of Bentham, that earlier theorist of jurisprudence rejected the idea of any rights outside of law. He argued that a good system of legislation would incorporate considerations of pain and pleasure of everyone and thus more effectively come to an optimal societal happiness. Rights would only serve to negate the greatest happiness principle by privileging unreasonable and unjustifiable claims on such a system.

Dworkin has two criticisms of Bentham's system. First, it gives the government too much power. Bentham's schema would seem to leave no room for law breaking in the form of civil disobedience. Dworkin argues that this needs to be tolerated in a liberal society. It is a way that rights get advanced. Rights are "constructed," they are not "natural" in the sense of falling from God or one set rational principle established once and for all.[41] Laws do in fact violate rights on occasion. On those occasions, civil disobedience is good for the society. We can perhaps understand what Dworkin is getting at best by considering Rosa

Parks's refusal to go to the back of the bus in Birmingham, Alabama. That refusal, which was a violation of the law, was good for American society. But where is the room for that kind of advancement of rights in Bentham's utilitarianism? If all rights were imbedded in law, and it was against the law for Rosa Parks to sit in the front of the bus, she had no right to sit there and thus deserved to be punished by the state.

The second reason that Dworkin rejects Benthamite utilitarianism is that it is deceptive in appearance. It looks like it is egalitarian in the sense of taking everyone's interests into account. In fact, he claims, it takes no account of the difference between "personal preference" and "external preference." External preferences, if I understand Dworkin, are not simply what I want but, rather, what I want for others. The example of the difference between the two kinds of preference that he offers is of a white law school applicant who prefers a policy of segregation because it improves his own chances of getting into the law school (a personal preference) OR because it keeps African Americans out and he is opposed to racial mixture (an external preference).[42]

Of course, neither of these preferences respect the principle of equality. But Dworkin's point is that utilitarianism fails to be egalitarian because it cannot find a way of distinguishing between preferences that are based on people's wishes for themselves and preferences that are reflective of what they want for other people, which often can be very negative. Therefore, Dworkin feels that he has shown the one form of liberalism that rejects the concept of rights to be incapable of protecting the principle of equality. In his view, only a rights-based theory can do so. Since he always speaks from inside liberalism, he does not discuss the possibility of rights-based nonliberal theories that might defend the principal of equality as well or better than liberal theories do. But then they might not respect the tight dichotomy that he draws between the "the right to treatment as an equal" and the "right to equal treatment," and indeed they might not find it satisfactory to privilege the "I want for myself" individual over people who might be altruistic and want *good* things for others, for example, white people who might want equality rather than discrimination for African Americans.

It is important to note that Dworkin writes from two traditional perspectives. The first is Western legalism. The second is Western individualistic liberalism, which gives equally distributed political rights priority over economic or social rights, which might have redistributive consequences. The hold of these traditions is less evident in the work of those theorists who approach the subject of rights through the concept of needs.

Needs

A significant number of theorists have come to look at human rights through the lens of human needs. Among the most prominent are Christian Bay, Henry Shue, and Johan Galtung.

Bay's use of "needs" as the basis of rights is particularly interesting because, while he consistently relied on the concept of needs, the position that he began with is radically different from the position that he ended up with. The book that Bay is best known for is *The Structure of Freedom*, first published in 1958. As the title indicates, this book is directed principally toward an understanding, and a prioritization, of the value of freedom. The last chapter of the book is devoted to the implications of what he has said about the value of freedom for human rights.

Like Rorty, the early Bay is influenced by Hume. He writes, "In the original version of his essay on the liberty of the press, Hume concluded that 'this liberty is attended with so few inconveniences, that it may be claimed as the common right of mankind, and ought to be indulged them [*sic*] in almost every government.' This statement expresses an important aspect of my approach too."[43] However, unlike Hume, for whom an ethics of social approval was sufficient, Bay does make a rational argument for prioritizing freedom over other values and for seeing it as the key element of human rights.

Bay argues that freedom, and more precisely "maximum freedom of expression," which he consciously substitutes for Bentham's "the greatest happiness of the greatest number," is crucial for the psychological development of the individual. Here he is talking not only about how an individual empirically might be constituted at any given point in time, but how that individual might grow over time, the potential of the individual.[44]

He admits that this entails a certain humanistic faith, but, in good Humean form, says that it is probable that his faith would gain a consensus. An additional reason for such prioritization of freedom of expression is that "a maximal freedom of expression is more conducive than other goals are to the realization of the social prerequisites for increasing satisfaction of the most important human needs. ... No matter what values men hold, the freedom to pursue these values is important to them."[45] They first do this by articulating or expressing those values.

Bay takes a psychological approach in this book. But this leaves him a bit uneasy. While it is crucial for the human psyche that individuals be able to express themselves, they still live in a material world.

Bay tries to address this, but he does so briefly and, in the view of this writer, inadequately:

> This position does not imply either a rejection or an affirmation of the materialist position that man's material needs in some sense "determine" his spiritual needs. I believe that a good standard of living is a prerequisite for the fullest attainment of freedom of expression, but I do not think that it guarantees a high level of freedom or even that it is necessarily a strong influence toward freedom. I do not affirm that free speech is more important than food in the stomach. On the contrary, if people starve, it is nonsense to expect them to care for free speech, except, at most, as a means to articulate their demand for food. Starvation can confine the freedom of expression more effectively than can political tyranny.[46]

This is the beginning and end of the discussion of such material concerns in the book. In the very next sentence of the text Bay continues on: "'Freedom,' my crucial value concern in this book, means expression of individuality, or self-expression."[47] The rest of the book looks at different dimensions of the value of expressive freedom. As indicated above, the book ends with a chapter in which the value of expressive freedom becomes the paramount value, the foundational value, for human rights. In a variant of John Rawls's "veil of ignorance," in which we must imagine ourselves in the position of the economically least favored,[48] Bay tells us that "by focusing on the value of the least free, we may one day be able to estimate differences in the levels of freedom between different countries in a nonpartisan spirit and with the authority of science backing up our findings."[49] This is the task of a humane social science for Bay. It is a task for the future. In the meantime, he counsels social scientists to concentrate on country studies and on historical trend analyses within countries.

In 1985, almost three decades after *The Structure of Freedom* was first published, and shortly before his untimely death, Bay presented a paper in Paris to the Human Rights Study Group of the International Political Science Association. This is a fascinating example of the interaction between the thinking of a scholar and changes in the external environment. In this paper, Bay argues that what he calls "the green ecological safety rights," should come first. They should be followed by the "red socialist safety and dignity rights," which in turn should be followed by the "blue dignity and freedom rights."[50]

Two things happened between the writing of his two texts. First, the problem of environmental degradation had posed severe threats to clean air and water for the entire planet. Second, conservative governments had come into power in the United States, Canada, and Great Britain. They were not particularly sensitive to environmental concerns, especially if they conflicted with the prerogatives of private economic activity. Bay thus was forced to confront the "materiality" of the situation in a way that he avoided in *The Structure of Freedom*. It seemed to him very obvious that there was now such a threat to safety and health needs, that "the most basic categories of human needs [fell into a] natural or 'rational' order."[51] Here Bay is no longer prioritizing a psychological approach to needs, nor is he any longer focusing on the individual as the victim of rights violations. It is the survival need of everyone that gets priority ranking on Bay's needs hierarchy now.

Hume no longer holds the theoretical purchase on a theory of rights that he once did in Bay's estimation. Now Bay turns to Rousseau, whom he interprets as a rational humanist. The General Will is read as the "good of all," which poses no threat to the freedom of the individual. Bay sees Kant's categorical imperative as an elaboration of Rousseau's thinking in the "a priori realm of thought, rational rather than empirical, that he [Kant] called Practical Reason."[52]

For Bay, Marx and Engels added the element of moral solidarity of free and equal associated producers. Thus even though Marx criticized the "Rights of Man," as they were expressed in the documents at the end of the eighteenth century, because he saw them "as a symbol of selfish bourgeois individualism [Marx] was a rational humanist; like Rousseau and Kant, he was out to safeguard the basic needs of every human being without exception, even though he shunned the language of human rights."[53]

Operating clearly in the rational tradition now, Bay drops his earlier contention that he was beginning from a position of belief, to a language of "persuasive rational grounding of competing priority claims concerning rights-priorities."[54] After declaring that the green-rights claims are mainly security rights, that is, the ecological system is at risk for ourselves and succeeding generations, he offers a clear repudiation of the psychological-expressive position that he took in his earlier book. He writes, "Now, freedom may well be said to be the highest good; provided, as some of us would add, there is enough of it to go around. Yet a prior concern, if we are rational and if there is a threat, must surely be with the continuing health of the eco-system on which our very lives depend."[55]

Now it also no longer makes sense to contend that we should focus on the rights situation only within individual countries. The threat to the environment is an international one. One of the green rights is the right to peace, the right not to be incinerated in a nuclear explosion that would destroy people of this generation and leave planetary harm and genetic residues for future generations.

But the categories of green, red, and blue turn out not to be sufficient in and of themselves to establish a hierarchy of rights. There are certain rights within each category that threaten survival and health and others that do not and are thus less imperative. "Only the most basic green rights are of the same urgency as the older blue rights to protection from execution or torture."[56] The "red" rights are basically those contained in the 1966 International Covenant on Economic, Social, and Cultural Rights. Red comes second, before blue, because "without the respect and dignity of treatment as equals, liberty may be of limited value."[57] The blue rights, like the green ones, are divided into those that concern basic security (rights to be free of execution, torture, or cruel and unusual punishment) and those that do not and in fact that should be curtailed (e.g., the "right" to immigrate to the country of one's choice, or the right to acquire and dispose of property according to one's own will).

In the end, he confesses that the color-coded categories are a very rough ordering principle and that what we should really be looking at is "what categories of harm are at stake: collective security; individual survival and health; the dignity of being treated as equals; or liberties of self-expression and choice (within socially and ecologically responsible limits)."[58]

While Bay's paper is thus a very schematic exploratory attempt to probe the relationship between needs and human rights, it clearly represents a marked departure from his early attempt to prioritize the need of the individual for free expression.

Henry Shue gives us a much clearer conception of rights based on a needs hierarchy. Shue writes with the intention of countering three views that he sees as prevailing in what he calls the "North Atlantic" countries, that is, the West. The first is that civil and political rights take precedence over economic, social, and cultural rights. The second is that there is viability in Isaiah Berlin's distinction between negative and positive liberty, with a clear prioritization of negative liberties. The third is that rights are something completely separate from obligations or duties. In order to break such patterns of thinking, Shue wants us to think about rights in terms of basic and nonbasic rights. Shue defines what he means by "basic rights":

> Basic rights ... are everyone's minimum reasonable demands upon the rest of humanity. They are the rational basis for justified demands the

denial of which no self-respecting person can reasonably be expected to accept. Why should anything be so important? The reason is that rights are basic in the sense used here only if enjoyment of them is essential to the enjoyment of other rights. When a right is genuinely basic, any attempt to enjoy any other right by sacrificing the basic right would be quite literally self-defeating, cutting the ground from beneath itself. Therefore, if a right is basic, other, non-basic rights may be sacrificed, if necessary, in order to secure the basic right. But the protection of a basic right may not be sacrificed in order to secure the enjoyment of a non-basic right.[59]

While Shue himself does not specifically use the word "needs," the argument is structured such that human beings do indeed need certain things, and thus need to have rights to those things acknowledged and respected if they are going to have any meaningful rights at all. Shue makes clear that he is not establishing a hierarchy based on the enjoyment or intrinsic value of the rights themselves. The only criterion for a basic right is that it is necessary, that is, needed, for the enjoyment of all other rights.

Basic rights cut across the traditional categories of political/ economic, positive/negative, and even green, red, and blue "generations" of rights. The easiest cases to argue are those that involve security and subsistence. Unless our physical security is respected and protected, there is little point in our claiming any other right. This was Hobbes's emphasis, but he thought that one had to give up all political rights for this, something for which Shue does not see the need.

For Shue, it is not just a matter of ensuring that people are not physically attacked by others. The same argument applies to the right to subsistence. He writes, "By minimal economic security, or subsistence, I mean unpolluted air, unpolluted water, adequate food, adequate clothing, adequate shelter, and minimal preventive health care."[60]

Shue sees the distinction between positive and negative rights as destructive. In Berlin's thinking, positive rights require some action on the part of other individuals, the community, or the state to have force. Negative rights merely require that individuals be left alone, that they not be subject to interference by other individuals, the community, or the state. As indicated, Berlin prioritizes—thus sees as more basic—negative rights. Shue argues that this leads people wrongly to assume that they have no duty correlative with a basic right. On the contrary, we have a duty not only to avoid depriving others of their basic rights but also to protect them from deprivation, and to aid them when they are deprived of their basic rights. If rights are really basic in the sense that Shue contends, then it would be morally inexcusable not to take positive action to aid and protect people from deprivation. Thus, Shue argues that duty and obligation override arguments based on self-interest of "each responsible only for the self." Moreover, if people are deprived of the food and shelter that they need to live, it makes little sense to simply not deprive them of the right to vote as a remedy. This would be another way of avoiding individual and collective duty to others, to observe without intervention as the entire structure of rights falls away from some people.

As indicated above, Shue's major focus is on security and subsistence rights, because those are the ones that he feels are neglected by the wealthy "North Atlantic" countries in their conduct of foreign policy. But he does raise the issue of liberty, the one prioritized by the Western powers. He makes two important arguments. First, "the enjoyment of rights to some liberties depend [*sic*] upon the enjoyment of security and subsistence, but the enjoyment of rights to security and subsistence depends upon the enjoyment of some liberties."[61] In regard to the first part of the argument, we have already made reference to the lack of utility of the right to vote to a starving person. But, also, one might require liberty of movement to assure oneself and one's family, or indeed one's group (think of Native Americans deprived of their hunting grounds, for example), of the means to security and subsistence. But the situation is not symmetrical. All liberty rights are contingent on the enjoyment of security and subsistence rights, but security and subsistence is dependent on only some liberty rights.

Second, contrary to Hobbes, "it is not possible to enjoy full rights to security or subsistence without also having rights to participate effectively in the control of security and subsistence."[62] Benevolent— or in Hobbes's case, rational self-interested—dictators cannot be relied upon to deliver the goods on security and subsistence both because the empirical record of dictatorships is very poor in this regard and, more fundamentally, because a right is a demand, and the channels have to be open to those who want to make the demand known to those who ought to but are not acting in accord with it.

Shue thus ties respect for security and subsistence rights to political democracy. But he does not get into the argument over what kind of participation suffices. He does not advocate indirect participation through the electoral process that Rousseau would see as dooming recognition of security and subsistence rights and landing us in the West in exactly in the position that Shue is critiquing. Nor does he advocate the kind of direct participation that Rousseau advocates as the only assurance of that kind of recognition.

Shue admits that there is a "soft spot" to his argument at the theoretical level. That is, *if* in the empirical world it should happen that an authoritarian government or a dictatorship were to protect security and subsistence rights better than ones that respected freedoms of participation and movement, then he would have to grant Hobbes's argument that they were indeed more desirable. But, on the basis of the historical record, he is betting that this will not turn out to be the case.

The most fertile field that Shue leaves undisturbed might be the possibility that participation and democracy should not be confined to a realm of political liberty distinct from security and subsistence. Perhaps the most certain way to ensure security and subsistence is to extend democratic participatory rights into the very economic institutions that we hope will ensure those rights. Along this line of thinking, Robert A. Dahl has argued that every justification that can be offered for political democracy is also valid for economic democracy.[63] We will come back to this issue in Chapter 5.

Johan Galtung adds greater complexity to the discussion of the relationship between needs and rights than what we find in the writing of Bay or Shue. He situates the issue within a framework in which the movement from needs to rights is a process of norm establishment. There are four different elements within this process as it has traditionally worked. The first is the "norm sender." Galtung views the U.N. General Assembly and other specialized components of the United Nations, such as the International Labor Organization and UNESCO, to be universal (as opposed to regional) norm senders.[64] Galtung sees these groups as stipulating in documents what constitutes human rights.

Second, there are "norm receivers." For him, individual governments are norm receivers. Governments are supposed to read those documents and adjust their behavior accordingly. Third, there are "norm objects." These are individuals, the only holders of human rights in Galtung's view. Finally, there is the "norm content" that specifies which specific behaviors are consistent with the norm and which constitute violations of the norm. Traditionally this has been a top-down, hierarchical process. Galtung calls such hierarchical processes "alpha" processes.

Galtung then classifies the needs that have been fed into this process in order to become authoritatively accepted as rights. He first divides them into material and nonmaterial needs. He then divides them into actor-dependent and structure-dependent needs. This gives him the following fourfold table.[65]

Table 2.1 A typology of needs, with antonyms

	Actor-dependent	Structure-dependent
Material	Survival (violence)	Well-being (misery)
Nonmaterial	Freedom (repression)	Identity (alienation)

Source: Johan Galtung, *Human Rights in Another Key* (Cambridge, U.K.: Polity Press, 1994), 57.

The process is one that traditionally has been based on Western legal and hierarchical (Galtung calls them "vertical") norms. The norm sender is at the top and the ordinary people are at the bottom, objects of the norms. Individuals within governments are held accountable for the mistreatment of individual victims in violation of the norms. It is much more difficult, however, for this kind of process to come to grips with rights violations that are not intentional acts of individuals in authority against individual victims but are, rather, the results of structures that those in authority merely tolerate. But the toleration of misery and alienation,[66] which as we have already seen is justified by such notions as limiting the list of human rights to make those that are established as norms more effective (Cranston), focusing on negative rights as opposed to positive ones (Berlin), or rejecting the concept of social, economic, and cultural rights (the U.S. government), means a world of victimization and suffering.

Because it is so difficult for the legalistic, vertical alpha processes to deal with the structural roots of victimization and suffering, Galtung suggests another way of thinking about human rights, about the process of turning some needs into human rights. He proposes a decentralized process in which everyone would have the opportunity of becoming a norm-subject and a norm-sender as well as a norm-object.[67] This would be a way of meeting the need for active agency in the most fundamental process of deciding norms. It would pertain not only to individuals but also to nongovernmental agencies such as Amnesty International or Human Rights Watch. Galtung thus proposes a more democratic, more pluralistic process by which *some* needs—he readily admits that certain needs are not and should not be rights and that some rights are not needs—will become human rights.

He looks to consensus as the way by which these would be established. He is willing to sacrifice some element of universality in order to bring together human rights and human needs in a more horizontal, decentralized, and participatory way. He writes, "What we are looking for is the consistent translation of human rights thinking into local normative culture, but then emphasizing the basic needs entitlement rather than the universality found, for instance, in the four components of the International Bill of Human Rights. Particular human rights, made specific to local culture and historical context, may be as significant as universal human rights."[68] He thinks that recognition of this would permit local participation and solidarity within and between communities, something that is inhibited by a purely macro-level conceptualization of rights. But then he adds something that is crucial to establishing a kind of dialectic or mediation between universalism and particularism: "But one approach does not exclude the other. Both—and not either-or."[69]

Galtung's formulation is really quite imaginative. But there are some elements that are questionable or murky.

First, some have argued that rather than thinking of the United Nations or its instrumentalities as "norm senders," we should we think of the states whose representatives vote for and/or ratify human rights declarations, covenants, as the "norm senders." If this is the case, then the hierarchical systems would be intranational, between governments and the people they claim to represent.

Second, Galtung characterizes the clause in the Universal Declaration of Human Rights that stipulates, "Everyone has the right to take part in the government of his country, directly or through freely chosen representatives," as a "social justice norm," rather than an expression of needs. This is different from Shue, who argues that, since exclusion from the processes through which needs gain recognition risks that very recognition, participation itself becomes a need. There is not, in my reading of Galtung, a clear exposition of the relationship, whether of difference or of sameness, between the concept of "social justice" and that of "human rights."[70] I have already contended that while Liberation Theologians use the expression "social justice," they seem to be talking about human rights if we understand human rights as including economic, social, and cultural rights, and if both "social justice" and "human rights" carry with them positive moral obligations to attend to the needs of the deprived. But Galtung maintains that social justice norms are "hardly expressions of needs, but of values governing the construction of social structures."[71] And it is curious that he uses the assertion of a *political* right to illustrate the difference between social justice norms and rights norms. We usually associate social justice norms with economic, social, and cultural issues.

Third, Galtung's assertion that "only individuals can sense deprivation and satisfaction of needs" is curious, since he wants to open need expression to collectivities and give credence to particularism and social solidarity. Could not a tribe or an ethnic group, after an internal discussion including almost everyone or their legitimate representatives, express a need for recognition of political, economic, social, or cultural rights that cannot be reduced to the expression of individuals? Or take the case of national self-determination. Is it really just individuals who express such a need? Some would argue that it is, but then they would be unlikely to demonstrate the kind of openness to specific local human rights claims based on particular expressions of solidarity and particular historical contexts that Galtung does.

These criticisms of Galtung, while not unimportant, must be taken in the light of his book being one of the most imaginative, perhaps even the most imaginative, work on human rights in recent history.

Discursive Inclusiveness

In his tome on law and democracy, *Between Facts and Norms: Contributions to a Discourse Theory of Law and Democracy*, written in 1992 and first translated into English in 1996, Jürgen Habermas devotes a chapter to rights. He argues that in today's world, which can no longer rely on the authority of religiously sanctified natural law, or on the secularized version of this, contract theory relying on prepolitical absolute principles, what is left to us as a justifying principle in questions of law and politics is "rational discourse, that is, the reflexive forms of communicative action itself."[72] This is to say that the sole way of legitimizing norms, whether they be human rights, laws, or decisions made under conditions of popular sovereignty, is through a discursive process in which we must give good reasons to each other in our search for moral right.[73]

The major object of his book is the establishment of a justification for modern law. Modern law, he argues, can only be justified by two things: human rights and popular sovereignty. There is thus a triadic internal relationship between law, popular sovereignty, and human rights. By "internal relationship," he means that all three are dependent on, and in a fundamental way, a part of each other. Law must incorporate and raise to a sufficiently high level of generality the reasoned will of each consociate in the system that is being represented. That implies the equal recognition of the interest and expressed will of everyone. Popular sovereignty implies the right to participate in the law-making process that raises rights to more than a mere claim, to an officially sanctioned norm that forms the constitutional basis for people living together. Rights without law would only be claims that could be refused without violating a generalized norm, while rights without popular sovereignty would of necessity be partial, as they were prior to the great revolutions of the seventeenth century (e.g., rights of lords versus kings or of serfs versus lords—rights based on status).

The normative keys are equal consideration given to interest, and equal recognition accorded to one another as members of a community who live together under discursively arrived at norms that we call law. He writes:

> The key idea is that the principle of democracy derives from the interpretation of the discourse principle and the legal form. ... the principle of democracy can only appear as the heart of a *system* of rights. The logical genesis of these rights comprises a circular process in which the legal code, or legal form, and the mechanism for producing legitimate law—hence the democratic principle—are *co-originally* constituted.[74]

Habermas admits that thus far he has operated in the realm of abstraction, and it is a very formalistic abstraction at that. But when he tries to become concrete, he does so through the very concept of the "legal form." Through the prism of the legal code, he introduces "rights *in abstracto*" that define legal persons, and in doing so generate the legal code. He thus comes up with a very different ordering of "basic rights" than Shue.

The most basic rights are those assuring the "greatest possible measure of equal individual liberties." There follow two necessary corollaries, "rights that result from the politically autonomous elaboration of the *status of a member* in a voluntary association of consociates under law," and "rights that result immediately from the politically autonomous elaboration of individual *legal protection*."[75] These rights guarantee the private autonomy of legal subjects who recognize each other as "*addressees*" of laws (an example might be Rousseau's particularistic individuals) who can bring the weight of the law to bear in their relations with each other.

The next basic rights are those that are necessary to establish these legal subjects as authors (an example might be Rousseau's citizens when they are directly participating in the exercise of sovereignty), and not just addressees of their laws. These are those that confer "equal opportunities to participate in the processes of opinion- and will-formation in which citizens exercise their political autonomy and through which they generate legitimate law."[76] Note here that "autonomy" is *not* privatistic. It is a very public notion. It means that each is free to say what she really thinks is true or good in the public realm, and to change that opinion only when faced by superior arguments. Autonomy does not mean a monadic withdrawal from the public domain into private concerns. Habermas would not prohibit this, but sees it as a pathological alienation from the rational norm-establishing process.

The final set of basic rights are those "to the provision of living standards that are socially, technologically, and ecologically safeguarded, insofar as the current circumstances make this necessary if citizens are to have opportunities to utilize the [above] civil rights."[77] He tells us that this category, "which can be justified only in relative terms," will be dealt with further in the final chapter of the book, a promise that is not really kept and that constitutes an important theoretical lack.

Habermas easily elides from the discussion of human rights to a specification of rights that turn out to be civil rights. True, Rousseau went from natural rights to civil rights, but he did it as a deliberate exchange when people entered the contract. Habermas is very Rousseauist in his emphasis on the discursive community, but, as already noted, he rejects the idea of a contract as a secularized version of older natural law that is out of place in the modern world. This still leaves him with the problem of particularism and communalism. When we talk about human rights, we are talking about rights that defy the boundaries of sovereignty, of any given discursive political community.

Habermas was obviously criticized on this point, because he comes back to it in a postscript in the English edition, written a year after the German edition had appeared and after he had received reader reaction. His response was that as "enacted actionable norms," constitutional rights are valid only within a particular legal community but that does not detract from "the universalistic meaning of the classical liberties," and that precisely:

> the discrepancy between the human-rights content of the classical liberties and their form as positive law, which initially limits them to a nation-state, is just what makes one aware that the discursively grounded "system of rights" points beyond the constitutional state in the singular toward the globalization of rights. As Kant realized, basic rights require, by virtue of their semantic content, an international, legally administered, "cosmopolitan society." For actionable rights to issue from the United Nations Declaration of Human Rights, it is not enough to simply have international courts; such courts will first be able to function adequately only when the age of individual sovereign states has come to an end through a United Nations that can not only pass but also act on and enforce its resolutions.[78]

In the above quote, Habermas shifts from a conceptual argument to a practical concern without a sufficiently bridging argument. Such an argument would have to deal with some severe impediments, given the positions he has committed himself to in the main body of the book. First, he has embedded rights so deeply in discursively enacted positive law within sovereign communities that he risks falling into Bentham's position that there are no rights outside of law. Indeed, he is more bound by the confines of law than is the legal theorist Dworkin, who sees both law and antilaw behavior (i.e., civil disobedience) as important in the establishment of rights. In Habermas's earlier writing, especially those dealing with the "new social movements," there was a notion of struggle as groups fought to establish rights against dominating systems that threatened their "lifeworlds."[79] Here the concept of struggle for rights gives way to a discursive concept that today is manifested in the representational-legislative processes of nation-states. While Habermas does have a utopian vision of a much more vital public world of discourse outside of that legislative or parliamentary process that would actually be listened to, it is just that—a vision of a possible future condition. In the here and now, Habermas is stuck with actual parliamentary processes being as close as we come to the operationalization of his discourse model in large, complex nation-states. While it might be a very good thing for the United Nations to exert the kind of power Habermas suggests, it boggles the mind to think of how that could be done according to the rational-discursive model that Habermas suggests.

Indeed, as some feminist theorists have suggested,[80] Habermas's universalistic hyperrationalism might just impose excessive limitations on a theory of rights applicable *both* to a complex society made up of particularistic differences based on race, ethnicity, gender, sexual orientations, and so on, and to an international order in which one finds radically different cultural norms. Affective qualities such as empathy and solidarity across lines of differentiation might be as important within and across state boundaries as are rational principles and rules of argumentation that Habermas holds to transcend social and cultural distinctions. He does not appear to see the bridging possibilities suggested by Galtung.

In sum, Habermas runs the contradictory risks of being trapped, on the one hand, by a Rousseauist vision of discursive communal sovereignty applicable to a small, agricultural, homogeneous society, and, on the other, by a Kantian universalism based on rational norms of will-formation that assumed that minds, when they are operating properly, completely transcend both culture and affect.

CONCLUSION

In this chapter, we have seen how in the twentieth century totalitarianism, world war, and genocide violated human rights in unprecedented ways. We also have seen how the victorious nations responded to these abuses, first through the Nuremberg trials and then through human rights norm-establishing documents issued through the mechanism of the United Nations. The key concept in these documents was human dignity. But, aside from the precise prohibitions and positive stipulations in the various agreements, there was no probing of the grounding of that notion. Nor did there have to be, because the authors were national leaders coming together in an international forum. They were not theologians or ethical and political philosophers writing treatises.

Nevertheless, the issue of grounding was important for many. The enormity of the violations contributed to a climate in which the idea that "God is dead" made a great deal of sense, as did the calling into question of the Enlightenment's commitment to the potency of human reason.

Grounding human rights thus became a real problem. Some harkened back to religious faith or secular belief as the best, or at least a sufficient grounding. Others gave more elaborate theoretical reasons for their adherence to something called human rights but did not have recourse to rationalist grounding. Finally, a third group attempted to offer rationalist grounding. These theorists tended to view human rights from the perspective of one of the elements of human rights: such as freedom and agency, equality, human needs, and discursiveness inclusiveness.

In the next chapter, I am going to suggest another approach to grounding human rights, an approach that I will designate as "holistic."

CHAPTER 3

A HOLISTIC APPROACH TO HUMAN RIGHTS

INTRODUCTION

The object of this chapter is to provide a propositional grounding for a holistic conception of human rights. It will attempt to do this without falling into idealist arguments such as the old natural law/natural rights formulation, without falling into a humanistic essentialism that sees human beings driven across time and culture by invariable characteristics, and without falling into a relativism that would see humans as nothing more than constructs of their own cultures at any given moment, a view that would strip human rights of all cross-cultural relevance.[1]

The argument in this chapter will take the form of a number of propositions and their elaborations.

Proposition 1: All human beings have the potential for development "Development" can go in many different directions. It can be intellectual, creative, and/or affective. Human beings can push themselves to understand things that are not obvious. They do this in everyday life experiences ("amateur" mechanics or naturalists, for example) as well as in the various academic disciplines. They can go so far in their understandings of nature that they are able to do rather incredible things when looked at in historical retrospect. They can send rockets into space, put people on the moon, and make it possible for me to write this on a computer that will actually remember and store, for better or for ill, what I am now writing. How many potential theoretical physicists and aeronautical engineers are there among us, going to inner-city schools and dropping out or being expelled, with a good chance of winding up in prison rather than in universities or institutes for advanced studies? How many children barely surviving at the fringes of the Sahara Desert in Africa have the potentiality of being one of those scientists or engineers, or of being a successful sociologist, philosopher, linguist, and so on? We do not know. All we know is that there is in all of us an intellectual potential, and much of that goes unrecognized and undeveloped at a high price to the individual, her society, and the world at large.

Similarly, we all have creative potentialities. As in the case of the intellectual potentialities, the precise nature varies. Many of us could be wonderful painters if our talents were recognized and we were given encouragement, training, and support. Others of us could be playwrights, novelists, sculptors, composers, film directors, and so on if only our potentialities were recognized.

There also is an affective potential. That is to say that we have the capacity to be introspective about our feelings, to try to achieve an emotional or spiritual balance in our lives, to become people of good character, to exhibit positive attitudes toward others so as to give them support, assistance, pleasure, friendship, and love.

At the risk of offending some of those in the animal rights movement who might view the notion of human rights as too exclusive and "speciesist" a concept, I would argue that the intellectual and creative potentials of human beings are so qualitatively different from other species, that they are indeed uniquely human. I do not mean to say that other species cannot "think." Experiments with chimpanzees show that they clearly can think and can manipulate language to some extent. But they cannot conceive of constructing laboratories and applying the same tests to humans. They cannot think of organizing themselves into schools, universities, or academic disciplines. Thus, while the DNA differential between the species of homo sapiens and other primates might be very small, the results of that in terms of intellectual potential are enormous. Chimpanzees, which are very social animals, nonetheless live substantially different lives than do humans. The lower complexity of their lives, which consist of constant repetition, undoubtedly is because of their lower potentialities. The difference was illustrated in the film *2001*, which begins with primates using natural objects as tools and moves to space rockets. We can say with certainty that chimpanzees will never put one of their own on the moon or on any other planet. If the chimpanzees get up there, it will be because humans put them up.

Similarly, there is no evidence that other species have the creative potential of humans. Humans organize their own space functionally and aesthetically. They assign certain spaces to agriculture, industry, leisure, commerce, and so on. They have architecture that varies with the different cultures. The dwelling spaces of other species tend to be the same whether in Africa, North America, Asia, or South America. Whales might use language to communicate with each other, but this is purely an instinctive biological expression rather than a cultural creation that can be manipulated for scientific, commercial, aesthetic, or cultural reasons. Could we imagine whales coming together to form something like the *Académie Française*, which would decide on whether a sound should or should not be given legitimacy in "whalese" in the North Atlantic? The creative potential of human beings, which leads to the larger cultural expression of societies and even the world, simply does not exist among other species.

I am less sure about the affective capacities of humans being so unique. As pointed out in the last chapter, Richard Rorty contended, "We [humans] can feel for each other to a much greater extent than they [other species] can." If what Rorty means is that we humans can think about or imagine other people who are human and who live far away from us as being in the same species, and conclude that we have obligations to them because of the sameness of our species-being, then I think that Rorty makes an important point. It makes possible something like human rights. But if Rorty means that other species feel less intensely about those close to them, then I don't know how Rorty can make such a statement. Anyone who has kept more than one cat or dog and witnessed the grief of the surviving one after the other has died, anyone who has seen the nature films depicting the obvious pain suffered by a mother cheetah or monkey after her offspring has been killed, must be dubious about this conclusion. In the *Discourse on the Origin of Inequality*, Rousseau made a similar point in regard to horses who come across a dead one of their species to demonstrate the naturalness of *pitié* (compassion) within a variety of species.[2] Of course, it is only human beings who kill other species for sport, as well as other human beings for a variety of motives (such as hurt pride after a real or imagined insult or as a demonstration of the pure power to take life) that make no sense among other species.

In regard to intellectual and creative capacities, the point is that these are uniquely human. In regard to the affective capacities, the point is that the potential is there, even if it coexists with a potential for cruelty in ways that it does not in other species. But we do not need to deny the capacity for cruelty in order to argue that there is a much better capacity that goes in the opposite direction and that this is important when we talk about the basis of *human* rights. We have the capacity to know that cruelty is wrong (indeed, the word itself is normatively laden, as opposed to the more neutral expression "infliction of pain"), even if we might commit cruel acts. We also have the capacity to know that we have a positive obligation to act to end or mitigate human suffering if it is in our power. Hence our solidaristic concepts of charity, generosity, and humanitarianism, which carry a moral obligation not to just desist from inflicting cruelty but to benefit others who are suffering whom we do not even know; for example, people who are victims of starvation, persecution, or natural disasters in faraway places. These concepts, unlike familial love, are at once affective *and* rational; they bring out our concern for others of our species and they reflect a utopian model or conception of a world without human suffering.

Some might say that not all humans have these potentialities, that there are some people who are mentally and emotionally impaired to whom they do not apply. It is possible that some people with physiological and emotional conditions that most of us do not have cannot think or create in the same ways that those do who do not have those conditions. But my former colleague at the University of Illinois, Michael Bérubé, who has a child with Down's syndrome, points out very eloquently and very poignantly that it is all too easy to dehumanize such people by wrongly assuming total intellectual or creative incapacity when what we are presented with is instead unfamiliar forms or expressions of these capacities. The case of someone in a coma, if such a state meant no consciousness as well as no communicative ability, would be different. But it could still pose human rights issues; for example, would it be a human rights violation to terminate the life of such a person by pulling the plugs of the machines keeping the person alive if the person had not given instructions to do so prior to falling into the coma? Is there a human rights issue that pertains to the family members and friends of such a person who might either want such a life terminated or want it prolonged even if this absorbs enormous resources in terms of financial cost and allocation of equipment?

One final word about other species. I fully support animal rights in the form of an injunction against cruelty to animals. But I do this because the other species are sentient creatures, and that is the only grounding of this right that I can think of. *Human* rights, however, have a wider grounding based on my understanding of the creative and intellectual potentials of human beings, as well as the more extensive affective potential for empathy with the entire species.

Proposition 2: Human potentialities are developed within a web of cultural, economic, and social relationships that are both

facilitating and constraining. **Such development entails a process of "co- and self-determination"** As Aristotle said, human beings are social animals. Both he and Rousseau saw the phenomenon of language by which human beings can communicate complex thoughts to each other as the proof of that sociability. What this means is that the monadic view of human beings, stemming from Hobbes's rejection of Aristotelian and Scholastic thought, and continuing through the predominant forms of liberal political and neoliberal economic thought, and social science (e.g., "rational" man self-interest presumptions), is simply inaccurate. Even a theorist as concerned about the unfairness of present forms of distribution as John Rawls bases his famous 1971 tome, *A Theory of Justice*, on pure individual self-interest.[3] In this theory of "justice as fairness," each of us remains behind a "veil of ignorance" as to where WE as individuals might fall in the economic distribution pattern. Thus, out of pure self-interested calculation, we do not want the range of possibilities to be too bad lest WE find ourselves at the short end of the stick. Rawls claims to make no appeal beyond self-interest, to altruism, for example, precisely because of the power and the normative sanctioning of pure self-interest in Western, and particularly Anglo-American, contemporary ideological presumptions.

The self-interested presumption underlying the veil of ignorance is far too constricted. Even the most "self-made" men and women had their potentialities developed within a web of social relationships. They grew up in a social institution called the family. This institution played a crucial role in their development. They went to schools in which teachers and nonfamilial peers played crucial roles in their development. As adults they became citizens of political entities that entailed both rights and obligations. They entered into work relationships with others, sometimes competitive, but often requiring professional assistance and cooperation. They developed friendships that impacted on them. They were likely to have belonged to a religious institution in which they shared spiritual development with others. They were exposed to the media, which had a formative impact on what they believed and to what they aspired. They were exposed to aesthetics that involved interaction with others, for example, going to concerts and discussing them with others, playing in concerts that involved cooperation with other musicians, and so on. They probably engaged other people in recreational and physical exercise activities in which appreciation for nature and mutual care for their bodies were exhibited.

To maintain this does not mean that each human being is not unique in some way. Just as we humans are all alike in being composed of

DNA but vary ever so slightly among ourselves, so, too, are we alike in having creative, intellectual, and affective potentialities. Each of us puts those together a bit differently as a result of different innate talents and different life experiences within our webs of social relationships. The commonality is that we all have had that web of social relationships.

Again, exceptions can be thrown out to disprove this. What about the "wolf-boy," the one who was lost in the forest and was raised by a pack of wolves, or Tarzan, who was raised by the apes? Well, so long as the wolf-boy or Tarzan were deprived of human sociability, the innate potentiality for development that they had could not develop in any human way. But they still had the potentialities. And when Jane showed up, Tarzan could at least demonstrate some of his affective potential in the form of caring and love for another human being. So cases of human isolation brought about by the freak occurrences of human imagination in no way destroy the points that (1) humans have these potentialities for development and (2) they require a web of social relationships for their development. It makes no sense to talk about human rights if one is talking about Robinson Crusoe before Friday showed up. But Robinson could indeed reflect on human rights as they would apply to those who were not so unfortunately stranded alone on an island.

This is precisely why I do not use the word "autonomy," so important in Kant's metaphysically based moral philosophy, in discussing human rights. I have no objection to the way in which Habermas used the expression "political autonomy" when he was talking about the equal opportunity of citizens to participate in opinion and will formation as part of the process of legitimate law-making. Here we are talking about an explicitly social/political process, trying at the same time to avoid the coercive potentiality of extreme communalism. But in an individualistic liberal society, "autonomy" is likely to be read as a separation or insulation from such social or political processes. It is for this reason that I prefer to represent the human rights subject as one of "co- and self-determination." The possessor of human rights is not an isolated self-interested monad with an interest only in being free from the interference of other people or institutions—what Isaiah Berlin calls "negative liberty"—but a being who is intrinsically part of his or her web of social relationships and has interests in and concerns for the people with whom he or she is interacting.[4]

This "co- and self-determination" view must not be read as obliterating the space for individual privacy. On the contrary, I see the need for such privacy as fundamental. Individuals need such spaces both for intellectual and creative work and for reflection on the quality of the web of social, political, and cultural relationships of which they are a part. Thus, I take the "self" aspect of determination very seriously and insist that it be given a reflective space. But it has a necessary internal relationship with other selves that I am calling "co-determination." We are active agents in the determination of ourselves, and we have a human rights claim to the space required for that. But this is part of a larger process of development that is social and involves cultural, economic, and political forms. It is not an either/or issue. Too much emphasis on the self (i.e., the isolated, autonomous, individualistic, privatized self) is both analytically incorrect and results in an egoism that would be difficult to reconcile with a recognition of human rights. Too much emphasis on "co" is also analytically incorrect in that it cannot account for the uniqueness of either individual personalities or creative and intellectual contributions, and normatively dangerous in that it could put at risk the spaces required for them.

Proposition 3: Developmental possibilities are materially and culturally conditioned over history While Marx perhaps put too much emphasis on the phenomenon of production at the expense of other phenomena, which he reduced to "superstructures," he was absolutely right in demonstrating how the evolution of our material context limits developmental possibilities. A nomad on the verge of starvation in the Sudan lives a material and cultural existence that is not very different from that lived by his or her ancestors hundreds of years ago. While the same affective possibilities (love, caring, solidarity) might be open to the nomad, the lack of control over a hostile environment precludes many other developmental possibilities open to someone who has lived in a society that has experienced the political, economic, and social changes that a North American, a European, a Japanese, or an urban middle- or upper-class Brazilian has.

Thus, even in our most technologically advanced age, the developmental possibilities of entire groups or categories of people are stunted. Both materiality and culture enter into this stunting. In sub-Saharan Africa, there is widespread poverty and very high rates of disease and mortality at an early age. Both government aid programs and private investment are minimal. In some Islamic countries, women are largely confined to the home. The most egregious recent example of this was in Afghanistan, when the Taliban were intent on reversing history. In Saudi Arabia, the stunting of the developmental possibilities of women is largely cultural, for there is plenty of oil-generated wealth there. It is thus similar to the United States, where there is such a tragic stunting of the potentialities of African Americans, Native Americans, and some Latinos despite the overall material abundance. In Afghanistan, there was both a material and cultural basis for the stunting of these potentialities.

But we also must take into account the historical development of both the West and the non-West. In the West, human rights talk was used by upper classes and the bourgeoisie after affluence had become more widespread than it had been in feudalism. "No taxation without representation," was a cry raised by those American colonists who were involved in significant economic activity. Their economic concerns were transformed into a political demand, which in turn was transformed into universal human rights language, which was not really universal in application. Class, gender, and race were determinants as to who would actually possess rights. The right of self-representation was restricted to a small minority. In France, the Revolution represented a political transformation of enormous importance, but it also represented the seizure of political power by a vastly enlarged nonaristocratic bourgeoisie that already exerted much economic power. Like the American colonists, they saw *their* possibilities limited by royal rule.

Historical phenomena of a grand scale do not occur "accidentally," if by accidentally we mean that they are unrelated to other phenomena. It thus "makes sense" that the cause of human rights was first articulated so explicitly, and was tied to successful political change, during the French and American revolutions. One would not have expected it under feudalism because developmental possibilities were fixed by one's position in the society. One would not have expected it under hunter-gatherer societies, because of both the low level of subsistence (scarcity itself stunts developmental possibilities) and the communalistic norms that ensured a certain distributional equity within the group.

Thus, human rights are a rather perplexing phenomenon. Their claims are presented as universals, but as specifically articulated they appeared at a particular point in history (at the end of the eighteenth century), within a particular culture (Western), and embedded in particular economic (bourgeois) and political (modern white male republican state) interests. In practice, they thus excluded most people.

Proposition 4: It is precisely this exclusion, and the developmental possibilities and aspirations of the excluded, that continues to provide the dynamic for the development of human rights When structures, institutions, and practices are outpaced by developmental possibilities and aspirations, we have what I will call *domination*. Domination is the exercise of power that frustrates the development of individuals, segments of societies, or entire societies. Domination confers benefits, whether they be economic, political, or the mere psychic satisfaction of controlling the fate of others, to the dominators. Domination usually manifests itself through a combination of raw force, complex institutional practices, and ideological justification in which the dominated "other" is characterized as somehow inferior or deserving of domination, while the dominator is deserving of the benefits.

I used the expression "developmental possibilities *and* aspirations" of the excluded. Possibilities, as we have already discussed, are historically and materially contingent. A child raised in a nomadic existence in a region devastated by drought is going to have very limited developmental possibilities compared with a child born to a middle- or upper-class French or American family. There is little reason to believe that *if* such a child had been born to a family in France or the United States, the possibilities would have not been the same as that of other children of French or American families of a given gender, class, and race. But the child was not born into such conditions and, thus, as an individual, does not have the same possibilities for the actualization of her potentialities. Aspirations for such a life would be completely unrealistic and it would not make much sense to call this limitation of developmental possibilities and aspirations domination. This is because the very mode of nomadic existence, which is culturally very important to nomadic groups and maintains them in a direct relationship to nature that most of us have lost, also is very limiting in terms of meeting basic physical needs and institution building. Nomads might not be aware of this difference, and might or might not make a choice of living differently if they had the opportunity. Their situation, as limiting as it may seem to outsiders, cannot be characterized as domination. Indeed, any attempt by outsiders to compel them to change their lives would itself constitute domination. Furthermore, it is difficult to argue that natural disasters, such as drought, constitute human rights violations. Intentional acts and structural effects can constitute human rights violations, but not natural causes. By contrast, it could be argued that victims can claim a human right to assistance when they are struck by such disasters.

Examples of intentional acts that constitute domination would be: the slave trade; conquest; colonialism; legal exclusion of women from politics and property-holding; and legal exclusion of women or an ethnic or racial group from political rights. Examples of structural exclusion would be: de facto exclusion of women from politics or control over property; de facto exclusion of racial or ethnic groups from the full range of educational, political, and economic opportunity; or vast regional disparities in wealth and opportunity, especially if they have followed and been at least partially a result of former acts of intentional domination (e.g., conquest, colonialism, slavery). Whether intentional act or structural domination (and it must be admitted that the line between them is not always clear), the dominators draw benefit at the expense of the dominated.

Proposition 5: Resistance to, or rebellion against, domination takes the form of struggling for new structures, institutions, and practices that will open up developmental possibilities for the dominated   "Human rights" can be used as a validating principle for such struggles in two contexts. First, it can be used within political systems against the domination of traditional structures, institutions, and practices that limit developmental possibilities and aspirations. Such is the case of women in some Islamic countries who are struggling for equal opportunities with men outside of the home. The Islamic authorities often respond to this struggle by contending that Islam has *its own* concept of human rights and that in Islamic countries women are physically protected, whereas in the West rape is a constant worry for women. It is almost always male authorities who offer this kind of response, since women are usually excluded from significant political and religious positions and voice even when they are not confined to the home.

A second way that human rights can be used is against external powers who verbally claim to be recognizing universal human rights but do not do so. Gandhi used both the first and the second. He argued—against traditional Hinduism—that the untouchable caste was a violation of the principle that all human beings were equal.[5] But he also argued against the British that their colonial control over India was a violation of the self-determining and democratic rights of the Indian people by a government that claimed to respect the principles of human rights. Gandhi's argument with traditional Hinduism entailed introducing a new legitimizing principle that ran counter to the caste system, the equality of all human beings. His argument against the British entailed simply using principles to which the British were already formally committed but were not abiding by in practice. In both instances, Gandhi was engaged in a struggle against domination in the name of human rights.

Human rights advance, in both conception and practice, through struggle. Gandhi advocated pacifistic or nonviolent struggle, feeling that violence itself, even if defensive, constituted a human rights violation. But often such struggles, like the French and American revolutions that gave rise to human rights talk, do entail violence. Whether nonviolent or violent, it is struggle against domination that is the substance of human rights advancement. It is within these struggles that the world is introduced to new dimensions and new applications of human rights. For example, it was only in 1979, after the struggle of the women's rights movement of the late 1960s and the 1970s, that the international Convention on the Elimination of All Forms of Discrimination Against Women was adopted.[6]

Moreover, in struggles against domination, there will almost always be illegality involved. This is why Dworkin insists that law not be the final word on rights, as Bentham would have it. It is only by acting against rights-violating law that change has any chance of coming about. When the Diggers illegally cultivated the land of the wealthy in seventeenth-century England; when the Boston Tea Party threw tea off ships into the harbor; when suffragettes in the United States tried to vote in legally male-only elections; when abolitionists formed underground railroads to help slaves escape; when the White Rose young people distributed tracts denouncing persecution in Nazi Germany; when the people of India began spinning their own wool in violation of British law; when Rosa Parks refused to move to the back of the bus, which was legally required in Birmingham, Alabama; when protesters tried to block the shipments of U.S. weapons to the murderous regimes of El Salvador and Guatemala in the 1980s—all of these people were acting contrary to some existing law code, but struggling for human rights in so doing. At any given moment, law is likely to legitimize domination of some sort. Thus, civil disobedience has historically been a key ingredient in the advancement of human rights.

Proposition 6: New forms, emerging from struggles against domination, can be dominating Within the West, where human rights talk began, the domination against which it was used consisted of absolute monarchy and what were regarded as exploitative uses of social and economic power by kings and aristocrats. These were replaced by the new structures of the constitutional state and of capitalist production and markets that drew strong support from the new constitutional state. As noted before, this is the basis of Marx's criticism of human rights as they were enunciated in the original French and American documents. For Marx, the historical conditions under which human rights emerged, and the practices of those who acted under the banner of human rights through the first half of the nineteenth century, meant that human rights themselves were inherently a tool of class domination.

Change in the name of human rights often entails moving from one form of domination to another. The movement from absolute to constitutional government and from feudalism to capitalism in some senses freed people from domination but in other senses introduced different forms of domination. Exclusion from the constitutional processes, as in the case of women, the nonpropertied, and slaves, was even more demeaning than it was under kingship where there was no pretense that everyone was equal. On the one hand, constitutional government with its legitimizing principles opened up the possibility for counterclaims against domination that were closed off under absolutism. On the other, it did away with the measure of material and status security and personalization of relationships offered by feudal economic and social relations when it "freed" people to offer their labor on the open market. During the Industrial Revolution the "masterless men," to which Hobbes referred in the seventeenth century, as well as their women and children, often found themselves working in mills or factories sixteen hours a day in unhealthy conditions for barely subsistence wages. The women were often sexual prey for employers and overseers. In England, children were used in mills and were subjected to physical punishments that we would today call torture if they did not work satisfactorily.[7]

Thus, the new political and economic structures that carried the banner of universal human rights also carried a double edge. They offered *some* people outside of the nobility certain possibilities for development and mobility that they had not had before. But they continued to exclude many from the political arena, and they no longer recognized the feudal code of rights and obligations that had existed between lord and serf that offered a paternalistic protection to the latter. "Free" men were responsible for their own survival, and that of their families. It was no longer the concern of others.[8]

A similar transition can be seen in the freeing of the slaves in the United States. Former slaves were legally free to make their way in the world but, as Tocqueville had predicted would be the case well before their "emancipation," one cannot say that they were freed from domination.[9] The domination assumed different forms, including exclusion from the political arena after Reconstruction and extreme economic exploitation without the exploiter having to assume the responsibility for housing and feeding the laborers. Even the lowest-class southern white could hire the labor of a black. And whites drove many a black from legitimately acquired land, through trickery, terrorism, and deadly force.[10] Of course, we could carry this story right up to the present where many things have changed but where there is still discrimination and domination, manifested in severely limited economic opportunity, education, and housing, and the differential behavior of police and the courts toward black people in the United States. While the history is different, a very similar situation exists in contemporary Great Britain, and if we add a large Arab population to a smaller black African one, a similar situation exists in France. In those two countries, the old direct colonial domination has given way to newer forms of domination of people of color who have immigrated to work.

Proposition 7: The core values of human rights emerge out of the struggles themselves The battle cry of the French Revolution—*liberté, égalité, fraternité*—gave us the historically new legitimizing values that encapsulate the developmental aspirations of people who had been mere subjects under the ancien régime. The problem is to interpret them in such a way that they complement each other, because a particular reading of each of them could cancel out the other(s). For example, certain measures to ensure equality or fraternity could lead to uniformity or a hyperpatriotism that might stifle all critical thinking and expression. Or, certain measures to ensure liberty could lead to economic domination and an egoism that renders fraternity impossible. Certain conceptions of fraternity could lead to an exclusiveness based on ethnic or national ties that would call into question liberty and equality and undercut the universality of human rights. And, as Carole Pateman argues, it did in fact lead to a gender exclusion as the literal meaning of "fraternity" implies, as in "all *men* are created equal [and] endowed by their creator with certain inalienable rights."[11]

Despite the difficulties in reconciling the three values, in virtually all subsequent emancipatory struggles against domination—whether it be against dictatorship, colonialism, racism, worker exploitation, or discrimination based on differences of gender or sexual orientation—these three values have been raised as the legitimizing principles of the struggle.

It would be a mistake to choose one of these values as *the* basic value, because doing so risks compromising the others. The cries for all three of these values arise out of concrete experiences of domination and struggle of real people, like Winstanley in the seventeenth century, Mary Wollestonecraft and Tom Paine in the eighteenth, Frederick Douglass and Elizabeth Cady Stanton in the nineteenth, and Mahatma Gandhi, Eugene Debs, Joe Hill, Martin Luther King, Jr., Rosa Parks, Nelson Mandela, Steve Biko, Rigoberta Menchu, Ken Saro-Wiwa, and Aung San Suu Kyi—and all the historically unnamed people who struggled alongside them—in the twentieth. The theoretical approach presented here roots human rights in the concrete historical experiences of people who have struggled, and who continue to struggle, against domination. It is thus not just a set of abstractions derived from philosophical reasoning or speculation. It is rooted in the active social processes that we refer to when we use that expression "human rights."

Proposition 8: The core values of *liberté, égalité, solidarité* all require "social recognition" Social recognition is a bridge back to the writers discussed in the last chapter who tried to ground human rights rationally along a single value or dimension. Social recognition ties together the values and dimensions on which they each rely. In fact, those values and dimensions parallel the core values we have been discussing. Gewirth stresses freedom or liberty, which is necessary for purposive or willed action. Dworkin stresses equality. Bay, Galtung, and Shue, who stress needs, and Habermas, who stresses discursiveness, all are dealing with aspects of what I think of as *fraternité*, or solidarity. Each of these core values require or entail social recognition.

The expression "social recognition" was introduced into philosophical discourse by Hegel, particularly as he elaborated the struggle for recognition between lord and bondsman (or slave) in the *Phenomenology of the Mind*.[12] There Hegel presents us with a dialectic of self-consciousness in which the identity of the person as a conscious being, rather than as a mere natural object, is established through mutual recognition. In the lord and bondsman, or slave, relationship, this obviously does not involve an egalitarian relationship that would be necessary for human rights. The lord is clearly the power and status superior of the bondsman. But recognition of the lord by the bondsman is still required in order for the lord to confirm in his own consciousness that he is indeed lord, and the bondsman is recognized by the lord and by himself as more than a mere material object at the service of the lord. The bondsman in his labor becomes a molder of nature, a creator of things, in a way that even the more powerful lord is not. Thus, each desires, and each gets, social recognition from the other.

The broader point is that we have a theory of internal relations here in which human beings require recognition from other human beings in order to function as human individuals, in order to have confirmation that they are not just inert or natural matter. The lord and bondsman relationships might be internal, but they are characterized by hierarchical domination. However, subsequent theorists of human rights, such as Lewis Hinchman and Alex Honneth, have attempted to make the connection between the concept of recognition and human rights. In Hegel, Hinchman argues, the struggle for recognition should be seen as the equivalent of the state of nature argument in Hobbes and Locke. Hinchman sees the lord/bondsman struggle in the *Phenomenology* as a prepolitical conception, similar to the state of nature. But, according to Hinchman, while Hobbes and Locke carry elements of the state of nature into the political world through their conceptions of natural rights, Hegel only uses the lord/bondsman dialectic to illuminate the dialectic of recognition that takes entirely different forms in political context. While Hobbes sees the struggle for power as oriented toward survival that ever remains the preoccupation of human beings (and Hinchman could have added that Locke saw the preservation of property in the same light), Hegel—by contrast—regarded the quest for power as a search for self-identity that required recognition and affirmation from others. Hinchman writes:

> As Hegel uses it, the term "recognition" means roughly a person's claim to be treated not just as a natural object, but as a self, independent and superior to natural things. Precisely the proof that one is "independent" of nature is displayed in one's willingness to die for the sake of recognition. In this way, a human being can manifest his or her power over the most powerful of all natural instincts, the desire for self-preservation [something unimaginable to Hobbes who treats humans as merely natural monads]. By risking their lives for recognition, people implicitly redefine their own identities. The ego, originally the seeming instrument of bodily desire, now takes on a dominant position in the individual's inner life, so much so that it masters the very passions that may have originally given rise to it. Here again, we see why Hegel rejects the reductionist tendency in the liberal tradition. The beginnings of something like self-consciousness do not necessarily tell us what it is. Just because the self was originally determined almost exclusively by bodily desire or instinct does not mean that this is what a human being "really" is, that one can overlook human self-development as though this were something merely contingent and inessential.[13]

As already indicated, Hinchman claims that Hegel sees the lord/bondsman relationship as a prepolitical one. In his reflections on law, there is introduced a formal political mechanism of recognition that attains greater universality. The mutual recognition offered by law in the modern state (Hegel was a great admirer of both the French Revolution and the subsequent code law spread by Napoleon over much of Europe) permits us to relate to each other as significant moral beings rather than as objects to be dominated (something Hobbes never gets beyond). This mutual recognition, codified into law and rights—not nature—is the origin of equality.[14]

Thus, we have in Hegel a teleological view of the development of individual human consciousness that requires immediate mutual recognition between particular human beings, as well as the mediated recognition of law and rights that give general recognition to the freedom and equality (understood as equality under law) required for the attainment of self-consciousness and the development of one's potential. The Hegelian insight that Hinchman gleans is that one would better understand human rights through the lens of complex human relationships through which people develop their potentialities and their identities than on the basis of their physicality and expression of urges and desires toward totally external objects, as is the case in Hobbes (the external object as other menacing people) and Locke (the object as property).

A more recent attempt to establish the relationship between recognition and rights is that of Alex Honneth. Honneth draws on both Hegel and George Herbert Mead, a major founder of the symbolic interactionist school of sociology and psychology who offers social psychological insights that are missing in Hegel. But Honneth goes beyond both Hegel and Mead in specifying the relationship between recognition and rights.

Honneth makes several crucial arguments. The first is that rights are "depersonalized symbols of social respect."[15] In and of themselves, rights create a form of consciousness in which people can respect themselves because they deserve the respect of all other people. They hold their heads high as rights-bearers. Rights are a recognition that people have a moral/developmental core, that they are responsible agents. It is interesting that both Honneth and Hinchman cite the same passage from Joel Feinberg to convey a sense of that self-respect and sense of dignity, vis-à-vis the self and others, that is inherent in being a rights-bearer:

> Having rights enables us to "stand up like men," to look others in the eye, and to feel in some fundamental way the equal of anyone. To think of oneself as the holder of rights is not to be unduly but properly proud, to have that minimal self-respect that is necessary to be worthy

of the love and esteem of others. Indeed, respect for persons ... may simply be respect for their rights, so that there cannot be the one without the other. And what is called "human dignity" may simply be the recognizable capacity to assert claims.[16]

Second, it is only human rights, not just rights accruing to a particular citizenship, that can assure us that this moral capacity that is so deserving of respect is ours by our very nature as human beings. Third, Honneth ties this to a theory of change in which society advances morally through the advancement of claims for social recognition. And fourth, he establishes a relationship between the importance of recognition and Habermas's reliance on discursive openness. In fact, he defines "self-respect" thus: "In the experience of legal recognition, one is able to view oneself as a person who shares with all other members of one's community the qualities that make participation in discursive will-formation possible."[17]

The relationship between recognition and rights is one of three relationships involving recognition that Honneth discusses. The first is the relationship between recognition and primary relationships, such as familial love and friendship in which needs and emotions are developed and in which one gains a basic self-confidence. The second he calls "solidarity," in which traits and abilities of value to the community are developed and recognized resulting in self-esteem for the individual. The third is that of legal relations, which involve rights. Here is where the development of moral responsibility of the individual takes place. And here is where self-respect, as a rights-bearer equal to all under the law, takes place.

But I think that Honneth falls into the same error here as does his mentor Habermas. He too tightly associates rights with rational legality. This is precisely why he dissociates solidarity from rights. Human rights require much more than an aggregation of citizens possessing merely formal/legal rights under positive law. As I have already argued, they also must entail an affective element that permits individuals to express solidarity and empathy with others who are not members of the same political entity and who are not subject to the same positive law. This affective capacity, along with higher analytical and creative capacities, is part of what makes human beings unique among the species and is an essential part of what makes human rights possible and obligatory.

Despite my disagreement with Honneth, which is really an extension of my disagreement with Habermas's hyperrationalism, both he and Hinchman have performed a very enlightening service in flushing out the relationship between social recognition and human rights. This is important because the aspect of social recognition not only ties together the three values of *liberté, égalité,* and *solidarité* but also clarifies the obligation side of rights. It says to each and every one of us that we have an obligation to recognize each other as free and equal beings, to recognize that we all have certain needs in order to be able to fulfill our potentialities, and to recognize that we must be willing to enter into empathetic dialogic processes with each other so that we can engage in practical projects of mutual enhancement. Social recognition is a theoretical concept that helps us understand why the rigid dichotomy between rights and obligations that some (particularly strong individualists) advance simply does not hold.

Proposition 9: The rights holders who can claim social recognition can be individuals but also can be a variety of kinds of groups or collectivities; recognition can be withheld by states, nonstate groups or entities, and even by individuals and families
In Hegel's *Phenomenology of the Mind,* social recognition is something that is claimed by individuals in the process of the development of their own consciousness. The presumption in Hinchman and Honneth is not any different. And, indeed, I certainly do not quarrel with the contention that social recognition is a crucial claim that individuals as rights bearers have on each other. Where I would differ from the above theorists—and from Jack Donnelly, who, in arguing against collective human rights denies that solidarity can be a source of human rights[18]—is in the restriction of such a claim to individuals. It is curious that Hinchman and Honneth do so restrict it, first because one of the points in making use of a relational concept such as social recognition is to break with the extreme rights individualism so prevalent in Anglo-Saxon thought, and because the specific form that the recognition takes in Hegel is indeed group specific. Lords and bondsmen, serfs, or slaves (however one translates Hegel's German expression for the less than equal) are all socially constituted groupings. The fact of being so grouped is crucial for their identities, for which they are demanding recognition. Thus, it seems to me, both Hinchman and Honneth have passed up an opportunity to fully exploit the concept of social recognition in their attempt to move toward a more holistic way of thinking about human rights.

Against Donnelly's contention that there are no collective human rights and that when collectivities are at issue we should think of the situation as one of an exercise of human rights "by individuals *as members of a collective group,*"[19] I argue that this is an unacceptable reductionism. This is not purely a quantitative issue. Yes, individual rights are involved when a people are targeted for genocide by a regime or when claims are made for a right to practice a religion or live life according to certain cultural norms. But these are not purely a sum of individual rights. These are rights of a people, a collectivity seeking to be recognized as such, to live a certain kind of collective life that is based on a certain notion of solidarity and community. Since the Lockean-liberal Donnelly chooses to eliminate the value of solidarity from the human rights equation, he cannot grant the kind of recognition that is being sought. Given my conceptualization, this is an arbitrary negation.[20] If some human rights violations are purely, or almost purely, individual,[21] others are best conceptualized as both collective and individual.

This position differentiates my work from another body of work that in some respects is close to my own, the "capabilities approach." It bases its understanding of human rights on the ability of people to choose various modes of living. In the work of Amartya Sen, the major concern is the impoverished people of the non-Western world, while in the work of Martha Nussbaum it is with the plight specifically of women in those areas. Thus, one can see that their concerns are similar to my concern over domination understood as the constraint of human developmental potentialities. Nonetheless, both of them confine human rights claims to individuals. This is not so strange in Sen, who is quite heavily influenced by Rawls, but it seems very strange in Nussbaum, because she claims to "ground the capabilities approach in the Marxian/Aristotelian idea of truly human functioning" but in fact winds up with a more liberal Kantian (with the concern for reason supplemented by a concern for emotion) individualistic understanding of rights.[22] At the same time, her approach shares with mine the refusal to prioritize a single value, while in Sen's work there is a clear prioritization of liberty and, because of his understanding of that word, of political and civil rights.[23]

We can think of the victims of human rights violations in four different categories: individuals, ascriptive collectivities and individuals, nonascriptive collectivities and individuals, and the entire earth's population. Ascriptive groups are composed of people who are collectively identified by dominant groups and the institutions they control as being intellectually or morally inferior. Their composition is fixed in the sense that simply by virtue of being of the group, one's social recognition is tainted by the imposed characteristics and identity. If not subjected to genocidal annihilation, the group is usually consigned to life at the bottom of the social, economic, and political ladders.

Nonascriptive groups are defined by roles or actions. While in some political and economic contexts it might be very difficult, it is at least theoretically possible for people move in or out of these nonascriptive categories, for example, by engaging or ceasing to engage in political activity or by entering or leaving the wage labor force to become self-employed or the employers of others.

At the same time, we can conceive of three categories of human rights violators: states, nonstate groups or entities, and individuals or families. Table 3.1 gives an idea of which sorts of practices fall under the different categories.

This visual tabular overview should indicate to the reader why I think that human rights are far too complex to be handled simply through the liberal individualist perspective that is so strong in Anglo-American thought and ideology. I will go into more detail in Chapter 4.

Table 3.1   Human rights violators and victims

Violators	Victims			
	Individuals	Ascriptive collectivities and individuals	Nonascriptive collectivities and individuals	Everyone
States	denial of right to habeas corpus; denial of due process of law; use of torture to extract confessions	genocide; racially discriminatory laws or enforcement and punishment; criminalization of homosexuality; denial of vote to women; racial, ethnic, or gender discrimination in public education	denial of right to organize politically; denial of right to political expression of opposition groups or parties; denial of workers' rights to organize or strike	nuclear tests
Nonstate groups or entities	terrorism where victims are random	genocide; racist, antisemitic, or homophobic violence; racial discrimination in private housing and health care	exploitation and/or denial of workers' rights by corporations; child labor	industrial pollution; deforestation; resource depletion
Individuals and families	selling children into prostitution	selling only girls into prostitution; forced female genital cutting and infibulation		

Proposition 10: Since the criterion for human rights violations is an impediment to development within a web of cultural, economic, and social relationships, social, economic, and cultural rights must have the same standing as political and civil rights Even though Articles 22 through 27 of the U.N.'s 1948 Universal Declaration of Human Rights covers a wide range of economic, social, and cultural rights, these rights were split off as early as 1951 in the subsequent drafting of legally binding covenants. This was because of pressure from the Western governments that dominated the U.N.'s Commission of Human Rights.[24] As we have seen in the last chapter, the United States had been a major supporter of economic and social rights under the Roosevelt Administration and Eleanor Roosevelt continued that support when she represented the United States on the Commission during the Truman Administration. But the political climate in the world and the United States changed in the early 1950s and the 1960s. There was the emancipation of former colonies, the Cold War, and an attack on the Roosevelt Administration's internal and external policies, especially its conception of the relationship between freedom and economic rights or entitlements. Thus, even though President Carter signed the 1966 International Covenant of Economic, Social, and Cultural Rights in 1977, the Senate has not ratified it. As I also indicated in the previous chapter, a similar hostility to economic and social rights was exhibited by Conservative governments in Great Britain. More precisely, they abstained from the Council of Europe's Social Charter, a strong statement in support of workers' rights, and after first successfully insisting on a weakening of the Protocol on Social Policy (usually referred to as the Social Chapter, but here referred to as the Protocol to avoid confusion with the Council's Social Charter) of the Treaty on European Union signed in Maastricht in 1992, they refused to sign even the weakened version.[25] The idea of the Protocol was to codify the earlier Social Charter into legally binding and enforceable treaty form.

A number of objections have been voiced against the concept of economic and social rights. In Chapter 2, we noted Maurice Cranston's point that if human rights are going to be something very special over and above other kinds of rights they must be restricted in number and kept close to the sorts of rights enumerated in the eighteenth-century French and American documents that addressed themselves to political and civil rights. He also argued that economic and social rights are applied to partial segments of humanity and thus are not universalistic the way political and civil rights are. Finally, he argued that political and civil rights are more easily translated into law and practice, especially in places of low development and resources.

Then there are the arguments of free market economists, extremely skeptical of the state's role in economic life, who became so influential in the United States and Great Britain during the Thatcher and Reagan years, and whose ideas retain an intellectual and practical influence globally. For example, both Friedrich von Hayek and Milton Friedman have argued that rights conceptions should be limited to protection of what Berlin called "negative liberty," that is, rights to be free of external compulsion in body and property as Locke had conceived them.[26] In addition to a general philosophical principle regarding freedom, they also both feel that such a conception is a necessary undergirding of the most efficient way of allocating resources, the unfettered market in which people are free to make choices on the basis of individual self-interest. This way of thinking about rights undercuts the consideration of economic and social rights because such rights mandate some action on the part of states to ensure or directly provide these rights. That action, both in the form of mandatory social ("social engineering") and fiscal (redistribution through taxing and spending) policy, is seen as a curtailment of individual freedom of choice. Thus, while the respect for "negative liberty" was seen as not violating any rights because the role of the state was purely protective of private bodies and properties, economic or social rights were seen as inherently violating the rights of some in favor of the entitlement claims of others.

Another reason advanced for rejecting such rights has been the fear of their use by developing, non-Western countries and by dominated minorities within the West. Both might assert a right to reparations for the past damage of imperialism, colonialism, slavery, and forced removal and confinement—especially in the face of continuing enormous gaps in wealth and living standards. An additional justification offered for denying the validity of economic and social rights claims has been that they would be used by non-Western political elites to justify the denial of political and civil rights. Thus, in 1992, during the presidency of the first George Bush, an introduction to the State Department's Country Reports on Human Rights Practices for that year expressed the administration's hostility to such rights, thus: "The urgency and moral seriousness of the need to eliminate starvation and poverty from the world are unquestionable ... the idea of economic and social rights is easily abused by repressive governments which claim that they promote human rights even though they deny their citizens the basic ... civil and political rights."[27]

Given my earlier propositions, I must reject the above arguments against economic and social human rights. The full development of human beings is every bit as contingent on their exercise of these rights as it is on the exercise of their political and civil rights. The arguments to the contrary are interesting but not convincing. Cranston's position would freeze human rights in the context of time, arguing that because documents written at the end of the eighteenth century did not incorporate the economic and social rights advanced in the twentieth century after World War II, the latter are invalid. Indeed, if human rights are social practices in response to dominating conditions, they cannot be frozen in time. They must be living and changing. Domination is almost never limited to the political. Domineering wealth and political power are perquisites of each other. Thus, so are political and economic rights.

Despite the absence of such economic and social rights in the eighteenth-century French and American documents, the relationship between economic and political power and rights was as true then as it is today, when this relationship is given recognition in a number of international documents to which most eligible countries subscribe. The 1986 United Nations Declaration on the Right to Development states succinctly in Article VI, 2: "All human rights are indivisible and interdependent; equal attention and urgent consideration should be given to the implementation, promotion and protection of civil, political, economic, social and cultural rights." But the same point had been made earlier in the 1948 U.N. General Assembly's Universal Declaration of Human Rights, in the 1966 Covenant on Economic, Social and Cultural Rights, and in the 1969 American Convention on Human Rights. It would be repeated the same year (1986) in the African Charter on Human and Peoples' Rights and, as we will see in greater depth later in this chapter, it appears in the authoritative documents of both the Council of Europe and the European Union. Thus, despite the Anglo-American positions previously discussed, there is now an international consensus on the viability of not only economic but also social and cultural human rights. This recognition represents a process of international social learning over time.

Moreover, Cranston's argument that economic and social rights apply to particular segments of humanity, for example, workers or the impoverished, and are thus different from political and civil rights that are universalistic, is not convincing. I have already made the argument for group rights in Proposition 9. But beyond that, and meeting Cranston on his own assumptions, the economic rights are more universalistic than he is willing to grant. For, while not everyone is a worker or impoverished at any given point in time, everyone runs a risk of being forced to sell his or her labor and/or to live in impoverishment or even to perish. This has been true in the past when there has been lower total world wealth, but is no less true in the present with the ever-increasing concentration of the world's wealth and control over land and resources and the resulting displacement of rural populations.[28] Indeed, these factors make it even more difficult for most of the world's people to avoid selling their labor.

Second, Cranston writes as though political and civil rights themselves are universal in the sense of being without categorical distinctions. Class, race, gender, age, citizenship, education, language ability, and criminal record have all entered into the question of determining who is to possess the right to vote. And the right of habeas corpus, while potentially applicable to everyone, is only applicable to people who have been charged with criminal behavior. But it is there for all to use when they do fall into the category of the accused just as worker rights should be there when people are in that economic position.

A final theoretical problem with Cranston's rejection of economic human rights has already been discussed in Chapter 2, that is, Henry Shue's point that if people are starving to death the political and civil rights are not meaningful. To be meaningful, we must recognize prior rights to subsistence and security. Cranston might be right that it is easier to translate political and civic rights into law and to enforce them, and that under certain conditions of scarcity one cannot do it, but that is not enough to rescue his theoretical argument. Under certain conditions (e.g., the U.S. Civil War), habeas corpus might be suspended by relatively rights-respecting regimes and it might be impossible to actually protect people's rights to speak and assemble. But that does not invalidate the right. Rights concepts are just more complex and relational than the political philosopher Cranston was willing to admit.

The arguments by economists such as Hayek and Friedman, who have been so influential on political leaders and economic institutions (especially the International Monetary Fund), begin with such strongly individualistic presumptions that any external impediment to the pursuit of self-interest imposed by a government in the name of social policy is not just more difficult but tyrannical. And that seems to be the only impediment that they are concerned with. There is no conception on their part that humans are not totally free monads, that they indeed develop through a process of "co" as well as "self" development. There is an exclusion of the values of equality and solidarity in favor of a conception of liberty that is constricted to a monadic pursuit to fulfill individual desire and self-interest, that is, a demeaning of so many interdependencies that constitute and give meaning to human life. Moreover, there seems to be no recognition that they are not living in the age of Locke. They are living in the age of bureaucratic corporations that have enormous power to determine the quality of life people live. Yet, they do not see this power as coercive. On the contrary, they use the legal fiction that these corporations are merely individuals deserving of equal protection with real individuals. It is extremely interesting that this fictional exceptional case in Western jurisprudence is offered to an economic entity in order to guarantee its economic rights claims, but that rights claims of other collective entities find it so difficult to get the same hearing.

In regard to the charge that economic and social rights can be used by regimes to claim that they are rights respecting while they violate political and civic rights, of course this is not only a possibility but also a factual practice in certain countries. But I have not argued for negating political and civic rights in favor of economic and social rights, and I do not see that there is any necessity to see these sets of rights as involved in a zero-sum relationship. In my holistic conception, both must be recognized, respected, and mediated, because domination entails the denial of both sets of rights.

Thus, the refusal to recognize egalitarian and solidaristic economic and social rights makes no conceptual sense given my prior propositions. Within nations, those who live lives of disproportionate poverty, malnutrition, high infant mortality rates, poor or no health care, low life expectancy, and low educational and employment opportunity have valid remedial human rights claims. At the international level, economic structures or willful economic actions, such as forcing austerity measures or impossible loan terms on poor nations or imposing economic blockades or embargoes, constitute as serious a blockage to developmental possibilities of the majority of the people in those countries as outright colonial domination did. Unlike misery because of natural causes or the isolation of some groups that live lives of extreme scarcity (nomadism, or hunting and gathering), structural or willed economic, social, or cultural deprivation must be considered human rights deprivations, because they result in a blockage of the developmental possibilities of masses of the population in these countries.

Proposition 11: You don't have to be a Western intellectual to understand the basic premises behind a holistic theory of human rights Thus far I have made reference to a number of Western philosophers or theorists and to texts drawn up by relatively learned political leaders. But perhaps the most poignant statement that I have read that expresses the complex nature of human beings consistent with my holistic view of human rights is a Zulu aphorism taught to Jordan Ngubane when he was a child. It is too long to include in its entirety, but a short segment will give the reader an idea of how ordinary people in non-Western societies can think of human rights holistically without using the expression "human rights." Sometimes we can look at analogous conceptions and be struck at how they get right to what we mean to say when we use a particular expression:

> I evolve forever, in response to the challenge of being human.
> I have a mind to light my path in the mazes of the cosmic order.
> This mind has many sides;
> It comprehends all things;
> It establishes my right to latitude; to being heard;
> It makes me feel at home in the cosmic order.
> My neighbor has a mind;
> It, also, comprehends all things.
> My neighbor and I have the same origins;
> We have the same life-experience and a common destiny;
> We are the obverse and reverse sides of one entity;
> We are unchanging equals;
> We are the faces which see themselves in each other;
> We are mutually fulfilling complements;
> We are simultaneously legitimate values;
> My neighbor's sorrow is my sorrow;
> His joy is my joy.
> He and I are mutually fulfilled when we stand by each other in moments of need.
> His survival is a precondition of my survival.
> That which is freely asked or freely given is love;
> Imposed love is a crime against humanity.
> I am sovereign of my life;
> My neighbor is sovereign of his life;
> Society is a collective sovereignty;
> It exists to ensure that my neighbor and I realize the promise of being human.
> I have no right to anything I deny my neighbor…
> I define myself in what I do to my neighbor.
> No community has any right to prescribe destiny for other communities…
> Equals do not prescribe destiny for each other;
> They hold conversations of minds.[29]

CONCLUSION

Conversations of minds across cultural boundaries represent the only hope for a conception of human rights that is truly universal. It has been argued that such a conception must be based on recognition of a universal capacity for human development. The actual processes of such development will take place within, and will be largely contingent on, material and cultural conditions. Not monadic individuals but, rather, people struggling for recognition and inclusion within webs of social relationships, that is, engaged in a process of both co- and self-determination, are the generators and claimants of human rights. If their struggles against domination are to avoid falling into new forms of domination and thus new human rights abuses, they must, as does Ngubane's aphorism, incorporate all three of the fundamental values—liberty, equality, and solidarity. In the West, but most especially in the United States, there is too often a sacrifice of the latter in the name of a hyperindividualistic conception of liberty. Outside of the West, it is more often liberty that is sacrificed in the name of a nationalistic or ethnic solidarity. Within both contexts, the ostensible reasons given to justify such options more often than not turn out to serve the political and economic antiegalitarian interests of dominating elites. While recognizing the complexity of mediating or negotiating among the three values within concrete situations, a holistic theory of human rights cannot accept the rejection of one in the name of another.

Having argued for this holistic conception, in Chapter 4 I will turn to a more detailed discussion of the rights holders and violators that appear in Table 3.1.

CHAPTER 4

THE HOLDERS AND VIOLATORS OF
HUMAN RIGHTS

INTRODUCTION

As we have already seen, two propositions in the last chapter have been matters of contention in the theoretical literature as well as in the practical political world. The first is that it is not only individuals who are human rights holders. Jack Donnelly argued that only individuals can be human rights holders and denied the relevance of solidarity to human rights. For him, collectivities such as groups or nations can have certain rights, but never human rights.[1] These are reserved for individuals and seem to be undergirded only by the values of liberty and equality. Donnelly challenges non-Western writers—such as Asmarom Legesse and Issa Shivji—who have advanced more collectivist or solidaristic conceptions of human rights.[2]

The second proposition that has been one of contention is that economic, social, and cultural rights are as important as political and civil rights, or indeed that they have any standing as human rights. We have already discussed Maurice Cranston's opposition to them and the facts that the U.S. Senate has refused to date to ratify the 1966 Convention and that State Department under the Reagan and first Bush administrations were overtly hostile to it. Furthermore, the almost universal consent to them on the part of other governments has been severely strained by the turn toward free market neoliberalism. In addition to these concerns, there is also the point that even if taken seriously, they are not as easily implemented as free speech or abolition of torture that require abstention from certain actions. The social and economic rights are "positive" rather than "negative," in that they require policies and action that some countries might find difficult because of their level of economic development.

But a third concept, presented in Proposition 9 and seen in the table on page 92, also might be challenged. That is that nonstate groups, and indeed even individuals and families, can be human rights violators. Usually it is the state that is seen as the potential human rights violator. Indeed, those human rights conventions and agreements that have the force of treaties do begin with the phrase, "The States Parties." So, in strictly legal terms, it could be argued that only those acting under state authority can violate such agreements, and thus that only those acting under such law can be human rights violators.

From my holistic theoretical perspective, I conceive of human rights from the perspective of the claims and struggles of victims of rights violations. These not only can be violations under state authority but also of others as well. In the latter case, states have the obligation to intercede and remedy the violations even if they are not the direct perpetrators. Indeed, sometimes it is difficult to prove whether the state is or is not a party to the perpetration, as in the case of some of the death squads that have been so prominent in the history of Latin America during the past century. Some might have been the creations of private land owners. But even if it could not be proved that a given death squad was a creation of a government or receiving support from it, the activity of these death squads would be a human rights violation and toleration by a government would constitute an additional violation.

I will deal in greater length with issues of economic rights, specifically workers' rights, in Chapter 5, and with cases of state violations of human rights in Chapter 6. In this chapter, I will defend in greater depth my own propositions that (1) it is not only individuals who are human rights-holders, and (2) that the state is not the only rights-violator.

Rights-Holders

If one admits the viability of the concept of rights, it would be ludicrous to deny that they apply to individuals. It would not be ludicrous but, rather, just mistaken to claim that every time there was a collective interest or desire that seemed to conflict with individual rights claims, the former should trump the latter. This seems to come close to the claims made by some non-Western leaders who are intent on maintaining authoritarian political systems, at the same time claiming that they respect human rights. Some rights usually pertain to individuals. They include rights such as the right to habeas corpus, the right to due process of law, and the right to not be tortured. These rights have been recognized as a result of an historical evolution of the conceptions of both the state and the individual. There was a time when people thrown in the Tower of London were never seen alive again and when Star Chamber proceedings took testimony under torture.

Similar practices of due process violations and cruelty continue in some instances, in the West as well as elsewhere, but there is an international consensus that they violate the human rights of the individuals on whom they are inflicted. When made public, as when from 1988 to 1991 police officers in Philadelphia manufactured evidence and lied before the courts in order to frame innocent people, the guilty verdicts are *usually* overturned.[3] The problem is that the abuses are all too often not even discovered, much less made public, because of the à priori credence given to the word of the police officers of the state in the state's own courts.

But even here the issue is not so simple. For example, the victims of the Philadelphia police officers were not just random people whom the police had identified as "bad apples" who needed to be off the streets. They were African Americans.

With this additional information, we move from merely the violation of rights of individuals by the state, to the nonrecognition and violation of the rights of a specific group, that is, the right of African Americans to receive due process from the police and the courts the way in which other people do. Had the problem been one in which the victims were random, it would have been a matter of purely individual human rights. Thus, *randomized* denial of habeas corpus, *randomized* denial of due process, and *randomized* torture or brutality (for example, if I, who am white and middle class, would stand an equal chance with Rodney King of being beaten by the police) constitutes individual rights violations in the pure form. But the nonrandom violation of due process is both a violation of the rights of the individual *and* a violation of the rights of the entire group that is harmed.

Similarly, in cases of genocide we see the violation of both individual and groups rights. In the 1951 U.N. Convention on the Prevention and Punishment of the Crime of Genocide, it is defined as meaning any of the following: killing members of the group, causing them serious physical or mental harm, inflicting conditions calculated to bring about the group's destruction in whole or in part, instituting measures to prevent birth within the group, or forcibly transferring its children to another group. Even those group members not physically harmed are forced to live intimidated and fearful lives.

There are other collective rights, such as the right to self-determination and the right to development, which in the U.N. Declaration on the Right to Development of 1986 includes the right to development of "peoples" as well as of "every human person" (Article 1). It makes no sense to talk about genocide, about the right of national self-determination, or about the right of "peoples" to development if one also argues that human rights only pertain to individuals. This entails an absurd reductionism.

In sum, rights claims of groups, which include but are not limited to the rights of each individual therein, have been triggered by instances of domination over specific collectivities (for example, genocide, discrimination), while purely individual rights claims (for example, right to due process, habeas corpus) have mostly been triggered by generalized patterns of what came to be seen as tyrannical and brutal behavior by governments.

BASES FOR GROUP DOMINATION AND RIGHTS

The United Nations has adopted documents that address discrimination on the basis of gender, religion, and race. Aside from these bases of domination, one could add language, nationality, sexual orientation, physical condition, mental or psychological state, and class standing or work situation. I will defer discussion of the latter until the chapter on human rights and the economy.

While the categories are overlapping, it might be useful to group them into three: (1) those where there are physical, biological, or physiological differences that are seen or perceived immediately on view, (2) those that are based on cultural differences, and (3) those that are based on nationalist aspirations. The categories are not just overlapping; they often flow into each other in consecutive order.

Physical, Biological, or Physiological Differences

Visible difference from the norm has for centuries been interpreted as inferiority. To use a Sartrean term, the "look" immediately establishes socially relevant differences.[4] The definers of the social meanings of these differences are usually, but not always, the majority. There is thus constructed a relationship of domination in which the dominated group or category is recognized as having less of a potentiality for development, or is indeed stripped of any potentiality, by the dominating one.

One example of such a difference is gender. This is a physical/biological difference. The bodies of men and women are different in terms of genitalia and general body frame. Recognition of women is made easier in virtually every culture by difference of dress and ornamentation. Thoughts, words, and behavior are adapted accordingly. In contrast to Plato, who was willing to make women philosopher kings in *The Republic* (although he was convinced that women at any rank in that society would be a cut below the men in capability), Aristotle thought that women were incapable of reason and thus incapable of rulership over rational beings. They were therefore depoliticized. The only beings they could rule over were prerational children and household slaves. This view of women was often justified by physical or physiological rationales (for example, smaller size, less physical power, menstrual cycle, the conviction that the uterus could dislodge and produce irrational behavior—hence the word "hysteria," as in hysterical women). Imagined women who departed from this were thought of as monsters, as in the "Amazons." This is despite the fact that Spartan women did in fact participate in many of the activities that the Athenians thought of as exclusively male, and served as a model for Plato's thinking about gender relations. But it was Aristotle, not Plato, who proved to be the more powerful ideologue for thinking about gender relations in the Western world. Once a newly born child was recognized as a female, her possibilities for future development were very different from that of a male child. Of course, this was true in most cultures. The perception of the physical/biological difference between the female and the male immediately turned into a social recognition of very differential developmental possibilities. Thus was Marx led to remark that the very first division of labor was not the productive one that he devoted his life to analyzing but the sexual reproductive and familial division of labor.[5] The domination involved in the stifling of the rational and creative potentialities of women was all the more powerful in that it was rooted in "nature." It was left to women to develop their affective emotional potentialities. These were the appropriate characteristics for giving emotional support to children and to husbands who faced the hardships of the world outside the home. These public activities required rational and creative qualities that were thought to be uniquely male.

The Western tradition squeezes women between two conflicting visions. One is that women, particularly mothers, are to be held in great respect. Thus, the old prohibitions on not swearing before them or discussing politics or other women in their presence. By contrast, women are dangerous. They gossip. This is not just a harmless activity of the idle but often is seen as malicious. They are self-indulgent, often a drag on the man who might otherwise do great things in the rational or creative realm. Thus does Plato—the very same Plato who would make women as well as men philosopher kings—blame women for the fall of his ideal state in his theory of state degeneration. For it was the "wife" who diverted the otherwise civic-minded husband into placing the honor and status of the particularistic family above the good of the state (the initial step in the degeneration of the ideal state, from aristocracy to timocracy). This Platonic rendition of the fall of the ideal state bears a strong resemblance to the biblical myth of Eve tempting Adam.

Myth and religion play strong roles in legitimizing the transformation of physical and biological difference into domination. One of the most interesting myths is that of the Kikuyu people in East Africa, which says that in the beginning women were physically stronger than men and used their physical power to dominate them. (It is such myths that gave rise to the fictitious Amazons.) The men came together and planned a strategy. They would use the women's bodies against them. They decided to impregnate all the women at the same time. When all of the women were in the late term of their pregnancies, the men revolted. Since the women's ability to defend themselves was severely curtailed by the burden of pregnancy, the men won easily. Thus, the women have no right to complain about their situation in life now. The men are only doing to the women what the women had done to the men when they held power—a perfect example of reciprocity and fairness, made possible by natural reproductive functions. Could a more powerful justification of domination, incorporating both historical reciprocity and nature, be conceived?

It is only much later in the Western world that the demands for social recognition of women as equals across the board were raised. As far as I can determine it began in the late fourteenth and early fifteenth centuries with Christine de Pisan, who challenged Aristotle's demeaning of women's rational capacities and pointed to the achievements of historical queens;[6] continued in the eighteenth century works of Mary Wollstonecraft, who challenged the acceptance of patriarchal domination by both Rousseau and Burke, and Olympe de Gouges, who protested that the French Declaration of the Rights of Man and Citizen were not being applied to women and offered her own "Declaration of the Rights of Woman and the Female Citizen";[7] and more recently manifested in the feminist and suffrage movements of the nineteenth and twentieth centuries. As we have seen, it was only in 1979 that women were given "official" international recognition by being encoded in an international convention. That convention takes note of discrimination specific to women. Women as a whole, women as a category, women as constituted groups, can make claims to the recognition of their rights under it.

Race is similar to gender in that it is physical and immediately recognizable and has been given social meanings that support domination. The negative attributions vary. One of the justifications used in the American South for slavery was an Aristotelian one. Aristotle criticized slavery for the way in which it was practiced in Greece. He thought that only those who were incapable of leading rational lives themselves ought to be slaves. Thus, slavery would be ideally a symbiotic rather than merely a dominating relationship. The slave would deliver labor to the slave-master and the slave-master would make the decisions requiring reason for the slave. In the American South, it was felt that the Africans and their descendants were inferior. They were lacking in reason (just as Aristotle had seen the tribes of northern Europe and the Asians as rationally inferior to the Greeks), and they were lazy because they never worked hard enough without supervision and the whip. Thus, teaching a slave to write, aside from being seen as dangerous to the institution of slavery (a point Frederick Douglass proved), also went against the natural abilities of the slave. It was, as it were, a crime against nature that was punished very severely. Both the teacher and the student could suffer for it, including having their lives taken. It is interesting that while there was no law against educating Indians in Guatemala in the 1980s, Indians who were known to be literate, for example, Indians wearing eyeglasses, were special targets of the U.S.-supported repressive forces of that country.

The claim that certain races are inferior is not dead. Unfortunately, some social scientists seem to feel the need to make the point that if one compares intelligence test scores between races, some do better than others. One could make of this "finding" that it points to the need to desegregate housing and schools, ensure proper nutrition and preschool health care and learning experiences, and to make sure that uniform skills and resources are devoted to the education of all of our children. That would be a valid rights claim under the 1966 Covenant on Economic, Social, and Cultural Rights. But one suspects that the motivation of these social scientists is the alleviation of guilt and social responsibility for the existence of such differential opportunities. If we recognize one physically identifiable group as having much less developmental potential than another, would it not be as cruel a hoax to offer these people better educational opportunities as to try to teach a slave to read? These contemporary social scientists writing about I.Q. differences between the races sound ever so much like Aristotle writing about women.[8] They all write as scientists, only interested in offering the legitimacy of science to confirm differences that are already visible to the dominators on the faces of the dominated. As always, claims of social recognition as free and equal beings run up against the intellectual justifiers, as well as the rawer instruments of power, of the groups that are withholding such recognition.

But racial otherness is not only seen as indicating inferiority as rational and creative beings. It is often also taken as a sign of evil or sin. Indian fighter General Philip Sheridan is quoted as having said: "The only good Indians I ever saw were dead."[9] That was the inspiration for the more popular expression in the mid-nineteenth-century United States: "The only good Indian is a dead Indian." The whites did what they could to make all Indians good. Nazi filmmakers equated the Jews with rats swarming all over German society. A good number of years ago, I had a very long conversation with a Mormon who telephoned to proselytize. Most of the conversation centered around the Mormon belief that black people had dark skins as a sign of God's punishment. This justified exclusion from church offices, an exclusion that was subsequently reversed after severe criticism from outside the church. In the United States, whites often associate African Americans with inherent characteristics of violence and criminality. Asians, by contrast, have been viewed as "inscrutable," tricky, cruel, not valuing life quite in the way Westerners do, or too aggressively smart and wanting to monopolize all the seats in the classes on science and technology in U.S. universities, or trying to buy their way into political influence through illegitimate campaign contributions. In France, the National Front has enjoyed important electoral success at the local levels and, even more important, success framing the issue for the other parties at the national level by blaming "immigrants" (a code word for Arabs almost exclusively until 1996, when the resistance of undocumented sub-Saharan Africans to deportation captivated French T.V. audiences)[10] for crime, lowering the quality of the French public school, and corrupting the true "French" way of life. Arabs and blacks are often accosted on the streets, purely because they are recognized as people of color, by the French police who ask for their identity papers. Arab men and boys also seem to die disproportionately in the hands of the French police and right-wing mobs.

There has been an internationalization of differential recognition. Just as most Americans conjure up an image of a black single mother when they think of "welfare recipient," even though most welfare recipients are white, so profiles of terrorists or suspected illegal immigrants at international airports are skewed toward people of color.[11] Long before the destruction of the Twin Towers, Middle Eastern people of color were recognized by many whites as sneaky potential terrorists. Initially, the rumor was spread by American law enforcement officers and the media that the bombing on the Federal Building in Oklahoma City was probably the work of Middle Eastern terrorists. The Clinton administration used that to gain more power to move against foreigners suspected of terrorism in the United States. Yet, two white male U.S. citizens were subsequently convicted of the crime.

In all of these cases of differential reaction to race or skin color, those negatively affected collectively have a human right to demand that the dominant perceivers, to use an expression of Sheldon Wolin, "re-cognize." Wolin writes: "When the system of representations that guides recognition is upset, re-cognition is possible. We might think of re-cognition as the radical revision in the culturally produced representations of a familiar being as when once current images of 'Negro,' 'Indian,' woman,' or 'sexual deviant' were shattered during the first half of the twentieth century."[12] That process, as we begin the twenty-first century, is far from complete. Because (1) the self-identity and self-image of those viewed negatively from the very moment that they are perceived by dominant Others suffers, and (2) the material circumstances of their lives are usually made more difficult, one can say that the fulfillment of their developmental potential is stunted. As a group, they thus have a human rights claim to be "seen" ("cognized") as beings equal with all others, and to be freed of intentional and structural discrimination.

One of the "seen" groups or categories least often recognized in the literature on human rights, including the formal international documents that are silent regarding them, are those who are differently formed, those who suffer from illness, or those who are subject to mental or psychological conditions. To be sure, severe cases of physical and mental illness can require institutionalization, and— Michel Foucault notwithstanding—not all institutions are simply dominators. Sometimes hospitals, nursing homes, and mental institutions are the only way of assuring that needed care will be given. But it is true that mental or physical affliction has been used as justification for stigmatizing and/or locking people up in institutions out of view of the general public, when this was not in their best interests and frustrated their development as human beings. The notorious case is that of people with leprosy. The disease was disfiguring and dreaded. It was dealt with as a social blight, and the victims were feared, ostracized, and placed out of sight. Cancer was a disease that a generation ago people did not talk about. It caused fear and shame. As in the case of leprosy, one wondered if the victims had not brought this upon themselves through bad thoughts or actions. Among certain people, AIDS is interpreted as the wages of sin and the people who have it are considered to deserve separation and ostracism.

In the *Republic,* Plato recommended that babies born with deformities or abnormalities be left out in the elements to die. While the situation has been improving over time, today in many settings paraplegics and hearing and sight impaired people still have difficulty in establishing themselves in the eyes of others as persons who have rights to what is required for them to lead full and active lives and to make important social contributions. The struggles of Helen Keller on behalf of the sight impaired and of Thomas Hopkins Gallaudet on behalf of the hearing impaired were in very profound ways human rights struggles. Theirs was a struggle for recognition of such afflicted people as free and equal with as much of a claim to developmental and educational opportunities as sighted and hearing people. The struggle to consider people with afflictions such as Down's syndrome as fully human and capable of learning and expressing themselves in ways that are worth listening to is a newer struggle. The fact that as yet these struggles of and for people with physical and mental afflictions are not in any international agreements does not make them any the less human rights struggles.

When I say that these differences are physical, biological, or physiological, I do not mean to say that the social consequences drawn from them are in any way "natural." I thus reject the terminology of William Felice, who refers to groups based on race, gender, and sexuality as "natural groups."[13] Quite the contrary, the relationships of domination, of the stifling of potentialities, are all socially constructed. I separate them from the cultural differences discussed below for two reasons. The first is that it is important to understand that power relations of domination and subordination are often established around physical differences from which there is no possible escape for the dominated. One can change purely cultural attributes either under pressure or if one wills to do so. Second, it provides a rubric for discussing some of the human rights issues associated with disease, bodily deformation, and mental conditions that are as yet ignored in the international consensus. It was not very long ago that a vice presidential candidate in the United States was driven from his candidature because it became known that he had sought psychological therapy.

Groups Based on Cultural Differences

Where race and color are concerned, there often is overlap between the physically visible differences and culture. But this is not always the case. It tends to be in the United States, where there are distinctive black and Latino cultures; or in Nicaragua, where black, Indian, and Hispanic cultures remain quite distinct; but such distinctions do not seem to hold in Cuba.

The two most often considered differences, which are not based on any physical characteristics, are those of language and religion or spiritual outlook. Often, French-speaking and English-speaking Canadians or Flemish and French speakers in Belgium do not look very different. The same is true of Catholics and Protestants in Northern Ireland, or of Hindus and Moslems in India before the creation of Pakistan. But such cultural differences often produce discriminatory practices that limit the developmental possibilities of some of these cultural groups.

More basically and more positively stated, culture is one of the crucial milieux in which we develop our affective and creative potentials, and in doing so create our identities. We cannot develop ourselves as individuals and relate to others without a cultural framework. Thus, Will Kymlicka has devoted much of his writing to trying to convince liberals that if they are really interested in the developmental possibilities of individuals, they cannot ignore the necessary cultural contexts of that development.[14] He thus argues that it would be wrong of them to leave the defense of culturally based group rights to more communitarian writers such as Charles Taylor (whose communitarianism is multicultural) or Michael Sandel (whose communitarianism is more unified and totalizing).[15]

Both Kymlicka and Taylor are Canadians.[16] Kymlicka, of Eastern European descent, is particularly interested in the rights of the indigenous populations and the survival of their cultures when presented with the dominant European populations. Kymlicka differentiates between voluntary immigrant groups and those that have become involuntary minorities, such as Inuits and Native Americans in North America, or African Americans who did not choose to come to the United States. They have been left out of the dominant modernizing culture and thus can make a claim to specific "group differentiating rights." But the ultimate grounding here is that they require shared values and traditions in order to establish identities and securities that are necessary for individuals to make choices. They are not comfortable with, and/or are excluded from, the dominant modern "societal culture," which itself is devoid of shared normative values according to Kymlicka. However, people who made a free choice to immigrate to the United States or Canada cannot make such a claim. They have given up their old cultures in exchange for entry into the new national "societal culture," which is probably less tradition-bound than their old former culture and will thus offer them much more freedom of choice in terms of their own ends in life. In supporting group-specific rights based on the need that individuals in certain collective situations have for a rooting that will ultimately permit them to make individual choices, and in differentiating between such people and immigrants who have indeed made free choices, Kymlicka offers "a distinctively liberal defense of certain group-differentiated rights."[17] It also turns out that all of the cultural groups to which Kymlicka would "grant" group-specific rights are groups that are physically distinguishable.

Not so Taylor. Taylor, born of a French-Anglo marriage, is particularly interested in the contestation of the two "voluntary," not easily distinguishable by sight, immigrant European cultures in Canada. The two major groups, of which Taylor is an amalgam, differ on the basis of language, religion, and historical tradition. Taylor is very suspicious of the claim made by Kymlicka that "societal cultures," that is, the dominant cultures of liberal societies, are truly neutral when it comes to basic values and goals. The problem that Taylor sees is one of a lack of recognition, the inability of the procedural-bound Anglo culture in Canada to recognize the value of a Quebec that has explicit collective values and goals. Taylor sees the Anglo culture as inhospitable to difference, and this inhospitality to difference threatens the very survival of Quebecois culture. While Taylor is usually seen as a communaritarian, he does not give up on liberalism entirely. Rather, he calls for a liberalism "that is willing to weigh the importance of certain forms of uniform treatment against the importance of cultural survival, and opt sometimes in favor of the latter," as opposed to a procedural notion of liberalism, in which the same presumably neutral rules apply across the board regardless of differences in substantive values.[18] He calls for a broader perspective, a "fusion of horizons," in which we suspend presumptions about our ability to be neutral and blind to difference. This would entail a recognition of the difference of others, and the importance or value of that difference. It also would entail recognition of the fact that we can be equal and different at the same time. But, reverting to a communitarian suspicion of rights even as he opens himself up to a kind of expanded liberalism, Taylor writes, "I am not sure about the validity of demanding this presumption as a right."[19] If he is suspicious of rights and its association with a certain kind of liberalism and a certain conception of freedom and of neutrality, how can the presumption of recognition of equal worth of the culturally different be grounded? He ends his essay with this reflection:

> Merely on the human level, one could argue that it is reasonable to suppose that cultures that have provided the horizon of meaning for large numbers of human beings, of diverse characters and temperaments, over a long period of time—that have, in other words, articulated their sense of the good, the holy, the admirable—are almost certain to have something that deserves our admiration and respect, even if it is accompanied by much that we have to abhor and reject. Perhaps one could put it another way; it would take a supreme arrogance to discount this possibility à priori.[20]

It seems that Taylor does not see the relationship between social recognition and human rights that I am proposing, that is, the concept of social recognition is what ties together the other values that underlie human rights. I would propose to Taylor that it is precisely a commitment to human rights, as I am conceiving of them, that should constitute both the substantive and the procedural (for example, due process of law and participatory processes adequate to codetermination) values and goals that bind peoples.

While Taylor does not feel as comfortable with rights-talk as the liberal Kymlicka, he in fact shares with Kymlicka a sensitivity to two issues that are indeed clearly rights issues: (1) individuals being crushed in a communitarianism that does not respect the rights of individuals to critique, dissent, or withdraw from a cultural context entirely or from certain aspects of the culture; and (2) the clash of cultural claims made by two or more groups that feel themselves dominated, as in the Meech Lake Accords, in which the Anglo/French Canadian agreement was opposed by some of the indigenous groups for failing to recognize their rights. Call it what you will, Taylor is concerned about those complex issues in which conflicting participants are making rights claims and his introduction of the concept of social recognition into the discussion is insightful to those of us who do not shy away from the connection.

Kymlicka advocates group-specific rights under the banner of a kind of liberalism that sees a fundamental and necessary relationship between culture and the development of the individual. But he restricts these rights to indigenous groups that have been dominated by the intrusion of outside people, or groups that have been brought involuntarily to a foreign place and dominated there. Outside of these instances, there are no group rights and Kymlicka reverts to a more traditionally republican view of an open and neutral society in which the same rights apply to all individuals. Taylor sees the latter as a delusion, and casts the problem as one of recognition rather than as domination and rights—again, a needless and mistaken separation of closely related concepts, I would argue.

Language and religion or spirituality have been discussed within the context of collective identity and human rights for many years. But another phenomenon has only more recently manifested itself as an open culture with a distinctive style of living. That is gay and lesbian life. I think that William Felice is correct in characterizing this a "culture," albeit one with some unique characteristics. First, it is more voluntaristic and more consciously constructed by the members than is the case with language and religion, which tend to be handed down through familial generations. Gay and lesbian people are usually born into heterosexual families. Second, as Felice points out, thirty years ago those who were gays and lesbians remained "in the closet," for fear of losing their jobs, their children, or their very lives.[21] The "coming out" of these people has been an international phenomenon with a network of hotels, bars, nightclubs, and so on all over the world. They run up against both the antisodomy laws of many secular states and the prohibitions of most religions. In March 1993, an international organization working for the recognition of the right of gays and lesbians to live their lives openly and without discrimination, the International Lesbian and Gay Association (ILGA), was given roster nongovernmental organization (NGO) status by UNESCO, an arm of the United Nations. However, this was subsequently rescinded because "the ILGA was unable to convince the U.N. that ILGA member groups did not condone sex between adults and minors."[22] More recently the U.S.-based gay and lesbian Human Rights Campaign has been created to continue the fight for equality and social recognition of gays and lesbians, but there is as of this writing no formal international recognition. Recognized by the United Nations or not, the point is that the claim for such recognition is one that cannot be reduced to just an aggregation of individual claims, because there is a formation of a collective identity around a subculture that has been repressed and continues to be repressed in many countries.

Groups Based on Nationalist Aspirations

To my knowledge, gays and lesbians have not declared their right to political independence or to political autonomy within a larger state.

But claims based on cultural identity, almost always involving feelings of domination at the hands of another language and/or religious group, have on numerous occasions spilled over into claims for recognition as a separate nation-state. Article 15 of the 1948 U.N. Universal Declaration of Human Rights declares that "1. Everyone has the right to a nationality. 2. No one shall be arbitrarily deprived of his nationality nor denied the right to change his nationality." Part II, Article 4, of the 1966 U.N. International Covenant on Civil and Political Rights, states that: "All peoples have the right of self-determination. By virtue of the right they freely determine their political status and freely pursue their economic, social, and cultural development." To be sure, this did not appear in the 1945 Charter because some of the major Western powers of the United Nations were still trying to hold on to their colonial empires. By 1966, the violent and nonviolent struggles of the colonized had led to at least formal independence in most instances. Once again, the recognition of the normative human right followed concrete struggle.

This is conceptually one of the most difficult human rights issues to deal with. First, one must, on the one hand, acknowledge that "peoples" do exist and manifest differences from others, while, on the other hand, one must avoid homogenizing those people.

I will relate what was for me a very poignant experience in that regard. I went to the Jewish cemetery in Berlin to visit the grave sites of relatives who died and were buried there before the Nazis came to power. As I was leaving I noticed a very prominent stone and statue that was engraved with quite a long message. The man buried there had died between the two world wars. The engraving related the man's trade and very proudly declared his dedication to the "fatherland." The "fatherland" was not Israel but Germany. He was a Jew, but he was also a German. It was clear that he considered his nationality to be German, and his stone was written in German, not Hebrew or Yiddish. It was Hitler who imposed the monolithic identity on his descendants and then killed them because they could not really be German.

Today, it is almost impossible to find a society that is not multicultural and multinational. We have to learn to live with and respect differences, to accord many of those differences a universal protection in the form of rights. We also have to accept people breaking out of old traditions and identities and forging new ones. Eastern European Jews often chided German Jews for assimilating and thus thinking that they were superior to the Eastern European who had less of an opportunity to assimilate. Blacks or Latinos who move out of the old neighborhoods are sometimes viewed as deserters or pretenders, as "Uncle Toms." In other words, there is often an assumption that someone who belongs to a certain national or cultural group has a moral obligation or duty to display certain characteristics that one associates with the group. That reflects more of a stereotyping mentality than a respectful one. It also can lead to a totalitarian atmosphere within the group in which the rights of some members are violated because of nonconformity.

Indeed, nationalist claims usually are divisive within the groups making the claim. For example, there is a very vocal Puerto Rican nationalist movement that wants to achieve Puerto Rican independence from the United States. But most Puerto Ricans have indicated in referenda that they oppose this. This is thus a fracture line in Puerto Rican politics. The same is true in Canada. The nationalists among the Quebecois might someday get a slight majority favoring the creation of a Quebec state independent of the rest of Canada. They came very close last time. But they will still have a society divided over the desirability of the move.

Another problem is that the nationalist aspirations of one group that considers itself dominated can conflict with the aspirations of another group that also considers itself dominated. Such a case was the one already referred to in Canada over the Meech Lake Agreement. Or take the case of Algeria, where one had the so-called Harkis, who collaborated with the French occupation and enjoyed benefits from French rule before the Algerians won their war of independence. After the war, when many of them went to France to live, there still were differences among the Arabs, the Berbers, and some elements of the old Jewish population that had been there since fleeing persecution at the hands of the Catholic monarchy in Spain in the fifteenth and sixteenth centuries. Many of the Jews left, but the Berber population was not in a position to do so and has expressed feelings of being a dominated minority. The situation is even more complex in sub-Saharan Africa, where the colonizers carved out very arbitrary states in terms of ethnicity and culture, encouraged ethnic antagonism as a divide-and-conquer technique, and thus bear a large responsibility for human rights violations associated with the Biafran War and the Rwandan genocide.

This is not to deny the validity of the right of self-determination. It is only to say that when the United Nations talks about "peoples," the situation is usually a complex one involving more than one ethnic and national group, and often more than one group that is feeling dominated by the majority or most powerful identifiable "people." But group rights determinations still can, and must, be made in the face of such claims.

As indicated, a variety of rights claims can be made by such groups. They can include rights to the teaching and use of their own language, the practice of a religion, the reservation of a certain number of political offices or economic or educational opportunities for them, the rights of local control through legislative or judicial bodies, the right to certain economic resources (minerals, water, and so on), or the right to secession.

Secession poses its own unique problems. After genocide, it is perhaps the most drastic resolution of cultural conflict within a given political unit. It is at one and the same time an act of severance and an act of creation. It says to others in a political association, *we* no longer want to be recognized as a part of *you*. *We* want to be recognized by *you*, and by the rest of the world, as self-determining. *We* want to be in charge of our own destiny. And, of course, the claim is made that *we* have a human right to do so.

Ernest Gellner claims that a linguist gave him the number eight thousand for all of the languages in the world.[23] Now, there is something on the order of two hundred nation-states. If every small group in the world made a claim to self-determination, it is obvious that there would be a radical disjunction and disruption in the everyday life of the world. Treaties, agreements, exchanges, conveniences, commercial relations, and so on would be radically changed. Indeed, with some exceptions like those of the Florida Keys ("the Conch Republic"), secession is usually recognized as a very grave matter, often entailing warfare.

Because of the disruptive effects of secession on those remaining in the original entity, on third parties, and on those who try to create a new political entity, Allen Buchanan argues that the burden of proof that secession is better than other approaches (for example, local autonomy or a group veto) always lies on the shoulder of those who claim the right to secede. He thinks that the following criteria are among those that must be used before such a right can be acknowledged: (1) the state refuses to cease serious injustices that can be violations of civil and political rights *and* "discriminatory redistribution, the state's exploitation of one group to benefit others";[24] and (2) the need to preserve a group's culture and physical survival against third-party aggressors when the group's own state is not doing so. Buchanan places strict conditions on the latter justification: the threat has to be real, less drastic ways of preserving the culture are unavailable or inadequate, the seceding culture must meet minimal moral standards itself (Nazis and Khmer Rouge need not apply), the seceding people are not doing so with the intentions of setting up a state that violates basic rights and prevents exit from itself, and neither the original state nor a third party has a valid claim on the territory claimed by the secessionists.

Here we see in Buchanan's thinking about the limitations on rights to secession a parallel with the way we have been talking about group rights in general. No group, whether secessionist or not, has a right to make a human rights claim on something that violates the basic human rights of either members of its own group (for example, stifling all dissent within) or that violates the human rights claims of other individuals or collectivities of individuals. But for Buchanan it is especially necessary to apply these criteria rigorously to secessionist groups claiming to be recognized as independent political entities, because the possible harms to others' rights are so great. One of the major concerns is with a situation in which the "haves" decide to secede from the larger entity in order to avoid sharing with the "have-nots." The attempted secessions of both Katanga (the mineral-rich province of what is now called the Democratic Republic of the Congo) and Biafra (the economically industrious area peopled largely by Ibos in Eastern Nigeria) have been read by some, including the national Nigerian and Congolese leaderships, as more of an attempt by the well-off to go their own way than of a genuine attempt to advance a cultural identity that was being repressed in the larger nation. The counterclaim, especially in Katanga, was that the region saw no return for the depletion of its resources and that this exploitation in and of itself conferred a right to secession. A parallel claim has been made by some in Scotland against Great Britain for the depletion of its oil reserves, although the concept of "devolution" and the establishment of a separate legislature seems to have undercut talk of outright secession.

Buchanan's view of the right of a group to secede is a remedial one. That is, the right to secession is contingent on mistreatment within the unified state. David Copp takes issue with Buchanan on this point. Copp argues that the "right to self-determination is not a remedial right any more than is the right of a people to democratic government. In my view, the right to secession is supported by democratic considerations, and is therefore a matter of political justice in the way that the right of a people to democratic government is a matter of political justice."[25] Copp does not argue that this right confers on secessionist movements the right simply to pull out regardless of the effect on the rest of the unified country. Secession would have to take place under "just terms" that would need to be negotiated. But the general point Copp makes is that simply the will to form a political entity confers an à priori right under democratic presumptions. Domination or ill-treatment may or may not be involved; that's not the issue for Copp. For Copp, a collectivity that desires to be a separate political entity has a right to so form itself as such.

Whether one agrees with Buchanan or with Copp, suffice it to say that in some cases a people will have a human right, under the collective right to self-determination, to claim the right to take themselves out of one political community and to create another without migrating elsewhere. If collective rights entail more complexity than individual rights, and I certainly admit that they are more complex, secessionist rights claims are the most complex of that subset.

In everything that we have said thus far after discussing clearly individual human rights, we are refuting Jack Donnelly's contention, one that I myself used to hold, that "Groups, including nations, can and do hold a variety of rights. But these are not *human* rights."[26] I have been trying to argue in a theoretically consistent way that there are group and collective rights claims that should be considered to be human rights. I am taking a position similar to Iris Young's, in which she argues "group-specific rights and policies should stand together with general civic and political rights of participation and inclusion."[27] Young is arguing from the perspective of a "culturally pluralistic democratic ideal" within a given political system. But I would submit that the same logic applies to internationally recognizable human rights. Because of system-transcending structural determinants, as well as specific exclusionary restrictions and laws within some countries, it is not just a matter of each individual woman, African American, physically afflicted person, or lesbian having her rights or not having her rights. The problem cannot be understood solely in atomized individualistic terms, nor can the resolution. The fact that there are indeed uniquely individual rights does not preclude, as Jack Donnelly would have it, the validity of group or collective human rights in instances in which groups suffer the intentional and structural consequences of distorted recognition. To borrow a term from U.S. jurisprudence, they then, as a group, have "standing" to claim human rights. In the case of Native Americans, this was given recognition in the 1970s when they were given official standing to represent such claims before the United Nations. Ever since, they have been articulating their group human rights, and validly so in my view.

Where I am in agreement with Donnelly is in his drawing the line at states. Donnelly writes, "Even if we allow the existence of collective human rights of people, societies, and families, we must draw the line at states, which are artificial legal and territorial entities."[28]

This would imply that Donnelly is perhaps willing to listen to my argument for group or collective human rights for nonstate collective entities that are crucial for identity formation and the development of human potentialities. And I agree with him that the state is inherently too abstract and coercive—and, I would add, too bureaucratic—an entity to be considered a repository of human rights. The most we can hope from the state, and this requires constant vigilance and struggle against contrary tendencies, is that it respect the human rights of individuals and substate collectivities. Thus, we must draw a distinction between the human right of a people to exercise self-determination by creating a state, and a claim that the state once created has human rights. Those reside in its citizenry and residents, whether individually or collectively.

But even if the reader grants the point that collectivities can have human rights, a reasonable question would be, "What are the criteria for determining what those rights are, particularly if there are conflicting rights claims by different groups, which is most often the case?" The criteria for validating group rights must include those to which Kymlicka and Taylor have been sensitive, that is, respect by the group for certain fundamental rights of individuals *within* the group, and respect for the rights of other groups. While pure "interests" can usually be settled by negotiations and compromise, rights disputes must be settled: (1) by normatively persuasive direct dialogue in which concerned parties both reason with each other and try to understand empathetically how the other party would be affected by worst outcomes for it; (2) by moral suasion from external parties (nongovernmental human rights groups, the U.N. General Assembly or Security Council, or governments that enjoy the confidence of both contending parties); or (3) by judgments from the International Court of Justice or the various regional or ad hoc international human rights tribunals. In certain cases, violence is needed to stop egregious human rights abuses, as in the case of the Nazis' attempt to exterminate Jews, Gypsies, gays, and political opponents. But this was not a conflict of rights claims. The Nazis had little respect for the concept of rights. Hitler's response to "the generation of our present notorious weaklings [who] will obviously cry out against this [his purification strategy], and moan and complain about assaults on the holiest human rights" was "No, there is only one holiest human right, and this right is at the same time the holiest obligation, to wit: to see to it that the blood is preserved pure and, by preserving the best humanity, to create the possibility of a nobler development of these beings."[29] This was an ironic mockery of human rights. Like Nietzsche,[30] Hitler saw moral claims that would limit the use of power as simply the attempt of the weak and less worthy to constrain the stronger and more worthy. He and his followers simply exerted power. In such cases, where the actions are so wrong and so repulsive and so little affected by any moral criticism, external power is the only alternative to the toleration of barbarism. It is to its shame that the external world waited so long to intervene in the ethnic cleansing of the Muslims in Bosnia.

INDIVIDUAL/COLLECTIVE AND POLITICAL/ ECONOMIC-SOCIAL-CULTURAL COMPLEXITY

William Felice sees a correlation between political rights and individual rights, on the one hand, and collective rights and economic, social, and cultural rights, on the other. I see the situation as more complex. First, as seen in the previous chapter, I distinguish between rights that are individual and rights that are collective *and* individual. The right of self-determination is a political right, but is obviously not *just* an individual right. It is a right of both a collective to determine its political identity, and of individuals within the community to live and participate within that political entity. The right to property is an economic right and is usually thought of as the private property of singular individuals, although this is obviously not so when it takes the form of stockholder-owned corporations (for which liberal legislation and jurisprudence has invented the "fictitious person" category), partnerships, cooperatives, or state property (as in a post office or court house belonging to the state). Thus, the most powerful forms of property are not individual at all. It follows that the rights claims and violations associated with them cannot be considered merely at the individual level. Similarly, most political rights claims operate at both the individual and the collective level.

Take the right to political expression. This is often given the most extreme individualistic interpretation in U.S. society. But if we take seriously John Stuart Mill's argument in *On Liberty*, the right to free expression is related to a collective civic enterprise in which we are engaged in a truth-seeking dialogue with our fellow citizens. Just as in Habermas, who is a curious mixture of German critical theory and Millsian liberalism, this dialogic process is an integral part of the functioning of democratic institutions. My right to free expression is in reality as much others' right to hear what I have to say and my right to hear what they have to say.

Because Mill's text is seen as the paramount statement on freedom of expression, it often is assumed by those who have not read it, or those who have not read it carefully, that Mill advocates free speech without any limitations. This is not so. While he argues that speech should have freer reign than actions, he immediately follows that contention with the following: "Even opinions lose their immunity when the circumstances in which they are expressed are such as to constitute their expression a positive instigation to some mischievous act."[31] Thus, for Mill, claiming that "private property is robbery" should be tolerated if written in the press but should not be tolerated if shouted to an excited mob before the home of a propertied person, or given to the "mob" in the form of placards. In this latter case, Mill sees it as a violation of the rights of the propertied person, because it poses a threat to his or her security.

By the very same consequentialist logic regarding the social effects of language that Mill uses, the 1969 International Convention on the Elimination of All Forms of Racial Discrimination includes the obligation of participating states to condemn and to render punishable by law "all dissemination of ideas based on racial superiority or hatred, incitement to racial discrimination, as well as all acts of violence or incitement to such acts against any race of groups of persons of another color or ethnic origin" and to prohibit such promotion or incitement on the part of organizations or propagandistic activities (Article 4).

Now, one may agree with this Article or not, or agree with the law in Germany against the dissemination of Nazi propaganda, or agree with laws in several European countries that in fact do make it a crime to incite racial hatred, or with the laws in some U.S. states that impose an additional penalty on a violent crime if the motive is racial hatred. But somewhere along the line, most of us would probably agree that there is a collective dimension to the right of free expression, both because it is a part of the civic process in which we all have a stake and because dehumanizing and inciting expression against peoples of other races, ethnicities, or religions have all too often been an integral part of the process of that most extreme human rights violation, genocide. Thus, we have, in the right to political expression, something that has both an individual and a collective element. If we cannot shout "Fire!" in a crowded theater when there is no fire because we think that the people in the audience have a right not to be put at risk, is it far-fetched to draw the implication that people of races, ethnicities, and religions that have few resources to defend themselves vis-à-vis the dominant group(s) also have a collective group right not to be put at risk? If our jurisprudence recognizes the doctrine of "fighting words" as a justification for the offended party to stop the abuse violently in one-to-one relationships, is it far-fetched to oblige the state to proscribe and punish the spewing forth of hatred and incitement against such groups?

Similarly, what about the right to organize freely? I, as an individual, may have the right to join whatever political or civic organization I wish. But there have to be organizations for me to join and these are collective endeavors. The like-minded people collectively have their rights, and the public at large has a right to hear what they have to say.

To take an economic example, workers, *qua workers,* have the right to organize themselves into unions. To be sure, this means that each worker has the right, and should have the actual possibility, to join a union. But it also means that workers as a group have a right to constitute themselves into unions, and unless that larger collective right is recognized, it makes little sense to say that each individual worker has such a right.

Thus, while Felice might be right in contending that the raising of economic, social, and cultural rights gave increased stimulus to discussion of group-specific rights, it is not correct to assume as perfect a correlation as Felice seems to. There are a good number of political as well as economic and social rights that need to be seen as having both individual and collective dimensions.

RIGHTS OF EVERYONE

There is a final class of rights that belongs to everyone in the world at a given point of time and to the as yet unborn generations. Henry Shue, who posited security and subsistence as the most basic rights in his 1980 book, posed the question in 1994 whether there was not a collective international right of the world's peoples and their descendants to be free from the effects of industrial pollution, deforestation, dangerous pesticide use, and civilian and military risks taken with fissionable material.[32]

It is obvious that all of our security is threatened when the ozone layer is harmed, when sun rays penetrate down to us in unprecedented strength, when radioactive particles are able to blow across a continent as was the case after the meltdown at Chernobyl, and when harmful pesticides such as DDT, produced but banned from use in the United States, are nonetheless exported to developing world countries so that they can contaminate the bodies of agricultural workers there and enter into the food chain and international food markets.

When faced with these phenomena, would it not strike one as strange to frame these as violations merely of *my right*, not recognizing the collective right that we have with all other people of our epoch and that of future generations? If our technological advances have brought us all some good, they also have brought boundary transcending dangers and a new set of human rights that we all collectively share. The boundaries crossed are not only those of nations occupying territorial space on the earth's surface. They cross the land/water boundary and penetrate to the depths of our seas, which are a crucial food supply and home to endangered species. And they cross the boundaries of "our" space (as in "our" airspace) and the atmosphere of the entire planet, as well as outer space.

RIGHTS VIOLATORS

When we think of human rights violations, we usually think of states as being the perpetrators of human rights abuses. However, there is nothing in our conceptual approach to human rights that would indicate that the offenders must be states. Other social entities and indeed individuals can be violators of human rights. If we examine the international rights documents, which were drafted by representatives of states and are supposed to bind states to respect human rights, there is nothing in those documents that says that only states can be violators. Thus, the specific prescriptions and injunctions in the 1948 Declaration of Human Rights begin with "All human beings," "Everyone," "No one," "All are." The Declaration stipulates what acts cannot be committed or what rights should be granted, not who or what entity should be abstaining from the action or granting something to people as a matter of right.

Nonstate groups can, and often do, violate human rights. It is not uncommon for organizations (for example, Ku Klux Klan and Aryan Nation in the United States, as well as skinheads in the United States and Eastern and Western Europe), and less structured mobs (usually stimulated and often led by such organizations), to target other racial, religious, and ethnic groups as victims of intimidation, terror, and outright violence. Victims in the United States have usually been African Americans, Jews (although Catholics sometimes qualify), gays, and most recently Arabs or Moslems. In Western Europe, immigrants from North Africa have been the major targets in France, while Turkish workers have borne the brunt of such actions in Germany. While economics is often stated as the cause of this by perpetrators or those who publicly try to understand their motivations, race and skin color are major motivators. For example, in France, there are more immigrant workers from Spain and Portugal than from North Africa, and I have never heard of an anti-Iberian immigrant worker organization or activity. Immigrant workers from Eastern Europe and Italy also seem to go unmolested. So, not only is it not true that immigrant workers are taking jobs that the French have been willing to do, it also is not true that "immigration" itself is the real issue in anti-immigrant campaigns and actions.

Racist, anti-Semitic, and homophobic groups do not have a monopoly on the nonstate violation of human rights. Corporations or other business organizations that exploit workers, refuse to recognize their rights to organize themselves for their collective protection, and employ young children in arduous industrial or agricultural production are human rights violators. States can be human rights violators by treating their own employees thus, or by refusing to protect the rights of people employed within their territories. But that does not mean that economic entities themselves are not guilty of human rights violations.

Just as states violate human rights of everyone when they engage in nuclear activities that harm, or that threaten to harm people, so, too, do economic enterprises violate human rights when they foul the air and water that we breathe and when they bring down the forests to such an extent that the atmosphere is damaged. Here again, the state that does not intervene fails in its rights protective function, but the economic enterprises are directly violating human rights.

Threats to traditional cultures also are posed by business enterprises in ways other than pollution or other environmental damage. For example, the Gold Rush in California spelled the end of the traditional existence for many Native Americans in the western part of what is now the United States. At present, there is a virtual war going on between indigenous groups in the Brazilian Amazon and gold prospectors and loggers who are encroaching on their traditional lands.

Businesses also can violate human rights by becoming complicit with government human rights violations. One of the most notorious examples of this is the use of slave labor in Germany during Nazism by firms such as Krupp and I. G. Farben. In El Salvador and Guatemala, large landowners paid military commanders in their districts to terrorize, torture, and kill hired peasants who tried to organize against their horrible working conditions and meager pay. In Nicaragua under the U.S.-imposed Somoza regime, there was little difference between the authoritarian state and business interests, because President Somoza had a share of all significant businesses. His share or cut was part of the cost of doing business there. In Guatemala, United Fruit and the U.S. government joined hands to destroy the elected democratic government of President Arbenz and turned Guatemala into a military dictatorship for approximately forty years. The overthrow of the elected government of President Allende in Chile, and its replacement by a military dictatorship under General Pinochet, was supported by International Telephone and Telegraph as well as by the U.S. government.

On the other side of the economic fence, the AFL-CIO, through its international operations, attempted to subvert labor unions that did not accept the complicity with business and government that the AFL-CIO was practicing in the United States. Perhaps the most extreme cases of the attempt to undercut unionizing attempts by workers who questioned the policies and/or legitimacy of their own governments, and who were putting forward more radical programs for economic, social, and political change, were perpetrated by the AFL-CIO's American Institute for Free Labor Development. This was funded by the U.S. government and operated in conjunction with it in Latin America. So, while government-controlled labor unions could violate the human rights of workers (for example, Eastern Europe, Mexico), so, too, could unions that entered into relationships with government on a voluntary basis.

In other instances, the relationship can be less voluntary. I once had a conversation with a former international Vice-President of the United States National Student Association (USNSA). The CIA wanted to use the association to counter the work of the government-controlled student associations in Eastern Europe. It thus covertly funneled money to the USNSA. After this student had been elected to the vice presidency of the USNSA, he was called to a meeting with CIA officials and informed that the USNSA was expected to perform information-gathering (that is, intelligence) activities for the agency. He also was informed that, if he revealed this, he would be subject to prosecution under the National Security Act. Thus, while the USNSA was acting covertly as an intelligence-gathering body, it was deceptive with the people from all countries with whom it was dealing. It also was deceiving students in the United States who thought that they were participating in an organization that was advancing their interests as students and establishing normal association ties with students around the world. Thus, the right to participate in organizations within civil society that were trying to get beyond the Cold War barriers was taken away and the leaders were placed in an impossible

Catch-22 situation—participate in the intelligence operation, resign and let someone come in who will participate, or blow the whistle and face the possibility of prosecution under the National Security Act. Journalists, also an essential part of a democratic civil society, were used in similar ways for both foreign and domestic intelligence gathering, and for propaganda purposes, undercutting the right of people to have access to information that represents the best journalistic judgment. But this was more voluntary and the responsibility of the press is perhaps greater than that of the younger and less experienced students who were coerced by the government.

Opposition movements also can violate human rights. Unlike my pacifist friends, I would not say that violence per se constitutes a human rights violation. As indicated earlier, human rights were born in the West as a result of two violent events, the American and French Revolutions. They were considered to be battles against tyranny. But in both of those, the treatment accorded to the Loyalists in the United States and the terror perpetrated by the Committee on Public Safety in France, there also were human rights violations. Some opposition groups feel that they have the right to kill anyone who disagrees with them, whether or not they are part of the military or political apparatus of the government or part of another oppositionist group. Some feel free to coerce people into their ranks, to use indiscriminate terror tactics, or to torture. Some that are ethnically based feel free to kill, torture, or rape members of other ethnic groups just because they belong to those groups. The fact that these people are not, or are not yet, operating as a government does not mean that their acts constitute anything less than human rights violations.

In some cases, families and individuals, often acting in conformity with cultural norms or economic pressures, can be guilty of human rights offenses. An example is the selling of children into prostitution. Clearly the human rights of the child are being violated. The child is denied recognition as a human being, is turned into a mere instrument for pleasure and money-making in a way that is degrading and devastating to his or her physical and psychological health. It may be true that parents who sell children into prostitution are themselves human rights victims of thoroughly unjust economic, social, and/or political systems. But looking at the issue from the perspective of the child victims, they in turn become perpetrators of human rights abuses against their own children. This is an instance, for example, among some of the poor segments of Indian and Thai society, in which there develops a chain of human rights violations, one leading to another. The poor parents are victims of social injustice and for the

rest of the family to survive they sell one or more children into prostitution. The resolution of the problem thus has to be both a recognition of the economic and social rights of people like the parents and
the state's prevention of such abuse of children.

The status of child is different from that of woman, racial minority, or gay. It is not an ascriptive category in that all human beings are
children in the early parts of their lives but cease to be children under
the control of adults as they age. In the case of the ascriptive categories, one is vulnerable to domination throughout one's life.

But ascriptive considerations are nevertheless important in child
prostitution. While some boys may be forced into prostitution by
their parents, the overwhelming majority of children forced into prostitution are indeed females. The rights of the individual children are
being violated, but so are the rights of females as a group. Female
children are being sacrificed as part of a gender-biased structure of
domination in which it is affirmed that women and girls are nothing
more than commodities to be traded for the pleasure of men. It thus
becomes part of the powerful patriarchal structure of gender relations
and devaluation of women that is so prevalent throughout the world
and that has led some Chinese parents to kill female babies under the
one-child policy.

Such killing is a human rights violation in my view, and it raises an
interesting issue. What is the relationship between human rights violations and just plain criminal acts? Why not just consider the killing
of female children murder? The answer is because it is part of a
general pattern of nonrecognition and dominating practices that literally
deprive specific groups or categories people of their humanity. This is
why, in my view again, it is important to distinguish between hate
crimes that involve violence and mayhem and cases of random violence or violence during the commission of a robbery or out of jeal-
ousy. True, the latter wrongfully deprives someone of health or even
life that the person could be said to have had a right to. But it does
not represent a *systematized* attempt to dominate and dehumanize an
entire category or group of people. Just as in the traditional relationship between Natural Law and Positive Law, where some laws actually in code books of states (positive law) are also natural laws, so, too,
will some specific violations of laws of states also be human rights violations, even though they will not be designated as such within the
text of the criminal code.

Let's consider killing. I see three categories of injustice possible in
killing. An individual who kills someone in the course of a robbery
or an act of fury is guilty of murder. One could argue—and perhaps

pacifists and others do—that it was a human rights violation because every person has a right to life, and this right went unrecognized. The victim is dominated in a very final sense having his or her life extinguished. But I am not sure that this illuminates the meaning of the act any further than the criminal definition and conception of murder does.

A second category involving killing would be illustrated by a lynching of a community member suspected of a horrible crime in a small homogeneous community. Here the meaning of the act is more interesting from a human rights perspective. The lynchers would be depriving that individual of the human right to due process of law. The motive of the lynchers is to punish someone similar to themselves who they believe has violated a law and crucial communal norms. The message such a lynching sends is to other individuals in the community who might be tempted to similarly transgress. One also might cite the lynching of horse thieves and rustlers in the old American West, which was intended to deliver a message that such behavior would be dealt with swiftly and severely. Again, this was a violation of the right to due process of law but was directed against individuals who were believed to have performed certain antisocial acts.

This could be differentiated from a third category, one in which the lynching is racially motivated. In that case, the lynching becomes part of a generalized pattern of domination. It constitutes not only a violation of the rights of the individuals who actually have been lynched but also of the group that is subject to and threatened by the practice of lynching. Within the target group, the specific victims of such killings are often random because in the minds of the lynchers they are simply standing in for the larger group itself. In the United States, in May 1997, murder convictions were obtained for neo-Nazi skinhead soldiers based at Fort Bragg, North Carolina, who set out in their car to commit such a random killing. They came on an African American man and woman out for a stroll, whom they did not know and against whom they had nothing personally.

Nor did the killers suspect that they had committed any antisocial act or crime. It did not matter, because they were using these two victims to strike out at an entire race of people. To be sure, this was a criminal act, but not *merely* a criminal act. It was a major violation of the group-specific human rights of African Americans to be free of the violence that so often accompanies racism.

This and the mind-set that led to it is part of the genocide complex that unfortunately seems to be simmering below the surface in too many multicultural societies. The message of each act of this nature is that "*I* or *we* would kill all of *you others,* if only *I* or *we* were presented with or could construct the opportunity." Within the target group, the individual victim can be random precisely because the target of the message is really the entire group. All three of the above instances of killing are crimes, but I think that the designation of human rights violations is meaningfully applied, or adds deeper understanding, to the latter two categories. The first is purely and simply a violation of the human rights of individuals; the second is a simultaneous violation of both individual and group rights.

One of the most difficult cases of possible human rights violations is one sanctioned by social custom but performed by individuals and family members. This is female genital cutting and/or infibulation, a practice common in parts of Africa and the Middle East. The practice itself is carried out by women in the group. From their point of view, it is a rite of initiation into roles within their cultures and a deterrent to adultery. Their perspective is that there is both an obligation and a right to practice the traditional rituals that have from time immemorial conferred the status of adulthood and strengthened communal bonds. But from the point of view of many Westerners, it is a deprivation of sexual pleasure of women, a health hazard, a needless infliction of great pain, and a part of the process of patriarchal control over women's behavior. From this perspective, it constitutes a human rights violation. It thus could be argued, and is by some, that this cultural practice should not be preserved under the general rule of respect for traditional cultures.

The issue of compulsion is important in deciding whether there is a human rights violation here. The act is done when the girls are quite young and find it difficult to resist. It can thus be considered to be a compulsory practice. Even so, some girls do object to it and try to escape the practice, sometimes by fleeing the country. Thus, even within the culture, there are those who oppose the practice, at least in its compulsory form.[33]

The issue of whether parents have the right to have the operation performed while they are in other countries also has been one of contention. The parental claim is that this is a part of the cultural tradition, and that the woman would not be recognized as a marriageable person within the cultural group if she were not cut and/or infibulated. This cultural rights claim has been rejected in the United States, where such acts can no longer be legally performed.

These are difficult issues. But where (1) a practice is committed on minors; (2) consent is not required; (3) the practice is accompanied by immediate serious pain and longer-term health hazards; (4) it is part of a system of control over women's bodies over which men have control, even if women are designated as the actual agents who carry out the operation; and (5) some women within those societies have objected to the procedure and tried to evade it, it is difficult to sustain the validity of this cultural practice even when parents wish to have it done. The fifth consideration is crucial. If it were merely Westerners coming in from the outside trying to stop a cultural practice over which there was no internal dissent, it would be more problematic to take such a position. The claims from people who favor the continuation of the practice that these internal dissidents have been influenced by outside Westerners are not convincing. The development of human rights involves, of necessity, communication across borders. If ideas, which were developed outside the context, such as the idea of "human rights" itself, resonate inside the culture that has been exposed to the ideas, those ideas are no less valid because of their point of origin. There is no such thing as a static culture. Cultures change, and they change because of both internal and external dynamics. It is extremely important to keep this in mind when defending cultural rights. To forget this risks leaving the least powerful people within the cultures at the mercy of the most powerful. At a certain point, even the wishes of parents to retain ancient rites and subject their children to them might have to give way to human rights claims coming from both within and without the culture concerned.

CONCLUSION

The foregoing discussion is a more in-depth explanation and defense of Proposition 9, that is, that rights holders who claim social recognition can be collectivities as well as individuals and the recognition can be withheld by nonstate groups as well as by individuals and families. While strict legalists might take the position that only states that agree to human rights covenants can be violators of human rights (a real problem, because then states could remove themselves from the category of rights violators by simply not signing onto any human rights agreements), ours is a bottom-up perspective on human rights and human rights violations. We look first at the domination and suffering to determine when we have a human rights violation rather than merely accepting a *de jure* list of normative rules already accepted by states (although we do not ignore such rules) and then at the power sources that inflict these things. One might argue with the positioning of some of the violations, but it is hoped that most people will be convinced by the discussion that (1) against some very strong currents in Anglo-American thought and ideology, groups and

collectivities can legitimately make rights claims *qua* groups and collectivities; and (2) against some arguments made elsewhere, particularly by leaders of authoritarian political systems or social groupings,
group or collective rights claims do not always trump individual rights
claims. This is the area in which transnational and transcultural
attempts to reason, understand, and empathize are most desperately
needed.

In Chapter 5, I will come back to the question of recognition and
economic rights. I will more deeply examine the issue of recognition
as it relates to the rights of workers within the context of the
contemporary global market economy and its dominating structures.

CHAPTER 5

TOWARD A POLITICAL ECONOMY OF HUMAN RIGHTS

INTRODUCTION

As we have already seen, some thinkers, including Maurice Cranston and many Western liberals, make the argument that to be effective the number of human rights should be very constricted. The categorization is also important. Human rights should be (1) civil and political, and (2) individual, that is, pertaining only to individuals and not to groups or collectivities. Thus, while the 1966 International Covenant on Civil and Political Rights is acceptable, there is widespread suspicion in this quarter that the covenant of the same year on economic, social, and cultural rights opens up a Pandora's Box and has nothing to do with human rights properly understood.

However, as we also have already seen, this position flies in the face of the international consensus on human rights norms.[1] Aside from a divergence from the key international documents and conventions mentioned in Chapter 3, it also is contrary to the core Conventions of the International Labor Organization.[2] It obviously is also contrary to the theoretical grounding for human rights that we have developed in Chapters 3 and 4. If the focus is on the recognition of potential for development that every human being has, the actualization of which is dependent on a process of "co- and self-determination" within a web of relations with others, and on an understanding that these possibilities are materially and culturally conditioned over history, it is absolutely crucial to consider economic processes both diachronically and synchronically, that is, over historical time and within economic structures dominant at particular points in time.

In this chapter, I want to delineate and discuss three kinds of social recognition as they apply to the economic domain. The first kind is distributional in nature. This is the kind of recognition that is most elaborately detailed in the 1966 covenant dealing with economic, social, and cultural rights. This is the recognition that people have a human right to an "adequate standard of," and a "decent," living. But there are requisites for this, such as jobs, income, housing, health care, and education, to which they also have rights. The covenant roots this ultimately in "the inherent dignity" of every human being.

The second kind of recognition is participatory recognition, or recognition as an active agent. This adds to the affirmation of the above distributional rights the right to some role in determining how the distributional rights will be recognized in practice. There are two dimensions of this. The first is the right of workers to be recognized as collective bargaining agents in the form of trade unions, and to strike within the legal parameters set by the state in order to ensure an adequate and decent condition of life. The second is a broader participatory right, which appears in both of the 1966 covenants (political and economic/social). They convey the idea that human beings have not only the right to claim specific rights but also to participate in the process whereby their rights claims are fulfilled.

The third kind of recognition is more empowering and applies specifically to workers. It is at best suggested or hinted at, but not fully recognized, in some of these documents. This is the recognition of workers as rightful direct owners of the means of their production and as determiners of the conditions under which they labor as well as of the distribution of the proceeds. This would represent a maximization of our basic idea of co- and self-determination applied to the economic realm. It does in fact exist in small cooperative pockets in both the highly and lesser industrialized world. But, as I shall argue, there is some basis in considering whether the generalization of this form of recognition might not be an important advance in how we think about human rights, as well as how we think about democracy.

DISTRIBUTIVE RECOGNITION

There are serious human rights problems posed by inequalities in the distribution of material resources within and between nations. Within most societies and nations, women and racial or ethnic minorities find themselves relatively deprived of the material resources for the development of their potentialities. Moreover, they find it difficult to gain the social recognition that would be necessary to oblige others to recognize this as a human rights issue. There is a circular deprivation of both goods and agency. Thus the effective attacks coming from members of dominant groups on affirmative action programs and the insistence that only individuals be considered, as though there were a level playing field in most societies for the actualization of the potentiality of all individuals.

The problem has a number of dimensions. One is the right to subsistence and security. As we saw in Chapter 2, these were posited by Henry Shue as the two "basic rights." From the perspective of my approach, it is a human rights violation that many people in the world today suffer from hunger and malnutrition and even starve to death when one-quarter of all the food produced in the United States in 1995 was wasted.[3] Here I would agree with Shue that it is not enough to say that this was not deliberate. Those who are advantaged, and governmental bodies dedicated to the larger public good—which in my conceptualization is understood as the maximum possible development of everyone's potential—have a duty to take positive action to protect people from deprivation and to aid them when they are found to be in a state of deprivation. Certain nongovernmental groups, such as Food First, based in Oakland, California, recognize this imperative and are far ahead of most governments in acting on this.

But I do not think that Shue's formulation of basic rights is sufficient. Gross inequality, even if all parties are ensured of subsistence, just does not qualify as a human rights-respecting situation. People who are deprived of decent housing, of quality medical care, of challenging educational experience, of access to effective professional formation or job training, and of employment opportunities while people on the top of the economic ladder are constantly improving their situation, are suffering a human rights deprivation. Thus what John Rawls refers to as "justice as fairness," that is, the idea that it is fair for those at the top of the economic stratification to benefit further only if those at the bottom benefit proportionately more, is in my view profoundly a human rights position.[4]

The root of the problem is not some aesthetic or morally abstract preference for equality in-and-of-itself. It is, rather, that great disparity, such as 1 percent of the families owning more economic assets than the entire bottom 90 percent, which was the case in the United States in 1989 according to Federal Reserve Bank data,[5] has the effect of a severe stunting of opportunity for development at the very bottom. Indeed, "a child whose father is in the bottom 5 percent of earners had only one chance in twenty of making it to the top 20 percent."[6]

They are very likely to be either unemployed, especially if they are African American males, or part of the millions of workers whose earnings keep them and their families in poverty and often without health benefits.[7] These people are written off as "the human exhaust of capitalism," in the words of the late Michael Harrington.[8] They are stripped of the economic and social requisites for the development of their potentialities.

Along with the "human exhaust" within capitalist industrialized countries, there also is the "human deprivation" and the "human exploitation" in many of the countries populated by people of color and that had been conquered, colonized, and economically exploited by the white Western nations during the last two centuries of the previous millennium. The differences are astounding:

> By the late 1990s, the fifth of the world's people living in the highest income countries had: 86 percent of the world GDP—the bottom fifth just 1 percent, 82 percent of world export markets—the bottom fifth just 1 percent, 74 percent of world telephone lines—...the bottom fifth just 1.5 percent. The world's 200 richest people more than doubled their net worth in the four prior years to 1998, to more than $1 trillion. The assets of the top three billionaires are more than the combined GNP of all least developed countries and their 600 million people.[9]

Since the fall of communism in the 1980s, poverty has become a major problem in Eastern Europe. It is also the case that, since that time, the people of the Middle East, Central Asia, and Latin America have experienced increased impoverishment. The lowest quintile of the world's population "lives" on the equivalent of a dollar a day or less. Almost half "live" on less than two dollars a day.[10]

While people might have experienced such relative economic deprivation in earlier eras of lesser total wealth accumulation without its being a human rights deprivation, we must consider the question in its concrete present context. As the opportunities for multifaceted development of human beings are opened up historically by advances in education, science, medicine, technology, and wealth generation, we must view as rights deprivation what might not have been viewed as such long ago in the same society. As we have already argued, when the burden of such deprivation falls most heavily on certain social groups because of ascriptive characteristics about which they can do nothing, then the issue of group rights becomes potent. From a human rights point of view, it would be meaningless for older white people in the United States who had perhaps experienced hardships such as being raised on a farm without indoor water or plumbing to compare their situation with African Americans in today's urban ghettos, or to make reference to their higher standard of living than people in most sub-Saharan African countries. Poverty-stricken nations of Africa, Asia, and Central America and the Caribbean and the poverty-ridden drug- and crime-infested American ghetto today are surrounded by unprecedented affluence. That makes for very stunted people who can neither realize their own inherent potentials nor compete for recognition or wealth within a highly competitive economic environment.

Claims made by many conservatives and neoconservatives that criticism of economic and social inequality is rooted in envy might be partially correct. After all, Frederick Douglass did indeed envy the little white boys with whom he grew up when he was a slave. But that was because those little white boys were going to be free to develop themselves into, and be recognized as, full-fledged men. As Douglass put it, they had rights and he did not. While slavery is no longer the issue, domination still is, just as Tocqueville warned in the 1830s that it would be if and when all of the slaves were emancipated.[11]

In sum, a radically skewed access to material resources that we all need to develop our potentialities in and of itself entails domination. To be sure, one response might be simply to recognize this maldistribution as a human rights problem and to take redistributive measures. The Swedish government takes a small percentage of the wealth of that country and redistributes it to the neediest nations. And some countries have relatively large foreign assistance programs. Agencies within the United Nations and NGOs have programs to alleviate some of the misery. But there is no comprehensive program designed to remedy the drastic international imbalance in access to resources needed for the actualization of human potential.

PARTICIPATORY RECOGNITION

As we have already indicated, as important as it is to redistribute to the most deprived, that does not do the full job of rights recognition. There is also the consensus on recognizing the right of people to have a voice, a say, a role on *how* their rights claims are addressed.

Thus are found the following words at the end of the preamble to the 1966 Covenant on Economic, Social and Cultural Rights: "*Realizing* that the individual, having duties to other individuals and to the community to which he belongs, is under a responsibility to strive for the promotion and observance of the rights recognized in the present Covenant." In the 1986 Declaration on the Right to

Development, Article I, Paragraph 1 reads: "The right to development is an inalienable human right by virtue of which every human
person and all peoples are entitled to participate in, contribute to and
enjoy, economic, social, cultural, and political development in all
human rights and fundamental freedoms can be fully realized."
Article II, Paragraph 1 stipulates, "The human person is the central
subject of development and should be the active participant and ben-
eficiary of the right to development." These documents infuse the
rights claimants, whether they are making fundamental redistribu-
tional demands on states or engaged in trade union activities such as
collective bargaining and strikes against state or corporate employers,
with entitlement and agency. As Adetoun Ilumoka stresses in her article on the economic, social, and cultural rights of women in Africa,
rights claimants cannot be mere beggars for rights, the entitlement
and effectuation of which is determined by others. "Rather, a people
must assert them."[12]

One of the most disempowering forms of "assistance" to countries
where the poorest people in the world live has been the austerity programs of the World Bank and the International Monetary Fund
(IMF). These programs have insisted on the slashing of whatever
modest governmental programs existed for the improvement of the
life of the people in poorer countries and taken the task out of the
public policy arena, precluding any possibility of democratic, grassroots participation. Social improvement is to be left to development
via the privatized market-driven economy in the hands of private
profit-oriented concerns. These are mainly powerful transnational
corporations, working in concert with tiny groups of indigenous
political and economic elites. In apparel production, a major area of
outsourcing, wages tend to be very low, working hours long, and
unionization forbidden or "discouraged" (sometimes by violence and
murder).[13] In the area of energy exploitation, such as Enron's power
projects in India or Shell's in Ogoniland in Nigeria, involuntary population displacement and environmental degradation is added to the
pillaging of economic resources.[14] Demonstrations or other forms of
resistance are met with repression by armed agents of the state and
the company. In addition, IMF and World Bank loans have burdened
the neediest countries with impossible debts, the servicing of which
makes it even more difficult for the countries to alleviate the suffering of their poorest citizens. But this combined exploitation of a
country's resources and disempowerment of its population does make
for huge profits for those at the very top of the economic heap, both
nationally and internationally.

It is claimed that in some unspecified long run all will benefit economically (the famous trickle-down effect), but the already deprived who are clearly the most negatively affected in the short and middle terms are denied any voice and any agency in the matter. It is people of color who are most deprived, whether at the national levels within Western industrial countries or at the international level between these Western countries and non-Western ones. Thus, this is an issue of both group and individual human rights violations.

There is another dimension to the group rights issue under conditions of contemporary liberal capitalism: that is, the rights of workers as both individuals and a group. I made the point in Chapter 3 that while the category of worker is not an ascriptive one in the sense that people are not born workers the way they are born female or black, and while workers can under certain circumstances gain their livelihood in ways other than wage labor, in many instances there are in fact no other viable options.

Here capitalism does not speak with a unified voice, but there is a trend fostered by "globalization." It is clearly favorable to ownership and managerial prerogative. It is also favorable to as much depression in wages and benefits as the supply of labor and the state will permit (if indeed *any* benefits are offered, which is not the case among most workers in the poorest countries and many low-wage workers in the United States), and to the "flexible" use of its labor force. Such flexibility concerns the number of hours worked, the arrangement of the shifts, levels of benefits if any, the conditions under which the labor is performed, and the techniques of discipline and grounds for dismissal.

Schematically speaking, there are three positions taken on workers' rights under conditions of global capitalism. In most of the poorer countries of what we used to call the Third World and in the Southeast Asian nations where economic power soared until the late 1990s (for example, Indonesia, Malaysia, and Singapore), workers are not considered to have rights that might conflict with the interests of the corporation and, if unions are permitted to operate at all, they are either government or management-sponsored. In continental Western Europe, there has been a subscription to the proposition that there are workers' rights, and that these rights are indeed human rights as specified by the 1966 Covenant on Economic, Social, and Cultural Rights. In Great Britain under the Thatcher and Major Conservative governments and in the United States from the Reagan and first Bush administrations, and to a great extent continuing through the "New Democrat" Clinton presidency and into the George W. Bush administration, there has been the proposition that corporations need the utmost flexibility in dealing with labor in the competitive international climate. This has been carried to such an extreme that legislation protecting labor has been severely weakened and even the right to strike has been curtailed. In the United States, this is manifested in the imposition of twelve-hour and sometimes even sixteen-hour workdays and the right of employers to hire replacement workers in the case of strikes and lockouts. (See Appendix A for such a case with which the author had direct experience.)

Under Proposition 10 discussed in Chapter 3, I have already made reference to the Council of Europe's Social Charter and the inclusion of portions of its worker rights provisions in the European Union's 1992 Treaty of Maastricht. Under Conservative governments, the British refused to accept the Social Charter and insisted on weakening its worker rights provisions when they were being considered for inclusion as a Protocol (otherwise known as the Social Chapter) in the Maastricht Treaty. Even after succeeding in their project of weakening the provisions that ultimately were accepted, the Conservative government refused to ratify the weakened Protocol. In 1997, the Blair government sent a representative to the European Union to state that the British would no longer opt out of the Protocol.

It is instructive to take a closer look at the earlier European Social Charter from which only the British distanced themselves. First, there is an affirmation of the validity and the interconnectedness of the entire realm of human rights stipulated by the two 1966 international covenants: "Recalling that the Ministerial Conference on Human Rights held in Rome on 5 November 1990 stressed the need, on the one hand, to preserve the indivisible nature of all human rights, be they civil, political, economic, social, or cultural and, on the other, to give the European Social Charter fresh impetus."

The second thing to note is that the document begins with a long list of workers' rights. The specific rights are too numerous to mention. But one right is worth mentioning for purposes of contrast, "the right to work" (Part II, Article 1):

"With a view to ensuring the effective exercise of the right to work, the Parties undertake:"

1. to accept as one of their primary aims and responsibilities the achievement and maintenance of as high and stable a level of employment as possible, with a view to the attainment of full employment;
2. to protect effectively the right of the worker to earn his living in an occupation freely entered on;
3. to establish or maintain free employment services for all workers;

4. to provide or promote appropriate vocational guidance, training, and rehabilitation.

This is followed by Article II, "The right to just conditions of work," which deals with working hours, holidays with pay (disdainfully ridiculed by Maurice Cranston, as will be recalled from Chapter 2), elimination of safety risks and compensation for inherently risky work, rest on traditional days of rest, and special consideration for night work. In all, there are six pages stipulating the rights of workers.

In addition to this document, within the body of European Union (EU) legislation itself there are directives on worker rights, including the rights of workers to be informed and the need for employers to consult with workers and to provide channels of worker participation in certain decision processes, such as layoffs and the moving of plants. We will return to these latter provisions and their significance toward the end of this chapter.

I do not want to argue that these European documents are sufficient to guarantee workers' rights in practice. Indeed, the ideological and institutional permeation of global capitalism was so potent as far back as the early 1980s that Raymond Williams, writing in Thatcherite Britain, saw it as a new form of totalitarianism—not a totalitarianism exclusively of the state as under communism or Nazism but one in which supportive states and quasi-state entities (for example, the World Bank and the IMF) function in concert with "private" economic institutions: "What is most totalitarian about the new dominant orientation is its extension beyond the basic system of extraction of labor to a practical invasion of the whole human personality."[15] I cite the European documents because, contrary to this hostile wave of aggrandizing global forces, they legitimize the concept of rights adhering to an economic group, that is, workers, and because they see them as tied to the totality of the picture of human rights. At least in the official documents that set the normative standards, there is a consensus on the importance of the indivisibility and interconnectedness of economic and political human rights among the industrialized countries of continental Western Europe and the countries signing the American Convention and the African Charter. There is *not* an East–West or North–South divide on the normative standards.

One of the reasons that the government of the United States moved so drastically from Franklin Delano and Eleanor Roosevelt's strong commitment to solidaristic economic and social rights to opposition to them is the current of excessive individualism within U.S. ideology that has at times been moderated by political leadership (for example, FDR's New Deal and Lyndon Johnson's War on Poverty) but was made hegemonic over national politics by the "Reagan Revolution." That individualism manifests itself in an interesting way in how the phrase "the right to work" has been defined in U.S. political culture and discourse. We have just seen how it was defined in the European Social Charter. It is a collective right of workers to have jobs available to them; to freely choose occupations; to enjoy the rights of free employment services; and to have access to vocational guidance, training and rehabilitation. In the United States, by contrast, "right to work" laws are those that protect individuals from being compelled to join unions, or to pay union dues, in a shop where there is union representation. Thus, even though the individual worker would benefit from the wages and working conditions negotiated or struck for by the union, he or she would not have to contribute to the sustenance of the union. Such laws, which encourage "free-riding," are clearly designed to break the sense of collective identity and solidarity and to foster a monadic individualism. The Europeans focus on the collective rights of workers, while the American supporters of the "right to work" laws focus on the individual worker's right to isolate him or herself, to break solidarity with the group for personal gain—in this case not associating or paying dues.

Exceptions to the Rule

If the current hegemonic ideology in the United States conceives of human rights as exclusively civic and political, there is an exception made for one economic right. That exception is the individual's right to private property, so heavily emphasized by Locke that he subsumed the right to life and liberty under it. Despite Locke's inconsistency and confusion on this, the right to property in land and goods is indeed what the dominant ideology in the United States takes to be *the* inalienable economic right.

Now couple this with another exception, this time an exception to the largely Anglo-American animosity to the concept of group rights. In the Anglo-American liberal tradition, it is only individuals—not groups or collectivities—that have human rights. But, alas, corporations are extended a right to private property. Here, common sense tells us that we are clearly not just talking about individuals. But in liberal jurisprudence, the corporation is considered to be a fictitious individual person. This legal ploy is indeed very handy for corporations, and perhaps partially explains why Charles Lindblom saw them as having unparalleled power in American political life, and why corporate power is overwhelming the ability of national governments to even keep track of their transnational operations much less exert any kind of control,[16] while unions have been sorely weakened in most liberal Western countries, especially the United States and Great Britain.

The corporation not only has the legality of the fictional person to protect its interests, which of course it translates into "property rights," it also has an even more potent weapon in its own version of the strike, the "capital strike." It usually does not have to use this. The mere threat of taking capital out of one country and moving it to another, causing unemployment and economic dislocation for which the government will have to pay the political price, is usually enough to convince governments that "probusiness" policies are required even if they exaggerate inequalities and unemployment. This was a lesson learned by the initially quite egalitarian Mitterrand government in France in the early 1980s. And as we have seen, in less powerful countries such as Guatemala and Chile, transnational corporations (that is, United Fruit and International Telephone and Telegraph) can act with more powerful foreign governments to simply remove by violent means annoying governments that insist on egalitarian economic policies more in line with the 1966 Covenant on Economic, Social, and Cultural rights. It might be that in the post-Cold War era, the withholding of World Bank or IMF loans or more direct attempts at economic strangulation—such as that being delivered on Cuba by the U.S. embargo—will be sufficient to bring recalcitrant economically egalitarian regimes into line if the capitalist countries can unify on the tactic, which is not proving to be the case regarding Cuba.

RECOGNITION OF WORKER CO- AND SELF-DETERMINATION

In discussing human rights declarations and agreements, I have up to now ignored those of the International Labor Organization (ILO). It is time to bring the ILO into the picture. As pointed out earlier, the ILO predates World War II, going back to 1919. Its operation was interrupted by the war. But in 1944, representatives from forty-one countries meeting in Philadelphia to reaffirm the mission of the organization declared "labor is not a commodity." This to me is an interesting normative position. I say normative because, in the dominant system, labor is, in fact, a commodity. It is bought and sold. That is why we talk about a "labor market." The worker is of purely instrumental value. She functions in an environment controlled by others to bring profit to others. She maintains her value only so long as she accepts and acts according to that. The market in labor, her need to buy in the market for goods and services, and the power of an ideology that inhibits imagining the possibility of any structural change in this relationship are disciplining forces to get her to accept these terms. So long as they persist, neither the commitment to a more adequate share in the distribution of resources, such as higher wages or better benefits, nor the commitment to the right to form labor unions in the 1948 Declaration and the 1966 Covenant to help attain these, would decommodify labor.

This has very important implications for our holistic conception of human rights that relies so heavily on the ideas of social recognition and co- and self-determination within a web of social relations. I propose that co- and self-determination models of economic relations offer the most fruitful ways to think about labor if one wishes to valorize the kind of social recognition that maximizes freedom, equality, and solidarity, the basis of human rights as I have conceived them.

The co- and self-determination model has three variants. Going from "thin" to "thick" manifestations, they are (a) worker participation in decision making *and* ownership shares in production or service operations in which they work; (b) complete worker ownership of, but shared decision making in, the enterprise; and (c) complete ownership of, and total decisionmaking power within, the enterprise. These are the models that come closest to maximizing the values of freedom, equality, and solidarity within the enterprises.[17] This entails a decentralizing redistribution of not just material resources but also of power over the conditions under which people labor. Here workers overcome commodification by becoming self-determining agents with crucial roles and voices in determining all of the major decisions made within the plant. In variants (b) and (c), all information would logically have to be shared. It should be shared in (a) if the shared decisionmaking and ownership scheme is genuine rather than merely a cooptive gambit. That, in fact, is the danger with (a), cooptation, even if shared decision making is accompanied by ownership shares, particularly if the workers own less than 50 percent of the shares. But it might still offer a site of struggle in which workers could assert their rights to develop their own potentialities by exerting some control over the conditions and processes of labor that is not possible within the present system of the prerogatives of constricted ownership and management.

The "thickest" manifestation is the one in which workers own the enterprise and alone have the final say over decisions. This is not a mere abstraction. Just as in political systems, the mode of participation is going to be heavily affected by scale. Thus, more direct face-to-face forms of participation can be accommodated in a small agricultural kibbutz in Israel or in one of the cooperative plywood mills in the U.S. northwest.[18] By contrast, more representative forms are required in the very large Mondragon complex of cooperatives in Northern Spain.[19] Even under these conditions, some inequalities will creep in, especially as the firm increases in size and complexity. There will be a difference in both technological and management skill levels. But within a setting characterized by a solidaristic ethos, they will have to be acknowledged and discussed by the entire workforce. They should thus pose less of a threat to both equality and freedom, but there is no doubt that there would be a tension and that a serious effort would have to be made to resist the possible threats to all three of the basic values posed by the acknowledgment of different skill levels. One way would be for such enterprises to have education and training programs that would attempt to spread knowledge and skills widely throughout the workforce. A more serious issue is the tendency, seen in some plants in the plywood industry, to employ nonowners as wage laborers. In this case, the employer, even though a collective, assumes the same relationship to the employee that an employer under the present dominant system does.

A problem with total worker ownership is that worker/owners in any given endeavor might make decisions that have negative external effects. These effects could violate the rights of others. I think that we would all agree that even if workers owned and controlled a plant, polluting air or water in order to less expensively make a product would constitute what we have called in the table on page 92 a violation of the rights of everyone else by a non-state group. Worker/owners in a plant should not be able to produce products that are unsafe or technological devices that facilitate the transmission of computer viruses. Workers in a plant should not be permitted to apply ascriptive discriminatory criteria for entry into the plant or task assignment. One way to deal with this is purely and simply through external governmental regulation. Another, which could complement government regulation, is for representatives of groups within civil society that have specific interests and knowledge about such things to have some representation within the decisionmaking process of the firm itself. This would bear some relationship to the situation that we have now where human rights groups are attempting to monitor rights violations within plants suspected of being "sweatshops." But the roles that I am discussing would be ones in which these nonowners are connected on a continual basis with the functioning of the plant and have full information about it. I am proposing an inside/outside mechanism whereby people working in nongovernmental groups within civil society would be given a role in informing and being informed, and in participating in the decisionmaking processes to prevent human rights violating external effects. This would ensure greater transparency than is now the case, and open up the decision process to informed participants who do not have an economic stake in the enterprise. There would be a net gain in both education and freedom, since workers would be constantly reminded of dimensions of their actions that they might not otherwise even think about. This would hopefully lead to decision processes with a more reflective balance between immediate economic gain and the rights of outsiders. And it would be both more inclusive in scope and less hierarchical than European corporatist approaches.

Another way that worker-owned and -controlled enterprises could be held accountable to consumer rights and interests is through the encouragement of consumer cooperatives. These would research not only price but also quality and safety of products, and through their buying power ensure a certain external accountability on the part of the associated producers. In England, there was a history of antagonism toward producer cooperatives on the part of socialist intellectuals, like the Webbs, who were advocates of consumer cooperatives.[20] But Peter Jay is quite right in arguing that there is no logical reason for such an antipathy, that the presence of both sorts of cooperatives could lead to complementary empowerment (since people are most often both workers and consumers) that would enhance both rights and the general quality of life.[21]

Like Robert A. Dahl in *A Preface to Economic Democracy,* I also would assume that government would continue to perform a number of crucial economic functions that it presently does, such as protecting contracts, preventing monopolies, printing money, and adopting fiscal and economic policies that would facilitate a healthy economic climate.[22] What would also be required would be for national and subnational governmental and international lending agencies to facilitate the extension of credit to worker-owned enterprises. While the very large Mondragon complex has created its own bank, there would probably have to be governmental (perhaps as well as nongovernmental, for example, workers' pension funds, the floating of bonds) provision for credit to the multiplicity of worker self-governing enterprises that I am talking about.

Moreover, I am not suggesting that this displace the need for some sort of wealth or income redistribution program. Such a program could be targeted at eliminating poverty or meeting basic needs (however those might be defined within and between nations), and at meeting some conception of justice or fairness that goes beyond basic needs or poverty as in Rawls,[23] or at meeting some other goal, such as the freedom to pursue diverse visions of the good life in the thinking of van Parijs.[24] Such programs would be necessary both to mitigate gross distortions of income and wealth that might develop between worker-owned and -controlled enterprises, and that might develop between people who can and do work and those who cannot or are retired. Nor am I suggesting that this displace the public provision of certain goods such as health care, transportation, education, and certain modes of communication (for example, mail, railroads, air waves, public radio, and television).

One objection that might be raised is that some people might not want to engage in joint decision making with others. That might be true. Some people may prefer to be self-employed, or to engage in smaller-scale businesses such as partnerships.[25] Others might prefer to be civil servants. While there hopefully would be some degree of participation of civil servants in the determination of their own working conditions, it would be unreasonable to presuppose that they should have the same degree of autonomy in determining their services that profit-making worker-owners would. So there would be space for people to avoid such collective decision making.

But it still might be argued that people just will not want to assume this sort of collective responsibility, that it somehow runs against human nature. First, if that argument is true, then the premise of political democracy goes along with it. As Dahl pointed out in *A Preface to Economic Democracy*, there really is no argument that we can use for political democracy that cannot be applied to this sort of economic democracy.[26] They both go back to the development of people's potentialities, the bedrock foundation for our conception of human rights. It would indeed be easier to let a dictator make the decisions for us. But even those of us who do not vote find something wrong with that. It strips us of even the possibility of having our voices heard if we should want to express them at some point. We would not feel quite whole as human beings in this day and age if we were presented with the specter of dictatorship. Why should we accept such an exclusionary distribution of rights and power in the economic realm?

One explanation often offered for why people are not very interested in politics is that it is distant, that there are too many other proximate and pressing things in their lives. What could be more proximate and pressing than our work situations? While a transition from externally controlled to empowered worker would present the same difficulties as any other transition of great magnitude, why presume that if people could have a role in determining the conditions under which they live their lives they would reject that in favor of a system of domination? Moreover, Dahl is also right in arguing that there is a common relationship between economic and political democracy. Both require human beings who have a confidence that they are indeed capable of growing and cooperating with others in molding the quality of their collective existences.

The perpetuation of the present economic system poses two threats to democracy, and thus to political and civil human rights. One is that a small group of people gain control over the wealth, natural resources, and political institutions and use them in their own interests regardless of the wishes of, and effects on, the vast majority of the world's population.[27] We have seen this graphically demonstrated in Enron's enormous influence over the U.S. political elite, in its financial devastation of the lives of former employees below the very top, and in its even more disastrous effects on peasants in India.

The second threat is that nondemocratic social relations in the workforce have a debilitating effect on people's ability to see themselves as ever being capable of political empowerment.[28] It is no accident that, in the United States, the percentage of industrial or service wage earners who run for office is extremely low and that in Britain and France even the Labour and Socialist parties have few such workers in the national legislatures. Thus, the easy equation between democracy, "economic freedom," and human rights that we hear today has it very wrong when "economic freedom" means the perpetuation of a system of worker domination.

The only model that would permit us legitimately to say that labor is not a commodity is one in which society recognizes working people as free and equal agents capable of co- and self-determination. True, such responsibility entails risk. Hegel saw risk, indeed risking death, as a key aspect of recognition. Here, workers would have to take the kinds of risks that owner/managers now take, which can mean the death of the enterprise. But when the owner/managers under the present system take the risks and lose, labor loses, too. Jobs are lost on the basis of decisions made by those superior to the workers. Labor also loses when owner/managers become risk averse, as when they choose massive layoffs or plant closings in order to avoid the risk of alienating present or prospective stockholders with diminished profits. Under the conditions of the sort of worker control that I have been talking about, while workers could not freely pose risks to public safety or a clean environment, they would collectively determine their own fates. There is a certain self-respect and a certain dignity in "co- and self-determination." That is why citizens of political democracies find it so hard to think of living under dictatorships or authoritarian regimes, even when they feel that they have elected the wrong people to office or made mistakes in referenda or town meetings. What is the logic of denying the relevance of that agency to the economic realm in which people have just as immediate a stake as they do in the political, and that itself is assuming an ever-greater determining effect over the political?

I have been arguing analytically and normatively. I am not arguing that the ILO in its conventions has advocated recognition as worker co- and self-determination. I am arguing (1) that if the ILO's contention that labor is not a commodity is to be taken seriously, we must think beyond the present forms of recognition accorded to labor; (2) that co- and self-determination is the form of recognition that would maximize liberty, equality, and solidarity in the economic domain; and (3) that there is a direct relationship between the maximization of those values, and hence of human rights, in the economic and political domains.

It is hardly surprising that the ILO does not incorporate what I regard as the logical consequence of their rejection of the commodification of labor. Neither the state of political/economic consciousness on the part of the leadership of most Western trade unions nor the representation of the business community along with the state and labor unions in the tripartite functioning of the ILO are conducive to such thinking.

However, while the vast majority of the 182 Conventions of the ILO (only thirteen of which have been signed by the United States) apply to very specific situations and often to very specific industries, such as civilian seafaring and fishing, there are some references that recognize alternative modes of recognition. While the emphasis is on unions when workers are referred to in collective association, in several instances the conventions make references to "elected representatives" of workers separate from trade union representatives (Convention 135, Article 5, and Convention 150, Article 2). Article 150, which deals with the system of "labor administration," that is, the "public administration activities in the fields of national labor policy," specifies that such an administration serve the needs of those who are not by law employed persons, specifying as one such category of people "members of co-operatives and worker-managed undertakings" (Convention 150, 7, c).

Two other aspects of the ILO's conventions are interesting. First, there is a concern expressed that where there are "elected representatives" of workers on decisionmaking bodies, they not be used to undermine the position of the trade unions (Convention 135, 5). This is to say that employers should not be free to create an alternative system of labor representation in order to break unions. This is a concern with which I am in full accord. It is essential to separate genuine worker control from the appearance of worker control that turns out to be worker cooptation or manipulation. The emergence of a plan to move toward worker participation when initiated by an employer during a dispute with the union is a sure sign that union-busting cooptation and manipulation are going on. The second interesting thing is that in at least one Convention, 158, employers within industries of a certain size are to notify "the competent authority," presumably a state body, when they plan to terminate employees, of the reasons for such termination, the number and categories of workers to be terminated, and the period over which the terminations are intended to be executed (Convention 158, B, 14, 1). The convention stops short of saying what the "labor administration" would do with such information. Still, there is the idea that employers must be accountable to someone else, but not to the workers themselves, if they plan layoffs.

However, both the Social Charter of the Council of Europe and its modified form in the Protocol of the European Union actually come closer to advocacy of worker co- and self-determination than does the ILO. Part I, Article 29 of the Council's Social Charter states, "All workers have the right to be informed and consulted in collective redundancy procedures." Article 22 states that "Workers have the right to take part in the determination and improvement of the working conditions and working environment in the undertaking." Article 2 of the EU's Protocol states that "the Community shall support and complement the activities of the member states in the following fields," two of which are "the information and consultation of workers," and "representation and collective defense of the interests of workers and employers, including co-determination."

I want to emphasize again the caveat of the ILO's Convention 135, 5, that some schemes presented as worker codetermination or worker ownership (the organization of United Airlines is a perfect example of the latter) do not entail any real transfer of control to the workers. They can and have been used to undermine unions. While we would have to rethink the role of unions under thick manifestations of recognition of worker co- and self-determination (for example, they might become advocates of the interest of certain sectors vis-à-vis the public and the government, facilitators of worker/owner communication at the national and international levels, establishers of quality norms of production or ethical codes of business conduct, educational and research institutions, guarantors of due process for the individual members of worker owned and managed enterprises, pension managers, providers of insurance and services such as leisure facilities and vacations), it is absolutely essential that in the here and now of global corporate capitalism, internally democratic and internationally solidaristic unions not only maintain but dramatically increase their protective and bargaining power to advance the human rights of working people. Without unions, the distribution of resources would become even more unequal and atomistic workers would experience much more draconian effects of domination.

CONCLUSION

In my holistic understanding of human rights, political and economic rights are interrelated. The denial of one set in favor of another, in either totalitarian communist or ultraindividualistic and privatistic capitalist modes, undermines human rights. As the star of the former mode has been extinguished in Eastern Europe, neoliberalism marching under the banner of public austerity, corporate privatization, and an enormous skewing of unprecedented private enrichment poses a severe threat to human rights and the only political form than can sustain them, democracy. While we can attempt, consistent with a declared international consensus, to attack the problem of maldistribution and the enormous human stunting that it entails, ultimately the only way to overcome the thrust to disregard or deprioritize economic human rights is to decommodify labor by decentering control over productive structures and empowering those who actually are doing the work within them. Just as political and economic human rights are interdependent, so are the political and economic democratic forms on which they must rest.

The principal economic form is the corporation. This form concentrates economic power in fewer and fewer hands. With this power it overwhelms political systems in both Western liberal and non-Western societies making democracy problematic, relentlessly pursues its own global expansion and rates of profit, defines efficiency only in terms of its market share and profit margin, disregards other quality of life values, and instrumentalizes both its own workers and communities of poorer people across the globe. Even if one were to limit one's conception of human rights to the political, as Cranston advocated, the corporation as we know it entering the twenty-first century would be inconsistent with human rights. But if we view human rights holistically, as I argue we should, the inconsistency is even more manifest.

But what about that other bureaucratic and powerful form, the modern state? What is its relationship to human rights? This is the question that we will address theoretically and empirically in Chapter 6.

CHAPTER 6

THE MODERN STATE AND
HUMAN RIGHTS

INTRODUCTION

A wide variety of political systems have existed in human history. There have been ancient kingdoms in Asia, Africa, and the Americas as well as in Europe; there has been the Greek polis; there have been empires that included conquered peoples over vast territories; there have been small political groupings coterminous with tribes or clans; there have been the American Indian "nations;" and there have been a number of relatively loose confederacies. The nation-state was distinctive because of its aggregative and assimilative capacity. What I call the "modern" state is those states that first appeared after the American and French revolutions and have continued to proliferate since then.

This chapter will examine the implications of the growth of this form of state and the implications for human rights in relation to a number of processes in which this relatively new historical form engages.

The state is curious. It is an abstraction, which is why the French write it with a capital letter, *Etat*. Yet, the effects of this abstraction on the lives of real people have been enormous. In terms of human rights, they have been quite contradictory. As already indicated, this modern state and human rights talk in the form of the Declaration of Independence, the U.S. Constitution, and the French Declaration of the Rights of Man and Citizen, began together as people transitioned from subjects to citizens. Modern states and human rights were born in the same violent revolutionary womb. But that has not meant that their coexistence since that time has been easy. Indeed, states view themselves as "sovereign," that is, as self-determining. But if human rights are to mean anything, it is that sovereignty must be qualified. There must be some things that states cannot do, and other things that states must do, in order to be in compliance with the demands or criteria of human rights.

In the following examination of the processes of the modern state, I am first going to present a general and theoretical discussion of the processes of aggregation, differentiation, and constitutionalization, and the problems they pose for the modern state's sibling, human rights. Then I am going to turn to the issue of violent and coercive practices of the modern state. Here the modern state bears similarities to the premodern absolutist forms of the state, formal constitutionalist constraints notwithstanding. And here we find some of the most egregious violations of human rights.

I am particularly going to scrutinize the coercive and violent processes of the governments of the United States for four reasons. First, the denial of social recognition and the devastating effect on the ability of people to develop their potentialities is so great. Second, I am more intimately familiar with these processes and the context in which they occur in the United States than in any other country. Third, the power and influence, including setting of example, of the United States outside its own borders is so great. And fourth, since the U.S. State Department takes on itself the role of monitoring and assessing the human rights performance of all other states, it is only just that the exemplar and judge itself be subjected to particular scrutiny.

Aggregation, Differentiation, and Constitutionalization

Aggregation

The modern state brings people together on the basis of a number of criteria, including relative power (conquest), territorial contiguity, shared historical experience, or shared cultural characteristics. In Europe, nation-states were constructed on the basis of territorial contiguity. The Scottish and Welsh people were on the same island as the English, and the more problematic Irish people were very close. After the expulsion of the Moors, and the conversion, expulsion, or killing of the Jews, the Catholic monarchs of Spain built a Catholic state of the various regions and peoples, with the exception of the Portuguese, occupying the Iberian Peninsula. France united the people of the Languedoc, some Basques and Catalonians in the Pyrenees, and the Bretons in the West, with the French-speakers who backed them up against mountains or seas. Much later, at the end of the nineteenth century, Machiavelli's four-centuries-old dream of a united Italy came to pass on the basis of territorial contiguity and language. So, too, did Bismarck's Germany, although there were greater variations in dialect than was the case in Italy.

The state we call the United States of America, as well as the states of Latin America, were built on the basis of conquest and colonization prior to their struggles for independence. Europeans conquered the lands of non-European peoples. Conquest and colonization are inconsistent with social recognition. The Europeans destroyed or severely weakened traditional forms of political organization. In South America, they often enslaved the indigenous people and delivered the most cruel punishments, including the severing of the hands of those who resisted working for them as slaves. In North America, most of the indigenous people were either massacred or forced into conditions in which they could not survive as the European-American state extended westward. In some instances, there was an attempt to westernize Indian children by sending them to boarding schools where they were forbidden to speak their traditional languages, enact their spiritual practices, and wear their traditional clothing.[1]

If the construction of the modern states in Europe and North America was virtually complete by the end of the nineteenth century, the creation of such states in other parts of the globe by and large had to wait until decolonization after World War II. The 1950s and 1960s saw the entry of many new states. Some of these, such as those in Africa and the Middle East, were based on nothing other than where Western powers decided to draw colonial borders. They thus disrespected precolonial cultural and historical tradition. Yet, with the demands for self-determination, there seemed to the Western powers to be no option other than to turn the states in Africa over to the people living within those rather arbitrary boundaries. In the oil-rich areas of the Middle East, the situation was different. There, the Western powers created states and installed elites whom they thought would protect their economic and strategic interests. Thus did Saddam Hussein claim that Kuwait was no real state but, in fact, a province of Iraq based on the historical experience prior to Western intrusion and control.

According to the *Europa World Yearbook 1999*, there are 194 nation-states in the world.[2] One reason that human rights applies throughout the world is that virtually everyone, regardless of their cultural traditions, is subject to the sovereignty and power of these states. Even most theocratic states, with the one exception of the Vatican, are still modern states in terms of the processes we are discussing. While representatives of these states drew up the U.N. and regional human rights declarations, we must not forget how Max Weber characterized the modern state: that entity that has a monopoly on the legitimate use of violence. On this point, the state is very different from the corporations discussed in Chapter 5. As we have seen, corporations are definitely coercive in both their internal processes and their external effects, and they sometimes call on the state to use violence in the defense of their interests and even become complicit with the state in violent action. But it cannot be said that corporations on their own can use violence legitimately. The modern state, by contrast, was born out of violence and continually uses it. It often uses that violence in ways that are inconsistent with human rights, even if its representatives have agreed to the international human rights declarations and covenants.

By aggregating the world's total population of over 5.7 billion people into 194 sovereign units, states gain in economies of scale and sometimes overcome differences that could be antagonistic among proximate but different peoples. As our discussion of secession in Chapter 4 indicated, states are not always able to overcome such differences. Aggregation does not always mean assimilation or even accommodation. Certain aggregated groups feel that they are not truly accorded social recognition in the state, that they constitute a dominated element within it. Their attempt to disaggregate themselves is often met by the state's use of violence.

In addition, even for those who do not feel singled out, the scale of the state poses severe problems.[3] The common reflection in the United States that Washington has become too distant from the people of the nation, or of the French that everything is controlled by *fonctionnaires* in Paris, is something that resonates not only with those who want to cut back on national social programs or regulations but also with those who are convinced that the scale is just too large for people to feel that there can be responsible and responsive government at the national level. Thus, aside from calls for local autonomy or devolution based on specific cultural identities, there also are more general calls for decentralization and for grassroots democracy in which a revitalized associational life at the local levels can give life to civic participation and the right to self-determination.[4] For some, it is idle to talk about this right without somehow coming to grips with the problem of scale.

What I have just said pertains to states that at least claim to be democratic. But that is only one subset of modern states. Many are not political democracies. These states do not respect the political and civil rights respected at least to some degree (and that varies considerably among the groups of states whose elites refer to their system as democratic) by democratic states. They usually justify the lack of democracy by the need to preserve the stability of their aggregation. Some, for example, Saudi Arabia, Singapore, Indonesia, or Brunei will recognize the right of private property and give wide freedom to commercial activity. Others, for example, China, North Vietnam, Cuba, and the Eastern European Communist countries prior to their implosions have placed constraints on both political rights and the right to individual private property. China has been backing away from constraints on private property but maintaining severe constraints on political rights.

The tightest form of aggregation is represented by totalitarianism. Under totalitarianism, unthinkable before the appearance of the modern state with its mobilizing and propaganda capacities, particularly in the area of communications technology, the state penetrates into the most minute realms of civil society so that there is no true separation between the state and a nonstate public associational sphere. There is no longer a right to privacy, even within the most basic unit of the family. What one thinks, says, writes, and does in one's home is always of interest to the state. The totalitarian state can be based on a variety of principles and needs. It can be based on the principle of a classless society and the need to prevent counterrevolution. It can be based on the principle of the revival of the true national *volk* and the need to eliminate all impurity from the national gene pool. Or, it can be based on the principle of moral/spiritual revival and the need to make the state subservient to the principles of a single religion that serves as the unquestioned "public good." Attempts at totalitarian aggregation sometimes do indeed deliver better than some political democracies when it comes to the recognition of most of the economic and social rights in the 1966 International Covenant. But by their very nature, totalitarian states are the most severe violators of political and civic human rights. In destroying the integrity of civil society, they go even further than Hobbes in rendering the people "subjects" while pretending to act in their name. Hobbes wanted to pacify the people politically in exchange for a large scope of economic freedom. Totalitarian states are not content with pacification. They want to mobilize people to offer visible signs of assent, like showing up at state-sponsored rallies or voting in one-party elections to ratify the leadership. They want to make people complicit in their own domination. Totalitarian states want to pretend that the laws that they proclaim are the "General Will" of the people, without giving the people the freedom of speech, association, and organization that are necessary for such a determination.

Fortunately, very few states are totalitarian now. The Nazi state was defeated in World War II and the Soviet state has collapsed. As of this writing, it appears that the exceptional antimodernist form of totalitarianism introduced by the Taliban in Afghanistan has been destroyed militarily. But there are still many authoritarian states that refuse to recognize political rights and mistreat dissidents, and many liberal democratic states that refuse to recognize or to take concrete actions to advance economic, social, and cultural rights. Social justice concerns, and rights claims based on them, seem to play less and less in terms of the aggregation processes of modern states.

Differentiation: The Flip Side of Aggregation

The modern state constructs territorial boundaries around itself, declares its sovereignty, and makes much of the difference between the "in-group" and the "out-group." The in-group are "citizens." The out-group are "foreigners." Thus, the state, under the ideological banner of patriotism symbolized by the flag and the national anthem, becomes a source of identity, a clear delineator of the boundary between "self" and "other."

Given what we have said about the problem of scale, some differentiation is going to be necessary if we are to have "communities," people who will either agree to live together despite differences in values (Kymlicka's image of the liberal state with no clear core of common values) or who share values (Taylor's vision). While I love to travel, make friends, and work internationally, I also want a manageable unit in which I am able to follow events and issues, take part in dialogue over them with people whom I know and who share the community with me, and have mechanisms of participating in decision-making processes when I wish to do so (without expecting that I will always convince others that I am right, and viewing the dialogic process as one in which I am ready for others to convince me that my original position should not have prevailed). While I have great respect for the United Nations, I could not have such a manageable unit if all political decisions that affected me were made in one international body.

But the sovereign state in today's complex societies is only slightly less aloof, and probably a good deal more bureaucratic. The state does not constitute a community. But it can contribute to a positive sense of identity. It can get us to recognize each others' civil rights, if not our human rights. It can get us to come to each others' aid in times of disaster. The particularity of the state, when it leads to recognition of each other as fellow citizens with reciprocal rights and obligations, can be a very good thing. Such recognition need not be at the expense of rejecting universal human rights or the capacity to empathize or come to the aid of others around the world. In fact, solid community bonds based on empathetic as well as rational dialogic ties can indeed serve as the basis for an expanded sense of interdependence and obligation. A concrete example of this is the "sister city" relationships that developed during the 1980s between cities and towns in the United States and those in Central America, in which attachment to civic values led to an obligation to assess critically the actual behavior of one's own government and to an empathetic and supportive relationship with others unjustly affected by its policies.

But sometimes it is at such expense. Sometimes a pride in one's own country leads to chauvinism, an exclusive respect for one's cocitizens (so long as they are also chauvinistic) and a disrespect, and sometimes a hatred, for the citizens of other nations or indeed for citizens of one's own country who are not sufficiently "patriotic." This lack of recognition of others has been a contributing factor in wars and domination, as in the dehumanization of foreign enemies or suspect fellow citizens, for example, Americans of Japanese descent in the United States and Canada during World War II.

There are other problems as well. Article 14, 1 of the 1948 Universal Declaration of Human Rights reads: "Everyone has the right to seek and to enjoy in other countries asylum from persecution." But states are very concerned about being overrun by "others" seeking asylum. Thus did Switzerland close its borders to Jews (but not to their expropriated money) trying to flee Nazi Germany. Thus did the United States government refuse to admit the 907 German Jewish refugees whose ship, the *St. Louis,* had landed in Florida. Almost all of them ultimately perished in death camps after their ship was sent back to Europe.[5]

In some cases, states play with the right to asylum for their own political ends. Perhaps the most cynical case of this was the way the U.S. government treated refugees fleeing persecution from the U.S.-supported repressive regimes of Guatemala and El Salvador. Despite the two hundred thousand-plus killings, tortures, and disappearances of people in Guatemala since the 1954 CIA coup that overthrew the democratic government of that country, and the proportionately similar story of tortures, killings, and disappearances in the smaller country of El Salvador, the U.S. government insisted that these refugees would be considered à priori economic refugees and thus not deserving of asylum. The vast majority were refused asylum. Most were either sent back to these countries during the bloodbaths, went underground in the United States, or made it across to Canada. But refugees from Cuba, where there was no such bloodbath going on, were welcomed with open arms. This was a clear manipulation of the right of asylum to meet the Cold War predispositions of the U.S. state. It even violated U.S. law that required asylum for people who had reasonable grounds for claiming a fear of persecution. If the people of Guatemala and El Salvador did not have such grounds in the 1980s, it is difficult to think of any people who did. They were simply foreigners who lacked the political influence of the Florida Cubans who had become citizens and wanted open immigration for their former conationals. The Guatemalans' and Salvadorans' rights as human beings seeking asylum, rights that were recognized by both the Universal Declaration of Human Rights and the U.S.'s own immigration law, went unrecognized by the U.S. state that bore much of the responsibility for the persecution in the home countries.[6] The official denial of the persecution was a way of denying that responsibility.

But there developed a movement in the United States, called the Sanctuary Movement, in which citizens acting on the basis of religious faith/and or conscience opposed the behavior of their state, while obeying the immigration law, by offering shelter to such people. The state sent spies into the religious institutions where the movement was based and prosecuted some of the participants for violating its laws. Despite this state action, there was established a people-to-people solidarity based on social recognition across national boundaries. As in the case of the already mentioned Sister City activists—and there was much cross-over between Sister City and Sanctuary activists—the participants did this in the conviction that where the state fails in its obligations to protect human rights, citizens acting together are morally bound to pick up the obligation and to come to the defense of the victims regardless of their nationalities. The tight exclusive communalism represented by the saying "my country [state] right or wrong" was replaced by a kind of social recognition that saw the rights violations directed against foreigners as trumping such patriotism. In fact, the participants made the argument that this kind of uncritical allegiance to the state actually undercut its legitimacy, that a true communal spirit must be more expansive in its recognition of the rights of others. They could point to the contradictions that the state was driven to in violating its own laws (for example, violation of U.S. immigration law in the cases of Guatemalan and Salvadoran refugees and violation of the law, commonly referred to as the Boland Amendment, prohibiting the arming of the Nicaraguan Contras, which was done anyway through the Iran-Contra scheme).

War also causes the state to differentiate between the citizens of an enemy state and its own citizens and those of nonenemy states, and even between its own citizens. The Nazis dehumanized the Slavs on their east and saw their future as agricultural serfs for the Aryans in the Thousand Year Reich. The Japanese dehumanized the Chinese, massacring the people of Nanjing and performing surgical medical experiments on nonanesthetized prisoners. They also dehumanized the Koreans by using Korean women as coerced sexual objects for their troops (the so-called comfort women). The United States adopted language to dehumanize the Japanese (the "slant-eyed Nips") in World War II and the North Vietnamese ("Gooks") in the war in Vietnam. Both the U.S. government and the military/oligarchic regimes it supported in Central American dehumanized those who criticized, resisted, or revolted. Where it is state against state, there is usually an accompanying propaganda on the home front that depicts the adversaries, making no distinction between the governments and militaries on the one hand and the people on the other, as less than human.[7] The long history of warfare between France and England led to the English referring to the French as "Frogs." I know of no reciprocally dehumanizing name that the French had for the English, but they did have a demeaning name for the Germans, les Boches. Fortunately, generational changes and the coming together of the European Union has lessened those old dehumanizing antagonisms.

During wartime, even members of the "we" state can find themselves designated as "others." Thus, U.S. and Canadian citizens of Japanese citizenry were placed in internment camps during World War II solely because of their lineage. This was clearly a human rights violation against both a group and the individuals therein. There were no charges of specific crimes, no trials, no due process, and yet a clear loss of liberty and property. Moreover, it was racially specific. People of German or Italian extraction were not so treated.

Foreign workers also raise serious questions concerning differentiation. In time of economic need, states open up their borders to workers from other countries who will do work that the state does not have enough citizens to do, or that the citizens of the state will not do. French citizens do not want to sweep the metro stations or the street gutters. So immigrant workers from former French colonies in sub-Saharan Africa are permitted in to do that. French workers do not like to do some of the more arduous or dangerous factory work. So workers from North Africa are permitted in to do that. French women do not like to work as domestic servants. So Spanish and Portuguese women are permitted in to do that. Most U.S. citizens will not perform back-bending agricultural fieldwork. So Mexicans are permitted into the United States to perform that work, just as Chinese were permitted into the United States to build the railroad lines out to the West in the nineteenth century.

But when the economy takes a downturn and unemployment and crime rates rise, it is often the formerly welcomed immigrant who is blamed and "urged" to leave, sometimes by the very people who had welcomed them in different economic times. Thus, Enoch Powell's name became synonymous with racism for many in Britain because of his anti-immigration stance, despite the fact that when he had been a minister of state (Housing and Local Government in 1955–1957, Health in 1960–1963) he bore major responsibility for bringing people of color into Britain to work cheaply in the public services.

More recently, toward the end of the last decade of the twentieth century, the National Front in France began to make very significant gains in local elections and in 2002 its candidate, Jean-Marie Le Pen, made the second round in the presidential elections. The National Front has really determined the positions taken by the major parties at the national level, by playing on the anti-immigrant theme. One of its major platforms is to bring back the death penalty. When tied to its view that rises in crime rates are due to immigrants with a moral system well below that of the white French, it is clear that the people it wants to put to death are these immigrants whose inferior cultures do not merit social recognition among the "true" French (that is, white Christians with long French ancestry). This is consistent with Jean-Paul Sartre's earlier analysis of why it was so difficult for Jews to gain such recognition among the French; they too were less than worthy "others" because they did not share the ancestry, ties to the land, culture, and religion of the "true" French.[8]

Constitutionalization

Constitutions are intended to limit the powers of agents of the modern state. The precursor to constitutional government was absolutist government. That is to say a king or a collective ruling body could simply decide what to do without any external restraint. Both Plato and Hobbes advocated systems in which the wisest (Plato) and the most effective manipulator of power (Hobbes) would be vested with this kind of unfettered authority.

It is difficult to think of rights without constitutionalism. Plato did not think in terms of rights. Hobbes did, but the logic of his argument led him to constrain rights to the sole inalienable right to *one's own* life. In Hobbes's *Leviathan,* one could not even intercede verbally to defend the rights of another against the sovereign. Indeed, Great Britain, with its "unwritten" constitution, walks a fine line here between having a constitution in any meaningful sense and giving to the government of the majority party the right to do what it wishes.[9]

However, constitutions themselves can also be rights violating. Slavery was written into the U.S. Constitution and stayed there until after the Civil War. Article I, Section 2 states, "Representatives and direct taxes shall be apportioned among the several States which may be included within this union, according to their respective numbers, which shall be determined by adding to the whole number of free persons, including those bound to service for a term of three years and excluding Indians not taxed, three fifths of all other persons [that is, slaves]."

The U.S. Constitution also mandated the return of slaves who fled from their servitude. Article IV, Section 2 stated, "No person held to service or labor in one State, under the laws thereof, escaping into another, shall, in consequence of any law or regulation therein, be discharged from such service or labor, but shall be delivered up on claim of the party to whom such service or labor may be due." This was despite the fact that the Declaration of Independence contained the famous words, "We hold these truths to be self-evident, that all men are created equal; that they are endowed by their creator with certain unalienable rights; that among these are life, liberty, and the pursuit of happiness. That to secure these rights, governments are instituted among men."

Thomas Paine was exceptional among the European founders of the United States in seeing a contradiction here. Indeed, Thomas Jefferson, one of the authors of the Declaration of Independence, believed that Africans and their slave offspring had very little potential for development, but that Indians were somehow innately talented people who would make important contributions to the new nation, *if* they gave up their institutions and culture and accepted those of the dominant Anglo-Americans.[10] Sadly, these beliefs continued for many generations, and are held by some even today.

The dominated people understood the meaning of this in human rights terms better than the drafters of the Declaration of

Independence, and they spoke up. It is important for us to resurrect their words, to let them speak for themselves rather than to always speak for them in academic language.

The former slave Frederick Douglass, one of those in whom Jefferson recognized very little potentiality, was taught to read and write secretly by the wife of one of his masters. He wrote of his condition as a slave:

> Once awakened by the silver trump of knowledge, my spirit was roused to eternal wakefulness. Liberty! the inestimable birthright of every man, had for me, converted every object into an asserter of this great right. It was heard in every sound and beheld in every object. It was ever present, to torment me with a sense of my wretched condition. The more beautiful and charming were the smiles of nature, the more horrible and desolate was my condition. I saw nothing without seeing it, and I hear nothing without hearing it. I do not exaggerate, when I say, that it looked from every star, smiled in every calm, breathed in every wind, and moved in every storm.[11]

For Douglass, the recognition of equal rights was something that was natural to young people, and it required considerable socialization to denature them into accepting racial inequality.

> Although slavery was a delicate subject, and very cautiously talked about among grown up people in Maryland, I frequently talked about it—and that very freely—with the white boys. I would, sometimes, say to them, while seated on a curb stone or a cellar door, "I wish I could be free, as you will be when you get to be men. You will be free you know, as soon as you are twenty-one, and can go where you like, but I am a slave for life. Have I not as good a right to be free as you have?" Words like these, I observed, always troubled them; and I had no small satisfaction wringing from the boys, occasionally, that fresh and bitter condemnation of slavery, that springs from nature, unseared and unperverted.[12]

Native Americans also understood their domination by a constitutional government of "others" in human rights terms. Ten Bears (Parra-Wa-Samen), of the Yamparika Comanches, said to the Anglo-American state, "You said that you wanted to put us in reservations to build us houses and make us medicine lodges. I do not want them. I was born on the prairie where the wind blew free and there was nothing to break the light of the sun. I was born where there were no enclosures and where everything drew a free breath. I want to die there and not within walls."[13]

Baron de Lahontan, a Frenchman who stayed with the Huron Indians of Canada from 1683 to 1694, quotes a Huron who told him long before the French Revolution and the Declaration of the Rights of Man and Citizen, "We are born free and united brothers, each as much a great lord as the other, while you are all the slaves of one sole man [the king]. I am the master of my body, I dispose of myself, I do what I wish, I am the first and last of my nation … subject only to the great Spirit."[14]

While the concept and language of human rights were often thought to be privileged domains of the European, African Americans and Native Americans clearly had hold of the concept, and understood how their domination violated it, even if they sometimes used analog expressions rather than the precise words, "human rights." Indeed, both Pierre Clastres and Jack Weatherford maintain that the social and political norms of the Native Americans were more egalitarian and far less coercive of individuals than the modern European state. Weatherford contends that the Native American served as the model for the free, inner-directed "noble-savage," with whom the "un-free" person under conditions of European civilization contrasts so badly in Rousseau's *Discourse on the Origin or Inequality*.[15] Weatherford points out that Thomas Paine, who was influential in both the French and the American revolutions, was "the first American to call for the abolition of slavery" and as a proponent of democracy "used the Indians as models of how society might be organized."[16]

Slavery was indeed outlawed by the Thirteenth Amendment, passed and ratified in 1865. The right of people to vote regardless of class or former state of servitude was afforded by the Fifteenth Amendment, ratified in 1870 (but often violated through terror, poll taxes, grandfather clauses, or literacy tests). And the right of women to vote was granted by the Nineteenth Amendment, ratified in 1920. The pitifully few Native Americans who have survived in the United States now have the choice of remaining on reservations, most of which are extremely poor, or melting into the larger cities and giving up most of their culture. The rights violations delivered unto the Native Americans in a determined Lockean move to take their "unproductive" lands is perhaps the most difficult to redress histori-cally through constitutional change.

With this major exception, the U.S. Constitution has been modi-fied from an exclusionary document quite at odds with the Declaration of Independence to an inclusive one consistent with the Declaration. Moreover, with the exception of rights to vote and run for office, most of the rights are extended to citizen and noncitizen alike.

Thus does the Fourteenth Amendment (1868), after declaring that no state can abridge the privileges or immunities of citizens, declare: "nor shall any State deprive *any person* of life, liberty, or property, without due process of law; nor deny to *any person* within its jurisdiction the equal protection of its laws" (emphasis added). Thus, when it comes to due process and equal protection of the laws, the constitution grants these to everyone regardless of their nationality. These are basic rights that every state in the union must grant to anyone who comes under its jurisdiction. Here there is supposed to be no differentiation between the former slave and born freeman, or the citizen and the noncitizen. But, as of this writing, the George W. Bush administration is preparing a precedent that runs counter to this. The proposed trial of captured *foreign* fighters and suspected terrorists before special military tribunals, where there are much more open rules of evidence than in courts trying U.S. citizens, where there is a lack of sentencing guidelines, where there is a curtailment of possibilities for appeal, and where the president has the final say on how a convicted person is to be punished raise, raises serious due process and equal protection of the laws issues for these noncitizens.

The issue of constitutionalism in Eastern Europe before the implosion of the communist regimes is particularly interesting. As will be recalled, Marx attempted to "deconstruct" the concept of rights in the Declaration of the Rights of Man and Citizen and in the constitutions of some of the North American states. He saw these rights as being simply the rights of bourgeois man, not of universal men as was implied by the documents. But that did not mean that those who claimed to follow Marx's teachings disregarded constitutionalism or the formal recognition of rights in constitutional documents.

On the contrary, such formal recognition was extended by the Soviet elite-to-be well back into the prerevolutionary period. The Draft Program of the Russian Social-Democratic Labor Party, written by Lenin in 1902, proposed a replacement of Czarist autocracy "by a *republic* based on a democratic constitution that would ensure" a whole host of rights, including, "inviolability of the person and domicile of citizens, unrestricted freedom of conscience, speech, the press and assembly, the right to strike and to organize unions; freedom of movement and occupation; the right of every citizen to prosecute any official, without previously complaining to the latter's superiors."[17]

The Constitution of 1936, written during the height of Stalin's use of physical terror against his real or imagined opponents, contains a contradiction. On the one hand, it pays tribute to the rights of free speech, press, assembly, and demonstrations. It also, "in order to develop the initiative and political activity of the masses of the people" guarantees them the right to participate in mass organizations not under the control of the state. On the other, it defines the Communist Party as "the vanguard of the working people in their struggle to build communist society and the leading core of all organization of the working people, *both government and nongovernment*" (emphasis added).[18]

Thus, this constitution talks about developing "the initiative and the political activity of the masses of the people," but it obliterates the distinction between state, public sphere, and civil society and places all under the directorship or dictatorship of the single legitimate party. The drafting of such a document was an act of pure and cynical formalism by Stalin and his associates.

The Constitution of 1977, as amended in 1988, repeated the same sort of contradiction and formalism when it comes to the issue of rights. Chapter 1, Article 9 states:

> The principal direction in the development of the political system of Soviet society is the extension of socialist democracy, namely ever broader participation of citizens in managing the affairs of society and the state, continuous improvement in the machinery of the state, heightening of the activity of public organizations, strengthening the system of people's control, consolidation of the legal foundations of the functioning of the state and of public life, greater openness and publicity, and constant responsiveness to public opinion.[19]

This statement, committing the Soviet Union to the principles of participatory democracy, is followed by a long list of articles guaranteeing fundamental rights to Soviet citizens. But the Constitution also contains Article VI, which states:

> The leading and guiding force of Soviet society and the nucleus of its political system, of all state organizations and public organizations, is the Communist Party of the Soviet Union. The CPSU exists for the people and serves the people. The Communist Party, armed with Marxism-Leninism, determines the general perspectives of the development of society and the course of the home and foreign policy of the USSR, directs the constructive work of the Soviet people, and imparts a planned, systematic, and theoretically substantiated character to their struggle for the victory of socialism.[20]

The Soviet constitution itself suffered from a kind of schizophrenia. On the one hand, it granted all of the political rights that one finds in

Western constitutions, thus conceding their legitimacy. On the other hand, it conferred exclusive legitimacy on a single party, and gave that party, which was constituted of only a small minority of the population, control over all aspects of public life in the Soviet Union. The constitution thus reflected two phenomena associated with modern states: constitutionalism and totalitarianism. Since the essence of constitutionalism is restriction of governmental power, these two tendencies can only coexist within documents. They cannot, and did not, in political reality. The price paid for the attempt is bound to be political and civil human rights. This does not, however, negate the fact that the Soviet Union respected certain economic and social rights to a much greater extent than most of the regimes that replaced it, and than many of the liberal democracies that survived it. Nor should it be taken to imply that the formal guarantees of due process and equal protection of the laws to all in liberal democratic constitutions are fully followed in practice.

VIOLENCE AND COERCION

Conflicting Visions of the Modern Liberal State

In classical liberal thought, beginning with Hobbes and Locke, the state's major function is a protectionist one. The state is there to protect the rights of individuals to their lives and their property from both foreign and domestic threat. As Hobbes argued most forcibly, in order to do this the state had to have sufficient compulsive power. Thus, it is not particularly surprising that the sociologist Max Weber would argue that an essential characteristic of the state is its monopoly over the legitimate use of force. Weber writes, "It [the modern state] is thus a compulsory organization with a territorial base. Furthermore, today, the use of force is regarded as legitimate only so far as it is either permitted by the state or prescribed by it. The claim of the modern state to monopolize the use of force is as essential to it as its character of compulsory jurisdiction and of continuous operation."[21]

Just as human rights were born in the violence of the French and American revolutions, and were both advanced and violated by those historical phenomena, so, too, the relationship between the rights-respecting modern state, which in a profound sense issued from those revolutions, and the force that those states continue to use has been a problematic one. After all, as has been pointed out, the modern state has engaged in wars of mass destruction, in genocide, and in acts of cruelty and torture that are at least equal to Western medieval practices.

There has been a public recognition of this kind of brutal behavior by states ranging from liberal to totalitarian during wartime. It also has been generally recognized in the internal dynamics of dictatorships and totalitarian states even in times of peace. But where it is less well recognized is in the normal dynamics of the liberal democratic states.

A prescient English activist and writer, Josephine Butler, wrote in her 1879 text *Government by the Police*, "What has become of the first principles of English law these days? Many even of the best of our public men do not seem fully impressed with the fact of the constant violation of the law in some of its highest principles by the Executive and their officers."[22] Butler was particularly outraged by the brutality of the police in breaking up Chartist meetings and by the brutalization of prisoners held in police jails.

At this time, when English society was much more ethnically homogeneous than it is today, there was a decidedly class bias to the brutality. The police were largely recruited from what Marx called the *lumpenproletariat* and were used by the upper classes to enforce a quite illegal and brutal form of discipline on working-class people who were trying to organize unions and political organizations. Despite their common class origins, the police also used it on other members of the *lumpenproletariat* who were defenseless against an organized armed power backed by political and economic elites. This kind of class violence would be repeated in the wars to prevent labor organization in the United States at the end of the nineteenth century and through the 1930s. In the United States, a specific national force was created and placed under the control of state governors to break strikes. This was the origin of the National Guard. But police continued to be used, as did private security forces such as Pinkerton's. The state extended the sanction of law to the actions of the latter as well.

Most middle- and upper-class citizens of contemporary liberal democracies do not come into contact with the police except when they are the victims of a crime, when they speed in their automobiles, or when they require emergency help in the case of an accident. Thus, among this segment of the population, which is the majority, the police (the human-physical manifestation of the coercive power of the state to which Weber refers) are indeed seen as providing the crucial protective function of the state. While such people might be angered by a police officer giving them a traffic ticket, the anger is usually directed toward the specific officer.[23] And the larger ideology kicks in, that is, that we have a basically just and rights-respecting political and economic system that the police protect from common criminals and political terrorists. During the Cold War, they also protected the good and decent citizenry from "subversives," who did not have to be "terrorists." In the United States, the "war on crime" replaced the "war on poverty" of the Johnson Era. Especially after the events of September 11, 2001, it is the "war on terrorism" that has taken center stage. Each of these "wars" has reinforced this ideology of a just and benign system offering everyone protection through the increasingly empowered state's police.

Academic trends and schools of intellectual reflection have minimized the actual amount of use of violence by the liberal state and especially its use in ways that violate basic human rights. Harold Lasswell, a member of the "Power School" of political science based at the University of Chicago in the 1930s and 1940s, argued in his *Politics: Who Gets What, When, and How* that a characteristic of the modern state's internal behavior is that in order to control masses (a function of every state according to Lasswell's "realism"), elites rely less on the use of violence and more on an increase in the use of rationing (distribution of money, goods, position) and signs and symbols (for example, ideological rituals, propaganda).[24] Moreover, at least in the United States, textbooks in American government either ignore or downplay the internal coercive/repressive aspects of state behavior. Secondary and higher education rarely exposes pupils and students to this aspect of what Allan Wolfe has called "the seamy side of democracy."[25]

But this deemphasis on the violent aspect of the state is also present in some of the writing of postmodernists who see their work as radical and hopefully subversive of the established order. A most influential figure here is the late French theorist, Michel Foucault. Like Lasswell, Foucault's major concern is power. Foucault's book *Discipline and Punish* is concerned with how a society "normalizes" its population, that is to say how modern liberal democratic societies ensure certain kinds of behaviors and deal with those behaviors and thought processes. There is both a more in-depth historical dimension and deeper methodological approach (which Foucault calls "archaeology" when he is being frank, and pure "description" when he is being coy.)

Foucault begins his book with a grisly description of the torture-execution of the regicide Damiens in Paris in 1757. He quotes reports of this affair: "[Damiens] taken and conveyed in a cart, wearing nothing but a shirt, holding a torch of burning wax weighing two pounds, then, in the said cart, to the Place de Grève, where on a scaffold that will be erected there, the flesh will be torn from his breasts, arms, thighs and calves with red-hot pincers, his right hand, holding the knife with which he committed the said parricide, burnt with sulfur, and, on those places where the flesh will be torn away, poured molten lead, boiling oil, burning resin, wax and sulfur melted together and then his body drawn and quartered by four horses and his limbs and body consumed by fire, reduced to ashes and his ashes thrown to the winds."[26]

Foucault carries on the discussion of the painful execution for three more pages and devotes the rest of this initial chapter to torture. The point of this is to show how the spectacle of torture carried out by representatives of the state against the bodies of those who resort to criminality, particularly fierce against those who would try to kill the very living symbol of sovereignty, the king, was carefully designed to control the population. At this point in time power is centered. It is in the hands of the sovereign, the living incorporation of the state (as in "*l'Etat, c'est moi*").

Foucault notes two moments of change in this centralized control through the public spectacle of the state's torturing and killing the criminal. The first comes after the fall of the monarchy and the coming of a more fully developed capitalist society and bourgeois class. Here punishment was still relied on, but it was subjected to more stringent rules. It became more representational and symbolic. The idea was no longer to stage spectacles that would fill onlookers of a torture-execution with fear (consistent with Hobbes's approach) but to use punishment to instill certain ideas in the public mind. For example, certain conceptions about private property could be represented more effectively in a system of law and punishment that observed more restraints and controls on its ferocity than did the former system. The final phase of this change is represented in the present. He argues that now there is a complete decentering of power, to the point that power is no more than a medium in which social and political interaction takes place. Here power is exercised through surveillance in all kinds of social institutions—educational, medical, social service, psychological, professional, and so on. He uses the term "the carceral archipelago" for this decentering and dispersion of surveilling (power) institutions and writes "the carceral archipelago transported this technique from the penal institution to the entire social body."[27] While all of the descriptive material is taken from French history, it is clear that Foucault is generalizing "this new economy of power, the carceral system," at least to the West. For he ends the book with this sentence: "I end a book that must serve as a historical background to various studies of the power of normalization and the formation of knowledge in modern society."[28]

Foucault's text is curious. While it is obvious that he saw a problem, there is nothing comparable to Weber's explicitly normative warning about society walking into an "iron cage." If power has become nothing short of the medium in which we all live, it is indeed difficult to specify what the problem really is and to look at it through a normative or ethical conception such as rights. But the one thing that Foucault is adamant about is that we should not look at sovereignty or the state as the major exerciser of power and violence over bodies. Power has become the observation and evaluation of bodies and minds that permeate our societies. If there is a "rights" problem given this analysis, and Foucault would eschew that word as much as Marx did although for different reasons, we would look everywhere *but* the state for its source.[29] What would be focused on are the ideological and cultural mechanisms of the society that are not seen as constituting systems but rather as decentered "moments" without a central core and without causation as we traditionally understand it.[30]

For many of us, this might appear quite reasonable, to match our life experiences as well as our intellectual understandings. But who is the "us" in such a statement? Joy James, an African American woman writer, criticizes Foucault's archaeology:

> Writing about the "disappearance of torture as a public spectacle"—with no reference to its continuity in European and American colonies where it was inflicted on indigenous peoples in Africa and the Americas—Foucault weaves a historical perspective that eventually presents the contemporary ("Western") state as a non-practitioner of torture. His text illustrates how easy it is to erase the specificity of the body and violence while centering discourse on them. Losing sight of the violence practiced by and in the name of the sovereign, who at times was manifested as part of a dominant race, Foucault universalizes the body of the white, propertied male. Much of *Discipline and Punish* depicts the body with no specificity tied to racialized or sexualized punishment. The resulting veneer of bourgeois respectability painted over state repression elides racist violence against black and brown and red bodies.[31]

Two points should be made here. First, false or arbitrary arrest, unjustified or excessive violence, torture, the planting of evidence, and lying in arrest reports by police are state-inflicted human rights violations regardless of who the victim is. But these are almost never random. They almost always tend to conform to social hierarchies. In Josephine Butler's time, the victims were working-class people, especially those who tried to organize politically to defend their class interests. It is still true in our time that lower-class white people (for example, those identified as "trailer trash" or "rednecks") are more likely to be subjected to such treatment than are middle- or upper-class whites with occupational, professional, and organization ties that can translate into political power. But Joy James is quite right, in the West by far the most frequent victims of human rights violations at the hands of such state agents are people of color.

Conclusion

Both the aggregation and the differentiation functions of the state pose problems for human rights. Aggregation overcomes extreme particularism manifested by clans and tribes and achieves certain economies of scale. But aggregation also fosters dangerous chauvinistic tendencies, that is, particularity on a larger and even more dangerous scale that can then be presented to the rest of the world as a universal (even if the actual practices diverge from the universal/particular image being presented). This is how many in other parts of the world see the Western claims to possessing the truth about human rights. Aggregation also can also lead to an absorption of virtually all of the politically relevant social space by the state. This is what we have in totalitarianism, which does not permit the assertion of either individual or group rights claims against the party/state.

Whether a state is liberal or totalitarian, constitutional provisions offer insufficient protection to fundamental human rights such as due process and equal protection of the laws. In fact, such constitutional provisions, are a double-edged sword. It is important that such statements exist as normative reference points, as criteria that those who advance human rights can point to in order to further legitimate their positions. But they also help create an ideological mask whereby people think that the practices of human rights are in fact being respected because they exist in such documents. The documents then take on mythical powers of their own. The struggle to actualize and expand human rights practices is a constant one, constitutional provisions notwithstanding.

In Chapter 7, we will take a closer look at the coercive and violent function as exerted by the most powerful modern state today, the United States, and the effects on human rights.

CHAPTER 7

PERPETUAL WAR AND HUMAN RIGHTS IN THE UNITED STATES

INTRODUCTION

Despite the birth of human rights in violent revolutionary processes, literal war is never conducive to respect for human rights. It means doing deliberate violence against the bodies of people designated as "others"; it means deliberately destroying the resources that they need to develop themselves; and it means dehumanizing them in the minds of one's own public. But if literal war poses threats to human rights, so does its figurative form, war as a trope. Since World War II, the United States has been intermittently at literal war a number of times (Korea, Vietnam, Dominican Republic, Grenada, Lebanon, Iraq, Afghanistan—and by proxy Central America and Columbia). But it has been consistently in a state of figurative war. The internal anticommunist crusade in the United States in the United States from the late 1940s to the early 1960s, which went by the name of McCarthyism, was part of the U.S.'s "War on Communism." In the 1960s, Lyndon Johnson took the trope in a more constructive direction when he declared a "War on Poverty," which was aimed at improving the social and economic human rights of those at the bottom of American society. But that was not to last. Beginning in 1980 with the victory of Ronald Reagan and a string of administrations that saw poverty as an individual failing rather than a human rights issue, the trope of war was returned to the more literally violent enterprises of the "wars" on crime, drugs, and terrorism.

The trope of war is very powerful on the public mentality. Once it is propagated, the insecurity of the public is aroused and politicians make a political investment in it from which it is very difficult to extract themselves. This crosses party lines. It is no accident that President Clinton signed the antiterrorism law, which greatly expanded the scope of the federal death penalty, in the election year of 1996, and that the presidential candidates of both major parties in the 2000 election were staunch defenders of the death penalty. Indeed, the winner, President George W. Bush, was the governor of Texas who had presided over almost 150 executions, with a U.S. record for any state of forty executions just in the year that he was elected. Given the way both parties have used the death penalty as one of the two symbolic indicators that they are serious warriors against crime (the other being more and longer incarceration under harsher conditions), they fear that it would mean political death to show a weakening in the resolve to prosecute this war.

But in the process, the trope ceased to be a trope and became a literal war long before the literal war against terrorism in Afghanistan. Moreover, it spilled over U.S. borders. Hence, the U.S.'s greater and greater engagement in the civil war in Colombia, ostensibly to fight drugs but also to fight leftist insurgents. And in the case of the domestic war on crime, it accelerated into armed occupations, raids, and checkpoints in certain minority neighborhoods.

I have been writing thus far in very general terms. I would now like to proceed to more precision regarding police violence, the death penalty, the state of incarceration, and the drug war to indicate how these have all involved grave violent and coercive human rights violations on the part of the U.S. and the individual states.

Police Violence

In 1994, Congress passed the Crime Control Act. It directed the U.S. Attorney General to collect data for research and statistical purposes on the use of excessive force by police officers. As of this writing, Congress still has not approved the funds to make it happen.[1] But on the basis of limited academic research, of Amnesty International reports on police behavior in specific cities and the U.S. as a whole, and a Human Rights Watch report on prison conditions, of systematic clippings from the *New York Times* and other press sources, it is obvious that there is an enormous difference between the frequency with which people of color are subjected to human rights violations at the hands of the state's police and detention officials and the frequency of whites experiencing such violation.

To paraphrase Foucault, I will just be descriptive for a bit while I relate some "archeological" data. This is important, because while the information I will present here has been in the public domain, few people would consult it, or if they chanced to see a portion of it in a newspaper, they would likely view it as a specific story about an aberration. There is after all a difference between reading with an attention and a focus (for example, reading for research purposes) and reading a newspaper or magazine for general information. So the fact that a liberal democracy permits newspapers to print articles about charges of police rights abuses does not mean that it will sink in, that people who are not so victimized themselves will notice that these are not just isolated incidents that they are reading about, or sad but inevitable and unrelated mistakes as the police execute the protectionist function of the state. Indeed, to the extent that it is specified that the victims are people of color, or that the names of the victims or their photographs reveal that fact, the racist perception that these people conform to a "criminal type" is likely to justify the attacks by the police in the minds of white upper- and middle-class consumers of the media. "Something" had to be wrong or the police would not have "reacted" this way. Or, "these people" are always "crying" discriminatory mistreatment. Or, the police have to be "tough" with "people like that" in order to survive in "those" neighborhoods.

But when one looks carefully, it is impossible not to come to the conclusion that the behavior of at least some of the police officers within a liberal democratic state constitutes anything other than extremely serious human rights violations. And while many police officers might well be rights-respecting, there is a devastating pattern to the lack of respect for law and the rights of certain categories of people, an egregious and violent manifestation of the withholding of social recognition by agents of the state.

Now to give some concrete examples. In Chapter 4, I made very brief reference to human rights violations by the police in Philadelphia. In Philadelphia, it was found that between 1988 and 1991 hundreds of people, many of them serving prison time, had been convicted on the basis of planted drugs, false police reports, and perjured testimony in the courts. The offending drug squad officers operated in a poor African American neighborhood where they often beat and robbed their victims before offering untruthful testimony that sent them to prison. There were seven proven cases of unjustifiable shooting. Hundreds of convictions were overturned. The city paid out $20 million to settle two hundred civil suits. In one of the rarest of occurrences, several police officers were actually sent to prison. In order to forestall law suits by several groups, the city did adopt some reforms. But this was after innocent people had been beaten, shot, robbed, and falsely imprisoned for considerable periods of time.[2]

In this instance, and in the instances that follow, people were denied their freedom, were denied equal treatment before the law, were denied a whole host of needs including the need to hold a job and care for their children or other dependents, and were denied discursive inclusion. For when one is subjected to perjured testimony by agents of the state, when one has legal representation in the court well below the level of more affluent people, when one is lacking in education, it is difficult to contend that there is any real inclusion of the people in the discursive legal proceedings that are about to have a devastating impact on their lives. No one of these is more persuasive than the other in terms of constituting a human rights violation. They all constitute a total denial of social recognition.

There also has been massive police violence, false arrest, and perjury in the courts on the part of the New York police. From 1995 to 1997, the amount paid out for such police misconduct in that city went from $19.9 million to $27.3 million.[3] And the same pattern is found—even if the city pays out compensation, the rights-violating police are almost always left on the streets to inflict more damage.[4] Again, the damage they inflict runs from death through brain impairment, paralysis, and loss of sight.

Between 1986 and 1990, Los Angeles paid out $20 million in damages. The payments in 1990 came to $1,300 per police officer.[5] In a detailed analysis of the behavior of the Los Angeles Police Department, Amnesty International found that department's use of violence to be in violation of Article 5 of the Universal Declaration of Human Rights ("No one shall be subjected to torture or to cruel, inhuman or degrading punishment"), of Article 7 of the International Covenant on Civil and Political Rights (which, unlike the Economic, Social and Cultural Covenant, the United States did ratify and is thus legally as well as morally bound to obey), and to the Code of Conduct for Law Enforcement Officials adopted the by the U.N. General Assembly in 1979, which stipulates in its third article that "force may be used 'only when strictly necessary and to the extent required for the performance of their duty.'"[6] The victims are not random, any more than they were in the nineteenth century. The report goes on to say that "the evidence suggests that racial minorities, especially blacks and Latinos, have been subjected to discriminatory treatment and are disproportionately the victims of abuse."[7] To cover themselves in these abuses, the police usually charge their victims with crimes.

To repeat, it is extremely rare that police officers are punished for their misdeeds against civilians. Indeed, Paul Chevigny, in his 1995 comparative study of the New York and Los Angeles departments, found that the police departments tended to not only disregard the validity of civil law suits and their applicability to police policy, but that the most violent officers tended to be rewarded with promotion and even to be made trainers of other officers.[8] The "code of silence" among police officers often means that there will be no other witnesses to testify against the offending state agents except the victims, if they are still living.[9] Even in the extreme case of the Haitian immigrant, Abner Louima, who in August 1997 was beaten and then sodomized with a broom handle that was then forced into his mouth with such force that it broke his teeth, none of the other officers in the New York City station where it happened tried to stop it or reported the incident. After he had been hospitalized and severe injuries to his internal organs discovered, a health care provider in the hospital publicly revealed the tortures to which Louima had been subjected. Only then was an official investigation begun, and did some officers speak of what they had heard and seen in the police station.[10]

In addition to the "code of silence" among police officers, there is the uncritical eagerness of prosecutors to get convictions of those whom the police charge, and the à priori assumptions that police officers tell the truth and that people charged with crime lie. Chevigny reports that not only do police officers regularly lie when they charge civilians with whom they have had face-to-face encounters or have chased in a car, but that such lying is actually taught in formal training sessions to "cover your ass."[11] Even when the cities pay out money for civil claims against police behavior, the cities usually do not admit guilt and the offending officers almost always escape significant, if any, penalties. Amnesty International writes: "In most cases reviewed by Amnesty International in which substantial awards were made for police misconduct, the officers had been absolved from any criminal liability."[12]

A 1994 federal law, passed after the beating of Rodney King and the riots sparked in Los Angeles by the acquittal in court of his police attackers, permits the Department of Justice to investigate racially discriminatory police behavior at the state and municipal levels. In 2000, after investigating the Los Angeles police for four years, the Department of Justice got the city of Los Angeles to accept a federal court agreement to change management and training patterns in the police department.[13] The Justice Department has pressured the city of New York to change police practices under the threat of similar federal court action. Los Angeles, Philadelphia, and New York are not alone among U.S. cities. The Department has reached consent decrees with the cities of Pittsburgh, Pennsylvania, and Steubenville, Ohio, as well as with the state police of New Jersey.[14] And both Chicago and San Francisco have paid out millions of dollars to settle wrongful arrest and mistreatment suits, some of them involving death or very serious and permanent injury to individuals.[15]

This is certainly not a problem unique to the United States among the countries that regard themselves as liberal democracies. In 1997, in both London and the West Midlands, large sums of money were paid by the police departments for assault (sometimes resulting in serious and lasting injury), unlawful arrest, and malicious prosecution of black people. Racist epithets were sometimes used by the police during the assaults and arrests. As is very often the case internationally, the officers involved in London were not punished.[16] But it was not the action but, rather, the inaction, of the London Metropolitan police that has drawn the greatest international attention and outcry.[17] The specific catalyst was the admitted failure of the police to thoroughly investigate and charge suspects in the 1997 murder by whites of an eighteen-year-old black man, Stephen Lawrence, who was waiting for a bus. An official inquiry concluded that "London police were plagued by a 'pernicious and institutionalized racism' that led to the failure of the force to investigate the murder and prosecute the men charged."[18]

Amnesty International issued reports in 1995 and 1997 charging the German police with brutally attacking foreigners, beating them to the point of breaking their bones. The 1997 Amnesty statements charged "a clear pattern of abuse by the police which appears to be racially motivated." In 1995, the beating victims were mainly Vietnamese. In 1997, many were Turks.[19]

But not all discriminatory violent or compulsory acts on the part of the police are rogue acts. Some are in conformity with deliberate policies that are either inherently discriminatory or are systemwide policies that are applied in discriminatory ways. The behavior of the police on the streets or roads is thus mandated by their higher officers and often condoned by civilian superiors and in the United States by state and county judges.

For example, while the crime statistics showed a decline of violent crime on the part of civilians from 1997 to 1998 (as we noted there are no national statistics on unlawful violent behavior of police officers), at the same time many U.S. police departments began to adopt a systemwide policy that was called "aggressive policing." It is widely practiced in the United States today. It sometimes includes stopping black motorists either on certain segments of the interstate highway system (state police jurisdiction) or within certain sections of the city without any violation or only a flimsy one and then searching the car. The sections of cities where such stops are practiced include both the minority community itself and white areas in which police are suspicious when they see a black motorist. Thus, a new expression has made its way into the American language, DWB. DWB is a play on DWI, or driving while intoxicated. DWB stands for "Driving While Black."[20]

This is very serious, both because it constitutes a deprivation of liberty to move about freely and because it has a further effect of extending the sentences of minority people. Many mandatory sentencing laws include stiffer sentences not only for the nature of the specific crime but also for having past convictions, sometimes even traffic convictions, but certainly for convictions based on what is found in the car. In some instances, in which there are "three strikes (convictions), you're out" laws, this can result in life sentences for relatively minor infractions. If minority people have their cars searched disproportionately, they logically stand a better chance of being caught with illegal possessions than do whites, and a better chance of spending more years in prison.

But one did not have to be in a car to attract differential police attention in Chicago. Before being successfully challenged in federal court in 1999, that city had adopted a policy of empowering police officers to order people to disperse on the streets if they had reason to believe that one or more of the assembled people were gang members. Failure to disperse or questioning the legitimacy of the officer's order on the grounds of a right to be outside in one's own community with other community members ("interference with a police officer acting in the line of duty") could bring arrest, conviction, and incarceration.

In one sense this resembles the British practices of the 1970s and 1980s under the British Sus law, as they are described by Louis Kushnick: "The Sus law is in fact a section of the 1824 Vagrancy Act, under which an accused person can be brought to trial on no other evidence than that of acting suspiciously in the eyes of two police officers. The evidence of independent witnesses is hardly ever called. It is used primarily against Afro-Caribbean males. In 1977, for example, young Afro-Caribbean males, who made up only 2.8 percent of the total population of London, accounted for 44 percent of all Sus arrests."[21]

A difference, however, is that in the United States aggressive policing and Special Weapons and Tactics (SWAT) teams are used primarily to control racially segregated ghettos, while in Britain, where poor whites and poor blacks tend to live in the same areas, the Sus laws were used against Afro-Caribbeans who wandered into more affluent white parts of London where they obviously did not "belong."

An important addition to policing in the United States is the above-mentioned heavily armed paramilitary SWAT teams. Dressed in either camouflage or black uniforms to symbolize their higher degree of militarization, they confront people in warlike fashion on the street or by entering domiciles violently. They burst in with automatic weapons drawn, physically subdue all people who do not resist, and fire on those who do. Once used mainly for hostage situations, these wartime commando tactics are now used more routinely in high-crime areas.[22] Timothy Egan argues that there are two reasons for the proliferation of the use of the SWAT teams. The first is that the U.S. government is making available a lot of surplus military equipment to police forces for the asking. They run from machine guns to armored personnel carriers. Second, there is a profit motive for the police in it. The forfeiture laws passed by the U.S. Congress in its "war on drugs" (on which more below) permit the police to seize assets such as cash, guns, cars, and boats and to use them to increase their budget or buy additional equipment. While a few states require that the cash or goods be returned if the person is not convicted, in most the police still may keep what they seized whether or not the arrested person is subsequently convicted.[23] On-the-spot resistance to militarized SWAT teams or to the more aggressive policing tactics used by teams of ordinary uniformed or nonuniformed police can literally be suicidal.

One need not even resist, just move in a way that makes heavily armed police nervous or angry, to stimulate heavy police firepower. An example is the tragic February 1999 killing of Amadou Diallo, an unarmed street peddler from Guinea who was the target of forty-one bullets (nineteen of which actually penetrated his body) from rapid-fire weapons fired by a team of four white New York police officers in front of the door of his own apartment building.[24] There is the presumption that one is "at war," and that the community in which one is on duty is "hostile territory" filled with the enemy. This is especially true when all the forces of occupation are of the "opposite" race from the inhabitants.

The combination of false and arbitrary stops, searches, arrests, beatings, killings, evidence planting, false police reports, and perjury before courts by the police would constitute human rights violations if they were done randomly or to settle personal grudges. Then they would be violations of individuals' human rights. But when they are done against specific groups of people living in specific communities, they also constitute a violation of the group right of those people to live in their communities while enjoying equal rights and protections from the state. The state must find a way to protect minority citizens from crime, without turning their communities into a zone in which they are all potential victims of state violence. The trope of war leads to a mentality in which such communities become a war zone for the police, a zone full of "others" who are all potential enemies, all internal "gooks."

The Ultimate Act of Domestic State Violence: Execution

The most extreme and least redeemable punishment levied against the body is, of course, death. The United States is the last major industrialized country to use the death penalty. Until 1998, when Amnesty International expanded its focus to include police brutality, prison conditions, and treatment of asylum seekers, Amnesty International's major human rights campaign in the United States was dedicated to the abolition of the death penalty. There has been intense pressure in the punitive climate of the United States to expand the number of crimes for which the death penalty can be given (many were added in the federal crime bill submitted by President Clinton and passed by the Congress after the bombing of the Federal Building in Oklahoma City) and to limit the appeal rights of those so sentenced.

As of July 20, 2000, of the nineteen federal prisoners who had actually been sentenced to die and were awaiting execution, thirteen were African American, one Latino, one "other," and four white. Thus, 79 percent were nonwhites.[25] In the same year, a U.S. Justice Department review of cases in which federal prosecutors sought the death penalty, found that in the previous five years, 75 percent of the defendants belonged to a minority group. Fifty percent of the defendants were blacks.[26]

Many more people are sentenced to die in state courts than in federal courts, with Texas holding the record. From 1976, when the U.S. Supreme Court permitted the resumption of the death penalty, to January 31, 2002, 758 prisoners had been actually put to death and many more awaited executions and appeals.[27] When people condemned to die by federal and state courts are taken together, 42 percent of them are black, while blacks account for only 12 percent of the population of the United States.[28] Moreover, a 1990 report by the U.S. General Accounting Office noted, "In 82 percent of the studies (reviewed), race of the victim was found to influence the likelihood of being charged with capital murder or receiving the death penalty, that is, those who murdered whites were found more likely to be sentenced to death than those who murdered blacks."[29] Nothing has changed since then. Through January 2002, 81 percent of the capital cases involved white victims.[30]

There is also a class bias, which is to some extent collapsed into race since a much higher percentage of African Americans than whites are poor. People who are executed are almost always people with few financial resources and are thus unable to afford the kind of legal defense available to more affluent citizens. Jeffrey Reiman writes, "Since the public defender is a salaried attorney with a case load much larger than that of a private criminal attorney, and since court-assigned private attorneys are paid a fixed fee that is much lower than they charge their regular clients, neither is able or motivated to devote much time to the indigent defendant's defense."[31] After studying cases of people on death row, Stephen Gettinger concluded that "'the single outstanding characteristic' of the people on death row was an inadequate defense."[32] Stephen B. Bright comes to the same conclusion in his article, "Counsel for the Poor: The Death Sentence Not for the Worst Crime but for the Worst Lawyer" in which he argues that incompetent and underpaid legal defense is particularly the norm in areas where the death penalty is most often imposed.[33] The state of Texas, which breaks the records on capital punishment, is the third lowest in spending for public defenders. The state itself provides no funds, leaving it to the counties. In addition, it is the only heavily populated state that has no organized system of public defenders in its major cities. Judges pay defending attorneys low flat fees, ranging from $50 to $350 per case, which is a disincentive for the attorney to spend much time on the case. In 1999, both houses of the Texas state legislature unanimously passed a bill that would have provided state funds for public defenders and raised the standards expected of them. Then Governor George W. Bush vetoed the bill.[34]

This impedes true equality before the law, and in this case the price of a hastily or just poorly prepared defense is a human life. Whether due to inadequate defense or a dishonest police or prosecutorial process, we know for a fact that a certain percentage of those executed are innocent, but we do not know what that percentage is. In my own state, Illinois, Professor David Protess of the School of

Journalism at Northwestern University, working in collaboration with the Center for Wrongful Convictions at that university's law school, has students in his investigative reporting class investigate cases of dubious death sentences. Within a three-year period, the fruits of his and his students' labor have resulted in five condemned men being released from death row. The latest as of this writing, Mr. Anthony Porter, was an African American man with an IQ of 51, raising questions of mental competence to stand trial much less being subjected to a capital charge.[35] Without this completely extrajudicial academic intervention, these five men would certainly have been unjustly killed by the state. In all, more than half (thirteen out of twenty-four as of January 2000) of the people sentenced to die in Illinois since the state reinstated the death penalty in 1977 have subsequently had their convictions overturned. Most have spent many years awaiting execution on death row. Illinois is not at the very top of the killing frenzy list. One can only imagine how many other innocents have actually been put to death in Illinois and in states with higher numbers of executions like Texas, Virginia, Florida, and Virginia.[36]

Just as the mentally retarded have been executed in the United States until the Supreme Court's June 2002 ruling against it (*Atkins v. Virginia* 00–8452), so have people who committed the crimes when they were juveniles (in violation of the explicit language of Article 6, section 5, of the International Covenant on Civil and Political Rights).[37] When the United States signed the civil and political rights covenant, the U.S. government stipulated a reservation that this provision could not trump U.S. law. The U.N. Human Rights Committee ruled that such a reservation is incompatible with the purpose of the covenant and therefore invalid. This is only one example of the U.S. state's being outside the international consensus on human rights. Also, quite in violation of treaty obligations, foreigners have been arrested and tried on capital charges without being informed that they have the right to see consular officials from their own countries. This right is granted by the 1963 Vienna Convention on Consular Relations, which the United States aggressively pushed to protect its own citizens and to which it is legally bound.

But the United States stands outside the Western consensus on human rights, and against a growing worldwide consensus that capital punishment itself, whether or not it is practiced in a racially or ethnically discriminatory manner, violates human rights. While in 1970, fewer than thirty countries had abolished capital punishment, by 2000, 110 had done so.[38] Indeed, given the importance placed on facilitating the development of the potentialities of people in my holistic approach to human rights, it follows that that those nations that see capital punishment as such as a human rights violation are correct. An individual who commits murder has done a terrible thing to a fellow human being. This is not an act that the state can ignore. I would argue that it must do three things. It must punish the offender. It must protect the community from further offense by the offender. And, third but related to the preceding, it must do what it can to facilitate the development of the better potentialities of the offender. Such facilitation might have to be done within the walls of prisons or mental institutions. Capital punishment aborts any possibility for betterment, any possibility for the offender to offer something positive to society in exchange for the opportunity to develop his or her better potentialities. It offers violent vengeance rather than reformative justice. And, of course, it is the one punishment for which there can be no remediation if the executed person turns out to be an innocent victim of the police and legal machinery.

A justice of constructive punishment, one concerned with the positive development of the potentialities of those who have harmed others and which leaves open the possibility of remediation for wrongful conviction, is the only form of justice that is consistent with my conception of human rights. Race and class disparities compound the problem, adding the dimension of violation of group as well as individual rights. But even if capital punishment were randomly distributed in the society, and even if all those convicted were truly guilty, it would still be a human rights violation for the above reasons. But if one thinks of the problem of crime in terms of "war," then is not the aim to kill the enemy? So capital punishment becomes the literal capstone of the figurative "war on crime."

Inequities of Conviction, Length of Sentences, Jury Selection, and Political Rights

True, one does not always kill the enemy in war. Sometimes one captures the enemy and puts them in prisoner of war camps. The "war on crime" has swelled the population of the prisons that already existed and given rise to an incredible increase in the building of prisons. State violence is manifested here in the involuntary taking of people from their communities and confining them in these institutions. The prison population is not a random representation of the total population of the United States. As in the death penalty, there is the class bias that was amply demonstrated in the 1970s and 1980s by Reiman in his book *The Rich Get Richer and the Poor Get Prison*.

Reiman writes, "Studies of individuals accused of similar offenses and with similar prior records show that the poor defendant is more likely to be adjudicated guilty than is the wealthier defendant."[39] Moreover, even if we look only at nonviolent crimes, the kinds of crimes that poorer people tend to commit (for example, theft, burglary) are more likely to get them jail time than the crimes that wealthier people commit tend to commit (for example, embezzlement, fraud, tax evasion) and the prison terms are longer for the poor.[40]

But the most striking skewing of the incarcerated populations in the United States in recent years has to do with race. A 1983 Rand study, commissioned and funded by the National Institute of Corrections of the U.S. Department of Justice, discovered statistically significant racial differences in both the types of sentences imposed and the length of the time actually served.[41] The same study showed that the self-reported reasons that prisoners gave for committing crime were that they had lost a job, could not find a job, or that they needed money for rent, food, or self-support. While these reasons predominated for the combined total of all inmates who responded, they were especially important for the African Americans.[42]

In 1997, 49 percent of the prisoners in state and federal prisons were African Americans. In 1995, one-third of all African American men between twenty and twenty-nine were either in jails or prisons, or on probation, or on parole.[43] The higher rate of felony conviction and imprisonment for people of color has severe implications for the exercise of political rights. In 1997, 14 percent of African American males in the United States were disenfranchised because of such convictions.[44] Such disenfranchisement also leads to exclusion from juries when they are selected from voting lists, as is often the case in the United States.

Alexis de Tocqueville was most struck by two manifestations of democracy when he visited the United States in the nineteenth century. One was the regionally specific New England town meeting. The other, the jury, was ubiquitous. Unlike in France where jurors are never permitted to debate the fate of a cocitizen without professional jurists being on the panel, one who is a criminal defendant in the United States has a right to have guilt or innocence determined by nonjurists who are his or her peers. Or does one?

Prior to the Civil War, only Massachusetts permitted African Americans to sit on juries.[45] Until 1986, the Supreme Court authorized the racially discriminatory peremptory challenges by prosecutors. It did so very explicitly in *Swain v. Alabama* (380 U.S. 202, 225, 1965), a case involving an African American convicted and sentenced to death (and ultimately executed) by an all white jury. There were a small number of African Americans in the jury pool, but each was disqualified. The Supreme Court ruled that the exclusion of the potential African Americans in the pool from actual jury service was acceptable as a "weapon of litigation."[46] In 1986, in *Batson v. Kentucky* (476 U.S. 79) the Court revisited the issue and decided that in any given trial instance, if a defendant can make out a prima facie case based on specific prosecutorial behavior or speech, and can persuade the judge that a nonracial reason offered by the prosecutor for striking a prospective juror is invalid, then the judge can refuse to admit the prosecutor's challenge.

It is interesting to note that the present Chief Justice, William Rehnquist, dissented from this decision and supported the earlier Swain decision that declared striking of minorities valid without qualification.[47] But Randall Kennedy contends that, even with the more restrictive Batson ruling, the actual behavior of prosecutors remains a problem. He cites a survey of all reported decisions of federal and state courts from the seven and three-quarter years following the Batson decision (April 30, 1986 to December 31, 1993), which revealed that judges found prosecutors guilty of violating Batson in slightly more than 10 percent of the cases in which defendants alleged racially discriminatory peremptory challenges.[48] Moreover, he contends and cites supportive cases that lying on the part of prosecutors, usually proven by taking the criterion stipulated by the prosecutor and showing that it was not applied in the case of white jurors, is a serious problem.[49] When racially motivated peremptory exclusion from juries is added to exclusion because of past criminal conviction (possibly creating a circular effect if those convicted indeed are not tried by a jury of peers), and to other criteria that the state can impose, such as a high school diploma—which is less frequent among African Americans than whites—and to lower voter registration among African Americans, one can see that there arises a very serious human rights problem for any individual African American defendant and for African Americans as a whole, that is, a violation of individual and group rights. The problem is compounded by the relatively small percentage of minority judges.

The exclusion of authoritative African American voices from the court systems through which such a high percentage of African Americans pass as defendants constitutes a very serious deprivation of social recognition. The exclusion of so many African Americans from the vote because they have been convicted of felonies and served time in prison constitutes an exclusion from the major political processes of co- and self-determination in a representative democracy, a severe deprivation of political and civil human rights.

Incarceration

Vivien Stern has written, "Imprisonment is a prime focus for human rights abuses. One set of human beings is under the control of another, dependent on them for food, the opportunity to perform their bodily functions, access to the outside world, work, exercise. When someone dies behind the high prison walls cover-up is easy; asking questions is hard."[50]

Extensive human rights deprivation takes place at all three levels of incarceration in the United States, the federal prisons, the state prisons, and the county or municipal jails. As of 1991, the federal government operated sixty-seven institutions of incarceration with an intended capacity of 38,584 inmates. But they actually contained 61,325 people, 59 percent over capacity.[51] With the increase of the number of federal crimes, particularly in the area of drugs, the federal prison population had swelled from 61,325 to 100,250 by 1995.[52]

This packing of people together in very cramped quarters led to increased tension among the prison populations. This resulted in a higher incidence of violence both between prisoners themselves and between prisoners and guards. While in the 1960s and 1970s federal prisons had a reputation of being more humane and safer institutions that those run by the states and cities or counties, in the 1980s the federal government decided that it had to create extremely severe conditions, ostensibly for rule violating or violent prisoners. The first of these institutions were the Marion, Illinois, prison for men and the High Security Unit in the Lexington, Kentucky prison for women.

In *Bruscino v. Carlson* (854 F. 2nd, 1988), the Seventh Circuit Federal Court, while ruling against the prisoners' complaints because of the violent nature of the inmates who had been sent there from other overcrowded prisons, called the conditions "sordid and horrible." The following description was offered by the court:

> As a result of the permanent lockdown, each inmate at Marion is confined to a one-man cell ... round the clock, except for brief periods outside the cell for recreation (between 7 and 11 hours a week), for a shower, for a visit to the infirmary, to the law library, etc. (Some inmates have more time outside the cell, as we shall see.) Recreation means pacing in a small enclosure—sometimes just in the corridor between the rows of cells. The inmate is fed in his cell, on a tray shoved

in between the bars. The cells are modern and roomy and contain a television set as well as a bed, toilet, and sink, but there is no other furniture and when an inmate is outside his cell he is handcuffed and a box is placed over the handcuffs to prevent the lock from being picked; his legs may also be shackled. Inmates are forbidden to socialize with each other or to participate in group religious activities. Inmates who throw food or otherwise misbehave in their cells are sometimes tied spread-eagled on their beds, often for hours at a stretch, while inmates returning to their cells are often (inmates of the control unit always) subjected to a rectal search: a paramedic inserts a gloved finger into the inmate's rectum and feels around for a knife or other weapon or contraband.[53]

A scholar at a British university who has interviewed lawyers of prisoners inside reported that some of the prisoners who have been placed in the punishment cells became so psychologically deranged that they took to eating their own feces.[54] In the mid-1990s, another such facility was built in Florence, Colorado. It is designed to be a more architecturally and technologically refined version of the older Marion prison.

The decision to send people to Marion or Florence is made by staff at the Federal Bureau of Prisons. While these institutions are there supposedly to punish rebellious or misbehaving prisoners and to serve as a deterrent for other prisoners, in fact people convicted of politically motivated offenses have been sent there directly. They include the Native American activist Leonard Peltier[55] and a number of Puerto Rican nationalists. While the United States denies that it holds any political prisoners, this extreme punishment was clearly because of the political nature of the offense.[56]

U.S. prison regimes at the state level have also hardened. Indeed, in the late 1990s, a number of states have created prisons on the federal Marion and Florence model. But even in the "normal" state prisons, those not specifically designed on the federal "supermax" models, there has been serious mistreatment of prisoners. Perhaps the most abusive state prisons are in Georgia where, the *New York Times* reports, the Commissioner of Prisons, Wayne Garner, watched "while inmates, some handcuffed and lying on the floor, were punched kicked and stomped until blood streaked the walls, said Ray McWorter, a riot squad lieutenant at the prison, in a deposition filed today in federal court."[57] A top aide to Mr. Garner touched off an attack on prisoners by the guards when he himself "grabbed an unresisting inmate by the hair and dragged him across the floor."[58] The guards, who went on a beating frenzy after seeing the

Commissioner's aide abuse a prisoner, were applauded by the Commissioner at a chicken dinner held to celebrate the beating of the prisoners. The guard lieutenant who submitted the deposition in federal court in Atlanta, where the Southern Center for Human Rights brought suit on behalf of the prisoners, described the celebration thus: "Everybody was high-fiving and shaking hands and congratulating each other and patting each other on the back and bragging about how much butt you kicked."[59]

This is one case about which we have graphic description. But Amnesty International and Human Rights Watch both report widespread physical abuse of prisoners in state institutions, including beatings and painful and permanently damaging use of restraints.[60] In a survey distributed to inmates in prisons in forty-one states in late 1989, seven out of ten inmates responded that they had witnessed prison guards beating prisoners. Of those seven, 40 percent said that they had seen this done routinely.[61]

But it is not only physical abuse such as beatings and painful use of constraints that are delivered on the body. There is, as in the federal institutions at Marion and Florence, the practice of isolating the prisoners so as to make them more acquiescent. In one of the New Jersey state prisons, African American prisoners have formed a group called the "Five Percenters." The members claim that the object of this group is spiritual, that it is to give the prisoners a greater self-esteem and self-confidence. The officer responsible for discipline in the prison calls it a "cult." The prison has established a 7-point system, and being caught on any two of the points gets one solitary confinement. Among these are simple membership, having Five Percenter literature in one's possession, writing about the Five Percenters, or talking with anyone about the Five Percenters. No overt action is required in order for one to be locked in solitary confinement with almost no time out of the very small cell for exercise.[62]

At the very local levels, county sheriffs, who run for election, have a relatively free hand in how they treat prisoners. Since their mandate is directly from the voters, they do not have to answer to other local civilian officials. Some, particularly in the South and the Southwest, have reinstituted the old chain gangs in which people work for long hours out in the hot sun while chained together. The idea is to punish through travail and shackling in the heat and through humiliation by exposing the prisoners in their prison clothes and chains to the general public. It is also supposed to teach young people a lesson of what awaits them if they break the law. Some convicts who have refused to work under these conditions have been placed in painful stationary positions, like the stocks of the colonial period, out in the hot sun.

Technology has also entered into this domain. Some, most effectively the Southern Poverty Law Center in Alabama, have protested against the chaining of prisoners. Enter Stun Tech, Inc. in Cleveland, which invented a stun belt, described in the *New York Times:*

> From up to 300 feet away, an officer can press a button to detonate an eight-second burst of 50,000 volts of electricity and stun a fleeing inmate for up to 10 minutes. Once stunned, prisoners also lose controls of their bladders and bowels. "It overrides the body's neuromuscular system," said Dennis Kaufman, president of Stun Tech, Inc. in Cleveland which makes the belts. "Normally you can open and close your hand twice in one second. This device makes it contract 20 times in a second. It wears the muscles down."[63]

After Amnesty International called for a ban on the belts, calling them "cruel, inhuman and degrading," Mr. Kaufman responded that they have rarely been fired (fourteen times) in the thirty thousand cases that they had been worn, because they strike such terror in prisoners.[64] In some cases, they are used to control the behavior of criminal defendants in court rooms lest they violate the rulings of the judges or engage in unauthorized verbal outbursts.

Other local sheriffs in Florida, Arizona, New Mexico, Idaho, and Washington State have been forcing inmates to live outdoors in tents regardless of the weather. There is also a move toward feeding prisoners substandard food (for example, military surplus), and charging them for their meals and for seeing a doctor.[65]

But it is not only in the South and West where jail inmates are abused. It also occurs in "urbane" New York, in the Nassau County Jail. In 1999, it came to public attention after an inmate of the jail, Thomas Pizzuto, serving a ninety day sentence for traffic violations, was beaten to death by guards. His offense was that he too loudly demanded his daily methadone treatment. After beating him, the guards made him sign a statement that his injuries, which would ultimately prove fatal, were the result of an accident. It has since come to light that there has been a long history of guards beating prisoners there.

Five years previous to Mr. Pizzuto's killing, Thomas Donovan, Jr., a mentally retarded man, was beaten by guards in the same jail. His father, a wealthy banker, tried unsuccessfully to get him medical attention in jail after the beating. He then sought redress in the courts. The comments made about the case by three people in very different positions are very telling.

Frank Quigley, the person in the district attorney's office who made the decision not to prosecute the guards after the beating, admitted his role, " 'I'm the guy who said no on Gemeilli [the guard who allegedly led the beating]. I'm the guy,' he said repeatedly, his eyes welling up with tears as he discussed the case. Mr. Quigley defended his decision, saying that the younger Mr. Donovan had given somewhat conflicting statements about his injuries and that his disability would have made him vulnerable on cross-examination."[66]

Thomas Donovan, Sr., father of the young man who had been beaten, responding to Mr. Pizutto's beating death and the ensuing investigation, said, "I was never a radical conservative, death penalty, hang-'em-all guy.... But I was a banker, I was a Republican, I tended to believe policemen, and when I heard minorities complaining about police brutality, I tended to discount it. I don't discount anything anymore. I'll never be able to serve on a jury again."[67]

Matthew Muraskin, president of the Legal Aid Society of Nassau Country, tells how his lawyers handle the situation when one of their clients is beaten by guards in the jail:

> We sit them down and tell them what might happen [if they file a formal complaint]. An assault charge might be laid against you, claiming that the inmate actually beat the guard up. Then it's your word against the correction officer's word. And it's another felony. And your plea negotiations might be adversely impacted on, because you're not cooperating, you're making a complaint. Besides, you've already been beaten up, so that you know that there might be more intimidation and retribution inside the jail.[68]

There is very little, if any, regular external oversight of penal institutions in the United States. Federal and state prison wardens, and even more so county sheriffs, are like kings in their domains. Like their fellow warrior agents of the state, the police, they are seen as performing a very difficult job on the front lines. But they are much more shielded from public view than are the police and thus have an even freer hand over how they treat people. This is leading the United States in the opposite direction from that of Western Europe and more toward harsh prison regimes that characterized the South African and Eastern European regimes prior to the falls of apartheid and communism, and that still characterizes many of the prison systems in the less industrialized countries of the world. Contra Foucault, it is indeed a system whose major objective is neither to merely normalize nor to merely observe. Nor is it a system designed to develop the better potentialities of the incarcerated. Rather, it has become a system of domination out to inflict maximum discomfort and pain on the body as well as the mind of the captured enemy in the war on crime. The captured enemy is disproportionately a person of color while the state agent inflicting the pain and even death is usually white. The techniques can be as crude as execution or the chain gangs, and as technologically sophisticated as the electric stun belt. It is a system that is very resistant to any external checks in the name of human rights, particularly when it appeals to the physical insecurities of the voting public and when those who come into its clutches are so racially and class specific.[69]

But it is as interesting to note where severe punishment is *not* handed out. It is rarely handed out against police officers who violate the law by abusing citizens. Even when municipalities in the United States pay damages to people, or to families of people, who have been brutalized or killed by police officers, it is extremely rare for police officers to be tried for these rights violations. Often they remain on the job with their clubs and guns to victimize other citizens. In New York City, Comptroller Alan Hevesi's office paid out $27.3 million to settle claims against the police in 1996. Brutality claims had tripled over the last decade in New York, and Mr. Hevesi said that he believed that most settlements constituted " 'an admission of some wrongdoing.' " But he also said that "the settlements do not trigger any investigation by the Police Department, not of individual officers or of general patterns of confrontation with the public. 'There is a total and complete disconnect.' "[70] In New York City, as in other metropolitan areas in and outside of the United States, unconditional support of police forces by politicians who curry political favor result in massive if largely hidden human rights violations. The financial settlements become blood money by which the victims or their surviving families are silenced. Only in rare instances, when a video camera is present (as in the case of the African American Rodney King, who has beaten by the Los Angeles police) or when the crime is leaked to the press by medical personnel (as in the case of the black Haitian Abner Louima, who was tortured and sodomized in a Brooklyn precinct station), is the public likely to hear of the human rights violations committed by officers of the state.

The Schizophrenic State's War on Drugs

The "War on Drugs" provides an interesting case of the intersection between war as a trope and war as reality involving the U.S. state's military, overt and covert, activity abroad. And once again, people of color within the United States have been disproportionately designated as the enemy.

As part of the "Drug War" that has been a preoccupation of U.S. administrations going back to President and ("Just Say No") Mrs. Reagan, much heavier penalties have been levied on the use and sales of crack cocaine than on powder cocaine. According to former "Drug Czar" Barry McCaffrey, "the median sentence for convictions involving 50 to 150 grams of crack cocaine is 120 months in prison; it's 18 months for like amounts of powder."[71] Moreover, crack cocaine is the only controlled substance for which there is a mandatory federal sentence for the first offense. There is none for powder cocaine.

There is another difference. Powder cocaine is a narcotic of choice of upper- and middle-class whites, of professional people, and those in the arts, whereas 90 percent of those convicted on crack cocaine charges are African Americans.[72] As in the case of unjust death sentences, we cannot know precisely how many African Americans are incarcerated because of illegitimate police behavior, because we only know about those cases in which it is discovered. But what we know is obviously the tip of a very nasty iceberg. Add to that the results of radically differential penalties for most white and black drug users and sellers, and we have a large part of the reason why U.S. ghettos and prisons form one complex of physical control over the bodies of African Americans.

Among industrialized countries, the United States holds the record in terms of the percentage of the population that it incarcerates. In 1996, the United States incarcerated 615 per 100,000. The figures for France were 91, England and Wales 120, Denmark 65, Germany 85, Greece 55, Italy 85, Brazil 95.5, India 23, and Japan 36.[73] The total (federal and state) U.S. prison population swelled from 501,886 in 1980 to 1,585,401 in 1995.[74] One cannot overestimate the impact of the "war on drugs" in this enormous swelling of the U.S. prison population. In the ten years between 1985 and 1995, the increase in the number of prisoners in state prisons for drug convictions went up by 478 percent. That compares with an increase of 86 percent for violent crimes, 69 percent for crimes against property, 187 percent for violations of the public order, and minus 6 percent for other unspecified categories of crimes.[75]

The state, however, has been of two minds when it comes to drugs. On the one hand, it has had the "War on Drugs." On the other, it has tolerated and even facilitated the entry of drugs into the United States in its "War on Communism."

The involvement of agents of the state in the drug trade is not a new story and it did not begin with cocaine. Indeed, the U.S. state was not alone among the Western democracies in facilitating the drug trade. In what they called "Operation X," French intelligence gained the support of three Laotian tribes and their drug lords, as well as the drug-trafficking Binh Xuyen in Vietnam itself, in exchange for their support of the French effort to retain control of Indochina after World War II. In collaboration with Corsican gangsters, the French agents facilitated the transfer of these drugs to Marseilles, whence they were sent all over the world.[76] Thus did Marseilles become the major transfer point for the worldwide heroin trade.

But even a bit earlier than that, from the late 1940s, U.S. intelligence was facilitating the commercial operations of Burmese opium growers and dealers because Chiang Kai-shek's Kuomintang had developed a cooperative working relationship with them in an attempt to prevent the Communists from gaining and maintaining control in China.[77] Thus, from the very beginning of the Cold War, the intelligence services of both France and the United States facilitated the international trafficking in hard drugs. U.S. intelligence continued the practice in Southeast Asia, after it took over the fight against the Communists from the French, and also used it in its attempt to shore up the forces in opposition to the Soviet Union in Afghanistan.

The most recent use of the practice that has become public, and the one that has contributed most to the devastating growth of drug use in the United States, was in the war against the Sandinistas in Nicaragua. For two years, the U.S. government was forbidden by the Boland Amendment from giving military support to the Nicaraguan Contras who were conducting a guerrilla war ostensibly against the Sandinista government but in reality against civilians (the approximately forty thousand people killed in the conflict were overwhelmingly civilian). Thus, the aid itself, being delivered in a clandestine manner by agents of the U.S. state, was a violation of law so long as the Boland Amendment was in force. This is what led to the Iran-Contra "scandal." The case of the Contras provides us with an interesting example of a nonstate group (albeit organized, financed, and trained by the U.S. liberal and Argentine dictatorial states) violating human rights, and to a much greater extent than the government that it was attempting to topple.[78]

Some of these Contras were also drug dealers. The Contra supply network through both Honduras and Costa Rica involved cooperation with the drug operations in both of those countries. Some of the same planes that carried military supplies in one direction carried drugs in the other and offloaded them in U.S. military airports. The documentation on this is voluminous and persuasive.[79] It indicates that the CIA was a central actor everywhere that U.S. counterinsurgency or attempts to bring down governments intermeshed with drug dealing. But it was not only the CIA. A U.S. Senate subcommittee investigation found that another executive foreign policy arm, the State Department, also was involved. The December 1988 report of the U.S. Senate Subcommittee on Terrorism, Narcotics, and International Operations stated that among other Contra drug links were "payments to drug traffickers by the U.S. State Department of funds authorized by the Congress for humanitarian assistance to the Contras, in some cases after the traffickers had been indicted by federal law enforcement agencies on drug charges, in others while traffickers were under active investigation by these same agencies."[80]

It was therefore nothing short of macabre when Ronald Reagan issued an executive order at the end of his first year in office, just when he began creating the Contra force, "drafting the entire federal-intelligence apparatus—including the Central Intelligence Agency (CIA)—into the war on drugs and ordering them to provide guidance to civilian drug-enforcement agencies."[81] Given the CIA's track record in Asia, it was little wonder that drugs, and their importation into the United States, became part of the CIA's Central American operations. Since the "War on Drugs" required greater repressive forces, more courts, and more prisons, the power of the U.S. state itself, which Reagan and his conservative followers were decrying, was increasing within as well as without its territorial borders.

The Noriega case is interesting here. Reagan's successor and former CIA director, George Bush the senior, ordered an invasion of the sovereign state of Panama to arrest Panamanian General Manuel Noriega. One of the charges was involvement in the drug trade. But if the drug charge against Noriega, who was found guilty in a federal court and sits in a U.S. prison, were true, it is unlikely that they were any the less true when he was anti-Sandinista and serving as a CIA "asset." He was not arrested until he shifted to a more positive position toward the Sandinistas. This is a clear instance of the U.S. state's playing politics with drugs. Making war on the Sandinista government and forcing the Nicaraguan people to "cry uncle" (Reagan's phrase) to the North American state was clearly more important than drug addiction and the devastation of lives that it was causing at home.

As discussed in note 79, the documentation on this is voluminous. The sources include the work of investigative journalists, scholars, and indeed of an additional official legislative committee. This is a report of a committee of the Costa Rican Legislature that found that U.S. intelligence operatives had indeed been shipping cocaine in and out of Costa Rica, in violation of their laws and sovereignty as well as U.S. law, as a part of the already illegal Contra support program.[82] Evidence also was presented in a 1998 video made by documentarist Barbara Trent, *COVER-UP: Behind the Iran-Contra Affair,* which included filmed statements by drug pilots admitting that they flew drugs from Costa Rica to military bases in the United States where they were offloaded.

Two things are very interesting here. Much of the information on drug trafficking was available while the Contras were still operating in Nicaragua. Indeed, there were even some news reports in the mainstream press. But there was little or nothing on mainstream television and that, for good or for ill, is where most of the people in our modern liberal democracies get their news. Moreover, papers such as the *New York Times* and the *Washington Post* carried some news stories but did not make much of the issue on their editorial pages. Indeed, when Gary Webb wrote his August 1966 *San Jose Mercury News* series on the relationship between Contra-related drugs and the distribution of cocaine by gangs in Los Angeles, the mainstream press excoriated the *Mercury News* for printing it. The *New York Times* ran a long story under the title "With Little Evidence to Back It, Tale of CIA Drug Link Has a Life of Its Own."[83] Under this internal media pressure, the editor of the *Mercury News* made a public apology for printing it. Even if, and I don't know that this is the case, Webb had made some misstatement of fact or had not followed this or that journalistic practice to the "t," one might have hoped that the press, while pointing these out or correcting them if they had better information, would have directed their critical energies toward the behavior of state agents and the repercussions in American communities. Instead, the press performed a suppressive function on behalf of the state against one of its own.

One characteristic of the press in Western liberal democracies is that it is critical of the government. But that has strict limits, and when a member of the journalistic club goes beyond those limits of "All The News That's Fit to Print," the slogan that appears in the upper left box of the *New York Times* masthead, the self-censorship of the liberal press kicks in. In this instance, what the mainstream press chose to ignore or mute were the human rights of the Nicaraguans to self-determination and to be free of killing and torture, the human rights of the Costa Rican people to determine how their territory is to be used and to hold state actors on it accountable, the human rights of North American people and especially those of color to not

have their communities devastated by drugs and drug-related violence and their people disproportionately incarcerated, and the right
of the people of the United States as a whole to have their state
respect its own laws.

CONCLUSION

While the end of Communism in Eastern Europe is indeed an
advance for political human rights, it also can lead us in the West to
an arrogant belief that all human rights issues have been resolved in
our societies and now the problem is to get those "backward" countries in the former Third World, now often referred to as the South,
to follow the lead of the North Americans and Western Europeans in
adopting practices that respect human rights. Since these are people
of color living in lands that have experienced Western imperialism and
colonialism, since they have access to information from and about the
West, they are usually quite aware of the fact that social recognition is
not accorded equally to all there.

The discrepancies, which are not capable of being reduced to mere
individuation, have become clearer in the domain of policing and
punishment during the closing two decades of the twentieth century
as immigrants of color have become less welcome in Western
European countries and as the "wars" on drugs and crime have been
intensified in the United States. Foucault notwithstanding, the bodies of certain groups in Western societies are subjected to kinds of violence at the hands of the state to which the bodies of the white,
middle- and upper-class "we" group are by and large immune.

The condition of the "they" groups is largely invisible to the "we"
group. This provokes two responses. One is a denial of any systematic
pattern. Here the liberal ideology renders anything but sporadic
errors or mistakes in the system unbelievable. The second is an admis-
sion of the pattern, but acceptance or mitigation of it. Thus, when the
American Bar Association commissioned a telephone poll of one
thousand adults in August 1998, 47 percent said that they believed
that the courts did not " 'treat all ethnic and racial groups the same' "
but 80 percent said that "in spite of its problems, the American justice system is still the best in the world."[84] Both responses, the denial
and the validation of the system in spite of its discriminating practices,
constitute a withholding of social recognition from people being
denied equality, freedom, basic needs, and access to the discourses of
decision-making bodies (courts, legislatures, and the editorial boards
of mainstream media) on anything like a par with the "we" group.

Indeed, there is a relationship in the United States between the rejection of the conception of economic and social human rights (and the refusal to ratify the 1966 International Covenant dealing with them) and the treatment of people accused and convicted of crimes. So long as crime is dissociated from some of its most fundamental causes, that is, the deprivation of social and economic rights, it will be dealt with as an issue of war against unredeemably evil individual enemies of state and society who need to be either killed or incarcerated for extremely long periods of their lives.

There is thus a certain irony in the transition from Lyndon Johnson's 1960s war on poverty, which can be seen as an attempt, however successful or unsuccessful, to deal with the issue of economic and social rights, to the wars on crime and drugs in the 1980s, which were coterminous with an official ideology that saw economic and social deprivation as issues of purely individual personal failing. There was thus no basis for mitigation and no ground for mercy. The function of the state was to use its coercive power and capacities for violence in an all-out war against the internal enemies of the state. The questions associated with the wars on crime and drugs are not the qualitative questions of how certain conditions of life affect crime but, rather, quantitative questions. How high or how low is the crime rate? How many acts can be criminalized? How many offenses can be made federal crimes? How many can be made capital crimes? How much time can we give to those convicted of crimes (of the lower-class variety to be sure)? How many prisons can we build to hold them? How many people can we execute to teach others a lesson? How many jobs will a new prison bring to our town? How much profit can we make if we go into the private corporate prison business? Whole communities of people are thus instrumentalized, for political and economic gain. Such instrumentalization, is social nonrecognition to the nth degree.

It was contended in Chapter 4 that nonstate groups can violate the rights of people. Drug gangs that debilitate and terrorize communities are one example of this. The question is whether modern multiethnic and multiracial states are up to the task of performing the protective and reformative functions that we ideally expect of them and that would be consistent with respect for human rights or whether they will continue to restrict social recognition to the already most powerful segments of the society. If Foucault was wrong in diverting our gaze from the state's continued use of violence against the bodies of some of us, perhaps he was right in declaring that the normalizing institutions required delinquents, that it needed their example to maintain its power over the rest of us.

A very poignant passage from Chevigny's *Edge of the Knife* offers a real-life instance of how the state can visit violence on the body of an "other" to normalize and discipline members of the "we" group who have gotten a bit out of line. The "bystander" in the story is someone who observed what he thought was improper police behavior, said something critical to the police, and got arrested. But the bystander, who clearly angered the police, was not an "other" from whom social recognition could be safely withdrawn:

> New Yorkers, those legalistic beings, not infrequently comment hotly to the police at the scene of arrests or summonses. The police are often exasperated and sometimes arrest the person, usually on the charge of interfering with an officer. The person is "run through the system," by being locked up, verbally abused, and left to wait hours for arraignment. In one of the worst of these cases, in 1989, such a bystander had been arrested and was languishing in the lockup; when he and other prisoners complained about not being able to use the telephone, the police beat up—no, not the bystander, as you might have expected, but instead a hapless black derelict, in the presence of the others, to intimidate them all into keeping quiet. Through this degradation the police wanted to teach the "liberals to keep your mouth shut," as one put it in that case.[85]

The police needed the black derelict, just as Foucault tells us that the systems of modern power need their delinquents and reproduce them. They thought that they could normalize or pacify members of the "we" community by a short-term stint in jail and verbal abuse. But they also had to demonstrate the Weberian essential characteristic of the state, violence. That's where the delinquents and the drug addicts come in very handy. The state and its agents have to be very careful against whom they use violence. Social recognition must first be withdrawn from certain segments of the society. The violence of both the state and private parties then flows as it were naturally. But only the state can claim that it was done legitimately and lawfully. Those seeking to gain or retain state office can claim that such violence is really delivered to protect the rights of all of us, our human rights. The vicious circle is closed. The innocence, bliss, and rights of the "we" group are maintained.

Alas, we have added two additional reasons to reproduce "delinquents." They are profit and jobs. The state, and the states within the United States, has decided to give private entrepreneurs a cut of the action. The private prison industry is one of the fastest growing in the United States, going from one or two prisons in 1984 to 163 as of April 1999.[86] For that industry to receive its cut, it obviously needs delinquents and criminals.[87] And the state devolves on these private parties its once-held monopoly on the legitimate right to use violence in its own name. In the mania to privatize virtually every-thing, the U.S. capitalist state and other states have in fact turned over to profit-seeking entrepreneurs and venture capitalists that one func-tion that Max Weber thought was such an essential and unique state characteristic—the legitimate use of force and violence. But the logic is hard to beat. If war against external "others" is legitimately prof-itable to private parties and corporations, then why should not the "war on crime" against internal "others" also benefit profit seekers among "us"? And since we now have economic "globalization," U.S.-based corporations in the "prison industry" have secured con-tracts abroad to manage or build prisons. This could become an inducement to less severely punishing states to buy into the "war on crime" fervor and to increase their rates of incarceration. After all, there is not just political hay to be made but also profits.

There is also a real and a symbolic payoff for political elites in terms of employment. First, there is the boom of jobs associated with prison construction, maintenance, and guarding. Smaller cities and towns with few other employment opportunities avidly compete with each other to attract prisons their communities. Very often these are largely white communities competing with each other to confine largely minority inmate populations. A second advantage to political elites of locking up such a high percentage of the least educated and minority population for long periods of time is that it makes it possible to claim success for a much lower unemployment rate than would be the case if these people were free. This is something that is almost completely overlooked when the U.S. unemployment rate is compared with that of countries with lower rates of incarceration. To the disadvantage of the minority and poor population for whom the "war on poverty" is long gone, it makes the economy look more "efficient" than it really is and political elites look better for simultaneously waging a "war" against crime and preserving an artificially low level of unemploy-ment. Whether done consciously or not, it still constitutes a massive human rights violation in a nation that prides itself on being the beacon of human rights in the world.

Conclusion

A Holistic Human Rights-Driven Twenty-First Century?

In the preceding chapters, I have attempted an admittedly ambitious and difficult task, to provide a grounding for human rights that was committed to certain values without ascending into a universalistic idealism. I have tried to provide a grounding that was sensitive to history and context, indeed one that extracted the relevant values from historical struggles to overcome domination and advance the cause of human rights, without falling into a relativism that would be incompatible with the very concept of human rights and that would at best relegate human rights to a purely strategic or tactical device to be used in power struggles against political or economic regimes that were being opposed on other more self-serving grounds.

After presenting a historical narrative of the development of the concept within the Western tradition, admitting that there are analogues with the non-Western tradition and offering the reader an aphoristic one from the Zulu culture, I analyzed some of the contemporary theoretical writing that attempts to ground human rights. I expressed the view that there is all too often the impulse to ground human rights on a single value, such as liberty, equality, or dignity. I presented a set of propositions and arguments that human rights must be thought of as a struggle against domination by potentially co- and self-developing human beings. Both the domination and the struggles against it are practices that take place within a web of social relationships. Those who resist domination are seeking recognition from others that the historically specific relations in which they find themselves do indeed constitute domination and that these relations strip them of the ability to actualize their potential as human beings.

Thus, I agree with Jack Donnelly that human rights are really a set of social practices. Whether they are God-given or not, I do not pretend to know. I respect, and indeed support and work with, those who are committed to human rights on the basis of such a faith. But what matters to me in this book, and what makes human rights so interesting to me analytically, as well as morally, is that they are embedded in the very fabric of our social dynamics over time. The values of liberty, equality, and solidarity, all of which are social values in terms of making sense only within the context of relations with other people, were put together in enduring textual and political form for perhaps the first time during the struggles of the French Revolution and its *Déclaration des Droits de l'Homme et du Citoyen*. They offer us criteria toward determining which claims for recognition of human rights are valid and which are not. The failure to recognize the importance of any one of these when assessing the negative accusations of domination and the positive claims to rights of co- and self-determination will lead us astray in our thinking and discourse on human rights.

I also have tried to clarify who are the holders and violators of human rights. In an earlier formulation, I had conceptualized three forms of rights-holders—individuals, groups, both individuals and groups, and everyone. After working with this and receiving comments over a period of time, I came to the conclusion that group rights should not stand in opposition to individual rights as a separate category but should be conceptualized as a composite of group and individual rights. My prior position was just too dichotomous, too lacking in complexity. Where there are violations of the rights of groups, there are always simultaneous violations of the rights of the individuals within the group. But I continue to steadfastly reject the position held by some, such as Jack Donnelly, that there can be no collective human rights.

This is one of the major debates in the theoretical literature on human rights, especially in the United States. Another is the debate over whether there can be economic and social human rights and, if so, how they rank with political and civil human rights, or if it is time that human rights are really only political and civil. The position that I have argued for is that political/civil and economic/social human rights must be seen as interrelated without any ranking between them. The prioritization of these rights has proven itself to be exceptionally dangerous in the twentieth century, with communist totalitarianism sacrificing political and civil rights in the name of economic and solidaristic rights, while liberal and neoliberal capitalism has been sacrificing equality and solidarity as values inconsistent with liberty.

I further reject the position stated in the Preamble of the African Charter on Human and Peoples' Rights that "the satisfaction of economic, social and cultural rights is a guarantee for the enjoyment of civil rights." My conception of a holistic human rights demands an acknowledgment of the equal validity of these values. It leads me to call for public policy that achieves balance between them. In this sense, excessively individualistic and privatistic neoliberalism is as radical as communist totalitarianism. It is "mean" not in the Aristotelian sense of balance and moderation, which is how its advocates see it, but "mean" in the negative sense of refusing to accept the egalitarian and solidaristic requisites for human rights and the real human suffering and stunting that this entails.

The state also poses a problem for human rights. As I pointed out, the modern state and human rights were born together. The modern state was supposed to protect human rights. Both because of the modern state's propensity to choose selectively from among the basic human rights values as just discussed, and because of the state's association with the use of violence both internally and externally, the modern state has been a major violator of human rights. This is a particularly serious problem because it is indeed states that sign and ratify the binding human rights documents, states whose representatives to the United Nations vote on the General Assembly's human rights declarations, and states that use the discourse of human rights to legitimize or delegitimize each other's regimes.

When the state exercises its violence externally it tends to dehumanize the enemy, and when it uses it internally it tends to target internal "others" who are usually of a minority race or culture and in a lower economic class position. The violence then becomes a violation of both collective and individual rights. We must move beyond Weber's view of the essence of the state as the legitimate utilizer of violence and coercion. It fits too comfortably with the liberal and neoliberal protectionist view of the state, and it begs the question of who and what are to be protected by state violence. It leads to a denial, à la the increasingly influential work of Friedrich von Hayek, that states have important roles in advancing human economic and social rights beyond merely those to private property.

Hence, if the new millennium, which we have just entered, is to be one of human rights advancement, we are going to need both a genuine acceptance of the imperatives of the full range of human rights and an understanding and struggle for the political and economic forms that will sustain them. In place of the essentially violent state, it will require nurturing democratic political forms that will understand that merely voting in elections does not do nearly enough to maintain liberty, equality, or solidarity among people, and that political and economic democracy are two sides of the same coin. It will require economic forms that manifest the values of equality and solidarity, the latter in active processes of co- and self-development. I have offered a sketch of what such forms and processes might look like.

Of course, these things cannot come about by my merely offering them as a wish list. Such things can only come about by the concrete struggles of real people who are dominated, alongside those who might not be suffering domination themselves but recognize the suffering and calls of those who are.

History is not linear. We tend to think of earlier ages as being the cruelest, but some of the worst instances of domination and genocide have occurred in the twentieth century. If we do not think, write, and talk seriously and self-critically across cultural boundaries about the meaning of human rights; if we do not recognize the imperative to act in association with others to advance the equally important values of liberty, equality, and solidarity; if we fail to establish forms and institutions that can sustain those values—if we fail in these tasks, then the new millennium could be worse than one we have just left behind.

Appendix A

A Case of the Violation of Workers' Rights in the United States: The Staley Lockout and Worker Replacement

In Chapter 5, I directed the reader to this Appendix as an instance of how workers' rights have degenerated in the United States during the last two decades of the twentieth century. I have seen at close hand some of the most devastating effects of the new power of international capital and the relative powerlessness of the people it employs in a city only an hour's drive from where I am writing—Decatur, Illinois. In Decatur, there is an enormous industrial complex that makes sweeteners from corn, called Staley. It had for many years been a locally owned operation employing almost a thousand residents of Decatur and the surrounding small towns and countryside. In 1988, Staley was bought out by Tate and Lyle, the largest European-based (London) transnational sugar refining corporation operating in over fifty countries.[1]

Corn processing is a dangerous operation because of the potentially flammable and explosive starch dust generated by the process, and because highly toxic chemicals such as propylene oxide, which took the life of worker James Beals in 1990, are used in the processing. While there were accidents prior to the Tate and Lyle takeover, the workers seem to feel that the management had a genuine concern for their safety. Bill Strohl, president of the local union for eight years, characterized the situation during those years as follows, "We had a lot of horror stories in the past. But we got them resolved. There was a fair amount of labor-management cooperation. We produced what were considered model safety manuals. Where it fell down was when Tate and Lyle took over. There was a big change in management's attitude toward safety."[2]

The death of James Beals prompted the Occupational Safety and Health Administration (OSHA) to investigate overall safety conditions at the plant. It found 298 violations and fined Staley $1.6 million. OSHA contended that the company "willfully failed to protect employees from live electrical parts, exposed workers to potential explosions [in fact, there had been a number of explosions in the plant's various buildings] due to use of non-approved electrical and spark-producing tools, exposed workers to unprotected rotating shafts and couplings, and did not adequately protect workers from exposure to fall hazards."[3] Beyond OSHA's findings, the workers charged that Tate and Lyle was significantly changing the environment at the plant by allowing burning and welding without permits, putting people on jobs with which they had had no experience, bringing in new supervisors with no experience in corn milling, increasing the use of contractors who were not experienced with similar conditions and who were not given safety orientations, and expanding compulsory overtime work.

Tate and Lyle claimed that it improved its health and safety performance after the OSHA findings. Some of the workers disagreed and claimed that it was devoting more to public relations than to changing the practices. Workers continued to file health and safety complaints. One worker who filed complaints said that he was reassigned to night shifts in violation of his seniority, forced to work every weekend, suspended several times, and threatened with dismissal if he continued to file the complaints.

In the summer of 1993, Tate and Lyle decided to move for a kind of flexible control over the workforce that would make complaints over working days or nights or weekends meaningless. They demanded that the workers sign a contract whereby they would work twelve-hour days, three and four consecutive days on alternating weeks, on rotating day and night shifts.[4] Overtime could be assigned to workers extending the working day up to sixteen consecutive hours. In the early to mid-1990s several corporations in the United States were forcing strikes, hoping to divide the workers and weaken or destroy the unions. Rather than the eight-hour day that labor had struggled so hard to get since the end of the nineteenth century, the only eight-hour guarantee for the workers in the contract was a minimum of eight hours of rest between the long working hours. Whether this was calculated by Tate and Lyle to force a strike and break the union or whether they thought the workers would actually accept such a conditions is uncertain. Despite their opposition to this change, the workers decided not to strike.

Instead, the workers decided to "work to rule." As one of the workers, Mike Griffin, put it, "We worked like machines."[5] If the workers were going to be treated like machines, he said, they were going to act like them. The workers held solidarity meetings in the plant, and disrupted and took over the meetings called by management to explain why they were imposing the twelve-hour workdays. Some workers would stand up while management was speaking and turn their backs. Staley claimed that the workers went further, that they engaged in sabotage by letting more water and product go into the sewers than was necessary. The workers denied this but the National Labor Relations Board found the company's charge credible.

On June 27, the company locked out approximately 760 of the workers. Following the example set by President Reagan during the air controllers' strike, it placed advertisements in newspapers in other areas of the country and hired replacement workers to take the jobs of the workers it had locked out. Some of the workers became "road warriors" and traveled around the United States, Canada, and even Europe publicizing what had been done to them and warning other workers that this is what they too could find themselves up against. They spoke in terms of human dignity and human rights. They came to this intuitively. They had read neither the international covenants nor the European Social Charter or Protocol discussed in Chapter 5. They pointed out not only that such long hours and rotating shifts were unhealthy for the human body and mind (many of the workers were men and women in their late forties and fifties, which made the physiological impact even more drastic) but that it would have drastic effects on their lives as members of families, churches, and other associations that were important to their lives and the life of the community in which they lived. Their off-work time would become unpredictable over longer stretches and their shifts would exhaust them. Their exhaustion would make their jobs even more dangerous than they already were. It also would increase the hazards of their drives home after work.

They sponsored meetings in Decatur that were attended by supporters from other unions, nonunion supporters, and trade unionists from other countries. They held marches and demonstrations, and their supporters—mainly trade unionists from other cities and spouses of locked-out workers, but also members of the clergy and political activists—blocked the truck entry gates of the plant. They were deemed by the state to be violators of the private property rights of the corporation. The police were sent to the scene where they sprayed those sitting across the entry with pepper gas. They also arrested a number of them. One locked-out worker, Dan Lane, conducted a hunger strike for approximately two months and his health deteriorated seriously. The lockout and militant resistance to it lasted approximately two and one-half years, until January 1996.

There was tremendous pressure on the workers to accept the company's terms. The transnational refused to budge on the major issue of the twelve-hour workday. The national union leadership, the UPIU (United Paperworkers' Industrial Union), was afraid of being shut out of the plant entirely, and pressured the local to accept the twelve-hour day. When the workers called on the national AFL-CIO for help, it informed them that there was very little it could do without being asked to intervene by the national UPIU leadership. The community was divided, some supporting the locked-out workers, but some maintaining that the strife was too divisive for the town and that the workers were lucky to have any job in difficult times for U.S. industry. The city council was composed largely of people who had management or executive positions in the large corporations. And there were linkages between the corporations. Archer Daniels Midland (ADM), the largest food processor and exporter in the world, and a major contributor to both political parties, had significant investments in Tate and Lyle, as did the powerful Illinois-based insurance company State Farm. There was a direct conveyor belt running from the Staley plant to the ADM plant a mile or so away. The Bridgestone-Firestone tire plant in Decatur, owned by a Japanese transnational, also decided to impose twelve-hour work days on its employees, but without the rotating shifts. The strike of workers there was short-lived. They saw what was happening to the locked-out Staley workers and capitulated without the same protracted struggle.

There were other pressures to accept the terms, negative effects that permeated the lives of the workers and their community. Mortgage payments had to be made to local lenders. Health benefits were at risk at the very time that the mental and physical health of the workers was being strained. Spouses of the locked-out workers were generally very supportive, but the strain on them was enormous as well, leading to a number of divorces.[6]

When the union's local bargaining committee rejected the contract offer of the company that contained the twelve-hour work days and refused to present it to the membership, the national UPIU president overruled the decision and forced a vote by the membership. The contract offer was accepted on December 22, 1996, on a vote of 286 to 226. While more compliant local leadership had been voted in, to the satisfaction of the national UPIU, which was trying to weaken the resistance, it had not yet taken office. Since none of the sitting local officers would sign the contract, officers of the national union signed it.

Although a slight majority voted to accept the contract, only approximately 180 of the workers decided to return and were accepted by the company. About thirty of those left shortly after returning. Some returned because they saw no movement in Tate and Lyle's stand after two and one-half years of resistance; they desperately needed income and would accept a job on virtually any terms. Some voted to accept the terms without any expectations of working under them for any long period of time. They were close to retirement and simply could not bear to lose their pensions after twenty-five or thirty years of working. Also, the company offered up to $8,000 in severance pay. But the contract had to be accepted before this would be paid out. As cruel choices led some to capitulate, the divisiveness and the hatred of the "scabs" by those who refused to capitulate became even more intense.

The immediate battle was lost to international corporate power. But some of the locked-out workers developed longer-term strategies. Some of the militant "road warriors" have become involved with the attempt to create a national labor party in the United States. They have formed an informational and mutual support network with groups fighting against such corporate power both in the United States and in other countries. Exchanges of visits and mutual expressions of solidarity, as well as fund-raising for labor battles, have taken place between these road warriors, trade unionists, and members of the national legislatures in Great Britain, France, Mexico, Brazil, Slovenia, and Bangladesh. They publish a newsletter called *The War Zone,* and there is an intense communications network via the internet. Other workers have joined in an attempt to change the composition of the Decatur City Council so that it would not be just an official forum and legislating body for the corporations in the city. The bitterness among many of the workers continues and the battle over the twelve-hour day and almost total labor flexibility has been lost at Staley, at least for the short term. But the feeling that basic human rights have been taken away persists. While in some it has led to alienation, cynicism, and pacification, in others it has led to action at the city, national, and international levels. But the psychological toll is still discernible on even some of those who continue to struggle.

It is interesting to note that the struggle between the workers and the management of Staley was at the same time a struggle for liberty (to protest on the plant floor and in the streets, to lead a full family and community life), equality (some degree of equality of power in determining the conditions of one's labor), and solidarity (a struggle for a discursive inclusiveness in which workers can collectively press their case within the workplace and the community, both in the instruments of government such as the city council and in the media). They had hoped that their articulations would not be met by the pure power of those who own the instruments of production, and by the police who, as agents of the state, might enforce their property rights regardless of the justifications of the workers' rights claims. They lost on all counts. Staley proved to them that the price of a job in their plants was for workers to accept the role of commodity, the ILO's proclamation to the contrary notwithstanding.

APPENDIX B

SEPTEMBER 11: AN ATTACK ON HUMAN RIGHTS*

People around the world are still in a state of disbelief. Children ask parents if this was real or a movie. We all walked around in a kind of surreal fog, asking ourselves from time to time if this was not a bad dream that we were having, hoping that we would wake up the next morning and find ourselves in a state of normality—planes flying overhead, teachers offering their normal subject matter, and discussion in the media of the tax rebate, social security, prescription drugs, and so on.

But the unthinkable was real. People in the United States had their sense of security from living in the most militarily and economically powerful country swept out from under them. They became afraid in ways that they had not since World War II. They became saddened at the death of so many people, so many "mommies, daddies, brothers, and sisters," in the words of the pupils of my cousin who teaches second grade. So many lives, so much future potential happiness and achievement lost because terrorists were convinced that their cause justified such a heinous taking of life. In some, anger overtook sadness and fear, or perhaps became a way of dealing with them. Many were angry that this had been done to American citizens and American property. America's pride had been damaged, and there were calls to fly the American flag and to retaliate on a grand military scale even though there was no conclusive evidence of who actually was behind the attack.

All of these reactions are understandable. How can any of us not feel the most profound sorrow for those of us who are no longer here and those surviving family members who are so impoverished by the loss of their loved ones? How can any of us not feel less secure knowing now in a way that we did not before that there can be no absolute protection against people who are clever and willing to die for their cause? And surely we can understand the anger at

* As indicated in the Introduction, this article was written approximately a week and one-half after September 11. It appeared in the October 2002 issue of the *Publici*, the monthly newspaper of the Urban-Champaign Independent Media Center; Website http://publici.ucimc.org.

such a callous use of other peoples' lives, especially civilian lives, to advance political objectives.

WHY A HUMAN RIGHTS ISSUE

The key here is what we mean when we say "us" and "we." The angry response is often channeled into an aggressive patriotism, a call for a vast and aggressive military response by the United States, that fails to see the real significance of this terrorism. This terrorism was an act against human rights, and as such it is a violation of the rights of all humanity. If one looks at human rights for the bottom up, that is from the perspective of the victims of human rights violations, then it makes sense to think of such violations as the failure to recognize the right of the victims to develop their lives and potentialities to the fullest extent possible. Political and economic domination impede this, but certainly the most immediate way of doing it is the termination of human life, especially when it is a collective act done for political motives such as terrorism or genocide. Thus, the appropriate affronted and violated "us" is not the partial "us" as U.S. citizens, but the "us" as humanity as a whole. If you have difficulty looking at this as such an affront, simply consider the victims. There were not only U.S. citizens. People from a wide variety of countries were on the planes that were hijacked and in the offices of the Twin Towers in New York. Indeed, the Bush administration is appealing to the governments of countries around the world for support precisely on the grounds that this is not merely an issue of concern to the United States but to everyone, regardless of nationality.

PROTECTING RIGHTS WITHOUT DESTROYING THEM

Certain conclusions flow from understanding the issue as one of human rights. One is that we must be sure that in trying to bring the perpetrators of this act to justice and in trying to eliminate terrorism generally, we do not use mechanisms that undermine civil and human rights. Sometimes it is difficult to reconcile such values as rights and security, but our dedication to rights and democracy must lead us to take precautions against intrusions into rights in order to secure rights. If we don't, then what are we really protecting and why? It is all too easy to fall into the mode of a garrison state in which dissent is no longer tolerated, some of our citizens are persecuted and even incarcerated, our right to support or contribute to political groups is compromised by the completely discretionary decision of the Attorney General to declare it a terrorist group, and privacy goes by the wayside as government monitors our phone calls and e-mails and even penetrates our homes with sound-detecting equipment.

In U.S. history, we have experienced the draconian Espionage and Sedition laws used during World War I (which was supposed to have been fought in the name of democracy), the incarceration of Japanese Americans in World War II, and the FBI's domestic counterintelligence (COINTEL) program through which there was infiltration and the attempt to destabilize both the civil rights and the antiwar movements in the 1960s and 1970s.[1] Patriotism understood as an inclusive and critical concern with the health of the body politic is a positive thing. But often patriotism is understood in intolerant and exclusive ways in which any difference and opposition is seen as being akin to disloyalty. Framing our understanding of the terrorist acts and our response to them in terms of human rights should help oblige our government to not repeat the repressive mistakes of the past and to protect minority people in our midst, in this instance especially Islamic people who have already come under attack in several cities.

The human rights understanding also has implications for how we react abroad. First, we must not react in a military way that would kill or injure many innocent people in other countries. To consider them merely acceptable "collateral" damage would be unacceptable. The perpetrators need to be brought to justice. But this is not a matter of some sort of patriotic need to seek revenge as Americans whose pride has been hurt. The terrorists have offended all humanity. Justice, not vengeance, requires that they be apprehended through an international effort that is as peaceful as possible. Finally, fitting the affront to all humanity and the interest that all humanity has in securing justice and discouraging further terrorism, the terrorists should be tried before an international court of competent jurists.

SETTING AN EXAMPLE

If the apprehension of those responsible and the bringing of them to justice must be an international matter, there is something that the United States can do on its own. That is to bring our foreign policies more in line with international standards of human rights than they have been. I have already alluded to domestic policies in the United States that violated rights. But the people and government of the United States need to take a critical accounting of U.S. policy during the past century. In that it will improve the quality of our civic life and our moral standing abroad, such a self-examination is patriotism in the most positive sense of that term.

Using human rights as the criterion, we need to reexamine our past policies in several areas. One is our government's refusal to accept the international consensus that there are economic and social human rights that go beyond the private property rights of corporations and individuals and are based on equity and social welfare concerns. A first important step would be the Senate's ratification of the 1966 International Covenant on Economic, Social, and Cultural Rights that President Jimmy Carter signed but that has languished in the Senate's Foreign Relations Committee. More concrete steps would include forgiveness of debts that poor countries have no hope of really paying off anyway and an end to the structural adjustment and privatization policies of the World Bank and the IMF. They are inconsistent with the many of the economic rights stipulated in the 1966 covenant.

A second desirable move would be in becoming more even-handed when judging the human rights records of other nations. The Middle East is a prime example of failure in this regard. Israel, which provided a heaven from anti-Semitism for victims of one of the most horrendous human rights violations in history, is the major recipient of U.S. foreign aid. The U.S. government has not hesitated to denounce the terrorism directed by some Palestinian groups against civilian targets in Israel, including deadly attacks on school buses. But it has either looked the other way, or simply give a friendly reprimand, in response to such rights abuses committed by Israel as the torture of Palestinian prisoners (which was only recently ruled to be illegal by Israeli courts), being quick to use deadly force against stone-throwing demonstrators and Palestinian police, the assassination of Palestinian political leaders, and the demolition of Palestinian homes either as a collective punishment or in order to make way for Israeli settlement. The fact that the U.S. government provides the funds for Israel's military imposes a special obligation on it to curtail such Israeli abuses of human rights. We will not gain respect in the Middle East until we are willing to condemn human rights violations, and adjust policies accordingly, on the part of both of the parties in this terrible conflict.

Perhaps most important, we need to examine critically the record of our own government in overthrowing more rights-respecting and democratic governments and supporting in their place regimes that terrorize, torture, and kill any opposition in their wake, as in Iran in 1953, Guatemala in 1954, and Chile in 1973. In the light of renewed media discussion of assassination as a possible tool available to U.S. decision makers after the New York and Washington terrorism, we need to look back at our government's past role in the assassination of foreign leaders—such as Patrice Lumumba in what was then called the Congo and became Zaire under the U.S.-supported dictator Mobuto, and General Rene Schneider who was loyal to President Allende in Chile. We also need to examine our government's history of training terroristic forces, such as the murderous Salvadoran officer corps trained in the School of the Americas, and in our creating, training, and supporting the anti-Sandinista Nicarguan Contras, the vast majority of whose victims were civilians.

It is very discouraging that the new Bush administration has brought into its ranks people who have been directly implicated in these policies, such as former Assistant Secretary of State in the Reagan administration Elliot Abrams who had been convicted by a court of lying before Congress about U.S. policy and John Negroponte, who as ambassador to Honduras when the Contras were being trained shares some responsibility for the atrocities committed by both the Contras against Nicaraguans and the Honduran military against its own people. Under Ambassador Negroponte's watch, the U.S.-trained and -financed Honduran army was killing human rights workers and people critical of the government's and the military's policies.

Especially disturbing was the approval by the Senate Foreign Relations Committee of Negroponte's nomination to be the U.S. ambassador to the

United Nations. It apparently only got through so easily (on a fourteen to three vote) on September 13 because the Senate Committee was eager to give President Bush virtually everything he wanted after the terrorist attack on New York. Republican senators supporting his nomination were reported by the *New York Times* to have told the Democrats that "it was time for the United States to put the past behind it" (*New York Times,* September 14, 2001, B3).

Finally, the United States government itself very recently targeted a building with civilian workers for destruction. At the same time that it apparently mistakenly attacked the Chinese Embassy in Belgrade, it also deliberately hit the building that housed the television studio in Belgrade, killing journalists and technical staff. A very bad precedent indeed.

CONCLUDING REFLECTION

It is never time to put terrorism and other human rights violations behind us, as urged by the Republican senators at Negroponte's confirmation hearing. Whether we are talking about terror inflicted by nonstate groups or terror inflicted as a matter of state policy, we are talking about human rights violations for which there should be no excuse, no forgetting, no putting behind, and no statute of limitations. Such human rights violators should be brought to justice whenever they can be apprehended, whether they are Chilean General Pinochet, the terrorists who just struck in the United States, or past or present officeholders in the U.S. government. The United States, once again the odd-man-out internationally, must stop blocking the attempt of other nations to create an international criminal court where such nonstate human rights violators could systematically be brought to justice.

An inconsistent commitment to human rights is no commitment at all.

NOTES

INTRODUCTION

1. Simone Weil, "Human Personality," in *Selected Essays 1934–1943*, trans. Richard Rees (London: Oxford University Press, 1962), 20.
2. Martha Nussbaum, *Cultivating Humanity* (Cambridge, MA: Harvard University Press, 1997), 140–1.
3. For example, Aristole's *Politics*.
4. Chapter 3 appeared in slightly modified form in *Papers in Social Theory*, No. 6, 2001, edited by Neil Stammers for the Warwick Social Theory Centre and the Sussex Centre for Critical Social Theory, 32–58.

CHAPTER 1 THE BIRTH OF THE HUMAN RIGHTS IDEA AND ITS DETRACTORS

1. Micheline R. Ishay, ed., *The Human Rights Reader* (New York: Routledge, 1997), 2–6.
2. Walter Laqueur and Barry Rubin, eds., *The Human Rights Reader* (New York: Meridian, 1989).
3. Carole Pateman, *The Sexual Contract* (Stanford: Stanford University Press, 1988).
4. The expression "masterless men" is from Hobbes's *Leviathan*, Part II, Chapter 21. It also serves as the title of the third chapter of Christopher Hill's classic work on the period, *The World Turned Upside Down* (London: Penguin Books, 1972).
5. Gerrard Winstanley, "A Declaration from the Poor Oppressed People of England," in George A. Sabine, ed., *The Works of Gerrard Winstanley* (Ithaca, NY: Cornell University Press, 1941), 272.
6. Ibid.
7. The most interesting discussion of these struggles in England at the time known to this writer is Christopher Hill's in *The World Turned Upside Down*.
8. Thomas Hobbes, *Leviathan*, Part I, Chapter 13.
9. Leo Strauss, *Natural Right and History* (Chicago: University of Chicago Press, 1953).
10. John Locke, *The Reasonableness of Christianity*, Section XXXIII.

11. John Locke, *Second Treatise,* Chapter XV.

12. Ibid., Chapter V.

13. Ibid.

14. Donnelly's argument is in Chapter 5 of his *Universal Human Rights in Theory and Practice* (Ithaca, NY: Cornell University Press, 1989). Macpherson's is in his *The Political Theory of Possessive Individualism* (Oxford: Oxford University Press, 1962) and in the Introduction to the Hackett edition of Locke's *Second Treatise of Government* (1980).

15. Louis Althusser, *Politics and History: Montesquieu, Rousseau, Marx,* trans. Ben Brewster (London: NLB, 1972), Part II, 113–60.

16. Rousseau's concept of the General Will is itself quite complex. What he really means is a subject of much dispute. We cannot get into that debate here. My understanding is, in brief, that the General Will is a rational grasping, after a process of dialogue, of what is in the best interest of the community as a whole. It is a holistic concept in the sense that the whole community has interests that cannot be determined simply by adding up the sum of the short-term individual interests of the members. Nor can the General Will be determined by a legislature that is bound to represent factional interests or self-interest of the legislators. It must be directly expressed by the members of the community themselves.

17. Jean-Jacques Rousseau, *The Social Contract,* Book I, Ch. IX, trans. G. D. H. Cole, *The Social Contract and Discourses* (New York: E. P. Dutton, 1950), 21.

18. Ibid., 20.

19. Mary Wollstonecraft, *A Vindication of the Rights of Woman* (New York: Norton, 1975), 45.

20. I do not go so far as Jacob Talmon in blaming Rousseau for either the Terror of that Revolution or subsequent totalitarian experiences. I am only talking about problems that aspects of Rousseau's thinking pose for conceptions of human rights. His thought is complex and could be used in a variety of ways, for good or for ill. The participants in the Terror used it for ill. See Jacob Talmon, *The Origins of Totalitarian Democracy* (New York: Praeger, 1960).

21. Immanuel Kant, *Metaphysical Foundations of Morals,* in Carl J. Friedrich, ed., *The Philosophy of Kant* (New York: Modern Library, 1949), 183.

22. Immanuel Kant, *Perpetual Peace,* quoted in William Ebenstein and Alan O. Ebenstein, eds., *Great Political Thinkers,* Fifth Edition (Fort Worth, TX: Holt, Rinehart, and Winston, 1991), 544.

23. Locke, *Second Treatise,* Chapter II, Section 6.

24. French Declaration of the Rights of Man and Citizen, reprinted in Laqueur and Rubin, *The Human Rights Reader,* 118.

25. Ibid., 119.

26. Ibid.

27. Ibid.

28. Edmund Burke, *Reflections on the Revolution in France* (Indianapolis: Library of Liberal Arts, 1955), 68.

29. Ibid., 89.
30. Ibid., 97–8.
31. Daniel Boorstin, *The Genius of American Politics* (Chicago: University of Chicago Press, 1953).
32. David Hume, "Treatise of Human Nature," in Henry D. Aiken, ed., *Hume's Moral and Political Philosophy* (New York: Hafner, 1948), 44.
33. Ibid., 45.
34. Ibid., 90.
35. Jeremy Bentham, "Pannomial Fragments," in Mary Peter Mack, ed., *A Bentham Reader* (New York: Pegasus, 1969), 257.
36. For example, see André Glucksmann, *Les Maîtres Penseurs* (Paris: Grasset, 1977), 107–9.
37. Karl Marx, "On the Jewish Question," in Robert C. Tucker, ed., *The Marx-Engels Reader,* 2nd edition (New York: Norton, 1978), 40.
38. Ibid., 42.
39. Ibid.
40. Ibid., 43.
41. Ibid., 44–5.

CHAPTER 2   SOME TWENTIETH-CENTURY REFLECTIONS ON HUMAN RIGHTS

1. For an excellent history of repression in the United States, see Robert Justin Goldstein, *Political Repression in Modern America: 1870 to the Present* (Cambridge, MA: Schenkman, 1978; reprint, Urbana: University of Illinois Press, 2000).
2. On the suffering and brutality in these camps, see Aleksandr I. Solzhenitsyn, *The Gulag Archipelago,* trans. Thomas P. Whitney (New York: Harper and Row, 1973).
3. Constitution of the Union of Soviet Socialist Republics, adopted on October 7, 1977 and amended on December 1, 1988, in Vadim Medish, *The Soviet Union,* 4th edition (Englewood Cliffs, NJ: Prentice Hall, 1990), 368.
4. One could question whether or not convicted felons should lose their right to vote—while they are in prison, for life, or both. These may or may not be rights violations. Where I do think that we have a human rights violation is where the penal system hits one race, religion, nationality, and so on in wide disproportion to its percentage of the total population. In the United States, where there is an enormous and growing disproportion of whites and African Americans, 14 percent of the total African American male population is disenfranchised because of a felony conviction on their record. CNN News, January 30, 1997.
5. Friederich Engels, 1891 Introduction to Marx's *Civil War in France,* reprinted in Robert C. Tucker, ed., *The Marx-Engels Reader* (New York: Norton, 1978), 618–29.

6. Leon Trotsky, *The Revolution Betrayed* (New York: Pathfinder Press, 1972).

7. The word "genocide" has had this broader meaning from the time it was first coined by Raphael Lemkin in his Carnegie Endowment for International Peace sponsored book, *Axis Rule in Occupied Europe,* 1944. For the definition accepted by the United Nations, see its 1951 Convention on the Prevention and Punishment of the Crime of Genocide.

8. Douglas Porporo, *How Holocausts Happen* (Philadelphia: Temple University Press, 1990), 3–13.

9. The 1948 Declaration took the form of a resolution adopted by a vote of the General Assembly. The 1966 covenants and most of the other norm-setting agreements required signatures and ratification by individual governments in order to be considered legally binding documents.

10. Karel Vasak, "Pour une Troisième Génération des Droits de l'Homme," in Christophe Swinarski, ed., *Studies and Essays on International Humanitarian Law and Red Cross Principles* (Geneva and The Hague: Martinus Nijhoff, 1984), 837–45.

11. There is some difference over just how to refer to the two 1966 covenants. In the previously cited Laqueur/Rubin and Ishay anthologies, the words United Nations precede the word Covenant in the title. While Steiner and Alston drop the United Nations from the title when they refer to them, they also write that: "the United Nations adopted two separate International Covenants" See Henry J. Steiner and Philip Alston, eds., *International Human Rights in Context* (Oxford: Clarendon Press, 1996), 256. Thus, either way of naming these documents would seem to be appropriate. Since the reader will understand that these are U.N. documents within the context of the chapters, I will drop the name United Nations from the titles of both of the 1966 Covenants.

12. United Nations International Covenant on Economic, Social, and Cultural Rights (1966), Article 15,I.a.

13. Ibid., 839. Translation from the French is mine. While Jack Donnelly titles his discussion of the third generation "Collective Human Rights?," it is clear from this passage from Vasak that he did not exclude the individual from bearing these rights. See Donnelly's *Universal Human Rights in Theory and Practice* (Ithaca, NY: Cornell University Press, 1989), 143.

14. Maurice Cranston, "Human Rights, Real and Supposed," in Morton E. Winston, ed., *The Philosophy of Human Rights* (Belmont, CA: Wadsworth, 1989), 126. Steven Lukes joins Cranston in arguing for a list of human rights that are "reasonably short and reasonably abstract," but would include economic and social rights. Steven Lukes, "Five Fables About Human Rights," in Stephen Shute and Susan Hurley, eds., *On Human Rights: The Oxford Amnesty Lectures* (New York: Basic Books, 1993), 38.

15. Ibid.

16. Bert Lockwood et al., "Rights of the Poor," *William and Mary Bill of Rights Journal,* II, 1 Spring 1993, 16.

17. Unger recognizes the importance of rights and offers a typology of rights: market, immunity, destabilization, and solidarity rights. See his *False Necessity* (Cambridge: Cambridge University Press, 1987), 508–37.

18. Among the more prominent liberation theologians are the Spanish-born Basque priest Jon Sobrino, who works in El Salvador, *Christology at the Crossroads* (Maryknoll, NY: Orbis Books, 1978) and *The True Church and the Poor* (Maryknoll, NY: Orbis Books, 1984), and the Brazilian brothers who are priests, Leonardo and Clodovis Boff, *Salvation and Liberation* (Maryknoll, NY: Orbis Books, 1984).

19. For a very interesting discussion of how the rights of women would be conceived in Islam if male interpreters of the Koran lost their monopoly on interpretation, see Riffat Hassan, "Women's Rights and Islam: from the I.C.P.D. to Beijing," unpublished, available from her at the University of Louisville.

20. Here I am consciously at odds with Aristotle's position in *The Politics* (Book VII, Ch. 3) that thought and theory constitute the highest form of action.

21. For another discussion of both Richard Rorty and Jack Donnelly, see Michael Freeman, "The Philosophical Foundations of Human Rights, *Human Rights Quarterly*, XVI, 1994, 491–514.

22. Richard Rorty, "Human Rights, Rationality, and Sentimentality," in Stephen Shute and Susan Hurley, eds., *On Human Rights: the Oxford Amnesty Lectures 1993* (New York: Basic Books, 1993), 116–17.

23. Ibid., 122. One wonders about the veracity of the claim when we see birds mate for life and the lack of abuse of their young among most other species.

24. Ibid., 125–6.

25. Ibid., 133.

26. Ibid., 134.

27. Jack Donnelly, *Universal Human Rights in Theory and Practice* (Ithaca, NY: Cornell University Press, 1989), 21–2.

28. Ibid., 18.

29. Ibid., 17.

30. Ibid., 22.

31. For an argument by a Westerner critiquing the overemphasis on individualism in "rights talk," see Mary Ann Glendon, *Rights Talk: the Impoverishment of Political Discourse* (New York: The Free Press, 1991).

32. Andrew Levine, *Liberal Democracy: A Critique of Its Theory* (New York: Columbia University Press, 1981), 127.

33. Ibid., 130.

34. Ibid., 131–32.

35. Alan Gewirth, *Human Rights: Essays on Justification and Applications* (Chicago: University of Chicago Press, 1982), 29.

36. Ibid., 5.

37. Isaiah Berlin, "Two Concepts of Liberty," in his *Four Essays on Liberty* (Oxford: Oxford University Press, 1969), 118–72.

38. Ronald Dworkin, *Taking Rights Seriously* (Cambridge, MA: Harvard University Press, 1977), 198–9. Of course, this was written long before the U.S. Supreme Court's ruling on the challenges to the presidential vote count in the 2000 elections in Florida. The decision against a recount has opened that issue up, even if the court attempted to limit the bearing of its ruling to that one instance.
39. The U.S. Supreme Court decision to stop the vote recount in Florida during the 2000 presidential election has opened up the issue in a very partisan way, unfortunately.
40. Dworkin, *Taking Rights Seriously*, 273.
41. Dworkin spends a good bit of time characterizing Rawls's theory of justice as a "natural" theory of morals, which must assume a natural theory of rights, and distinguishing his "constructive" theory from it. His discussion of the modest assumptions required for a constructive model is summarized thusly: "on the constructive model … the assumption of natural rights is not a metaphysically ambitious one. It requires no more than the hypothesis that the best political program, within the sense of that model, is the one that takes the protection of certain individual choices as fundamental, and not properly subordinated to any goal or duty of combination of these." 177.
42. Ibid., 234–35.
43. Christian Bay, *The Structure of Freedom* (New York: Atheneum, 1965), 371.
44. Ibid., 6.
45. Ibid., 14.
46. Ibid., 15.
47. Ibid.
48. John Rawls, *A Theory of Justice* (Cambridge, MA: Harvard University Press, 1971).
49. Ibid., 375.
50. Christian Bay, "Taking the Universality of Human Rights Seriously," paper presented to the Human Rights Study Group at the World Congress of the International Political Science Association, July 15–20, 1985, Paris, France, 2. The color coding of these rights was actually begun by Johan Galtung.
51. Ibid., 5.
52. Ibid., 8.
53. Ibid., 10.
54. Ibid., 16.
55. Ibid., 18.
56. Ibid., 23.
57. Ibid.
58. Ibid., 24.
59. Henry Shue, *Basic Rights: Subsistence, Affluence, and U.S. Foreign Policy* (Princeton, NJ: Princeton University Press, 1980, 1996), 19.
60. Ibid., 23.

61. Ibid., 70.
62. Ibid., 75.
63. Robert A. Dahl, *A Preface to Economic Democracy* (Berkeley: University of California Press, 1985).
64. Johan Galtung, *Human Rights in Another Key* (London: Polity Press, 1994), 19.
65. Ibid., 57.
66. Misery is the deprivation of well-being needs. Well-being needs are needs for: nutrition, water, air, movement, excretion, sleep, sex, self-expression, dialogue, education, protection against climate, environment, disease, and heavy, degrading, and boring work. Alienation is the deprivation of identity needs. Identity needs are those for: self-expression, creativity, praxis, work, self-actualization, realization of potentiality, well-being, happiness, joy, activity, challenge, experience, affection, love, sex, friends, spouse, offspring, roots, belongingness, networks, support, esteem, understanding social forces, social transparency, partnership with nature, sense of purpose, meaning with life, closeness to the transcendental, transpersonal. Ibid., 73. Galtung only states that these are needs. He does not say that all of them should be translated into human rights.
67. Ibid., 100.
68. Ibid., 113.
69. Ibid.
70. Ibid., 85 and 92.
71. Ibid., 85.
72. Jurgen Habermas, *Between Facts and Norms,* trans. William Rehg (Cambridge, MA: MIT Press, 1996), 98.
73. In his earlier work, this also held true for cognitive truth. See, for example, his *Communication and the Evolution of Society,* trans. Thomas McCarthy (Boston: Beacon Press, 1976) for probably the clearest exposition of his discursive approach to cognitive truth. But *Between Facts and Norms,* as the title indicates, focuses on normative, rather than cognitive, "truth."
74. Habermas, *Between Facts and Norms,* 121–2.
75. Ibid., 122.
76. Ibid., 123.
77. Ibid., 123.
78. Ibid., 456.
79. See his "New Social Movements," *Telos,* 49, 1981, 33–7. Habermas has used the expression "life-world" in at least two different ways. One is a conceptual way of thematizing the moral/practical capabilities of human beings. The other is a spatial metaphor, representing areas that are being defended against encroachment by exterior systems with a different and imperialistic logic and language. On this, see A. Belden Fields, "In Defense of Political Economy and Systemic Analysis: A Critique of Prevailing Theoretical Approaches to the New Social Movements," in Cary Nelson and Lawrence Grossberg, eds., *Marxism and the*

Interpretation of Culture (Urbana: University of Illinois Press, 1988), 141–56, especially 145–9.

80. For example, Nancy Fraser in *Unruly Practices* (Minneapolis: University of Minnesota Press, 1989), Chapter 6 and Seyla Benhabib, *Critique, Norm, and Utopia* (New York: Columbia University Press, 1986, Chapter 8.

Chapter 3   A Holistic Approach to Human Rights

1. In 1992, Wolf-Dieter Narr and I published an article entitled "Human Rights as a Holistic Concept" in *Human Rights Quarterly*, XIV, 5, February 1992, 1–20. The argument made in this chapter closely resembles the argument made there. I owe a great deal to Wolf-Dieter Narr— first, for getting me interested in making human rights an object of study and, second, for sharing his insights on the subject with me. This chapter reflects some of those insights but goes considerably beyond them.
2. Jean-Jacques Rousseau, *The Discourse on the Origin of Inequality among Men*, in J. D. H. Cole, trans. of *The Social Contract and Discourses* (New York: E. P. Dutton, 1950), 224.
3. John Rawls, *A Theory of Justice* (Cambridge, MA: Harvard University Press, 1971).
4. Isaiah Berlin, *Four Essays on Liberty* (New York: Oxford University Press, 1969), 118–72. It should be noted that Berlin himself is not writing about human rights and has a fairly nuanced view of the relationship between collective demands for social recognition or status and liberty.
5. Mahatma Gandhi, *All Are Equal in the Eyes of God* (New Delhi: Government of India Press, 1964).
6. For an excellent theoretical treatment of the role of social movements in this process, see Neil Stammers, "Social Movements and the Social Construction of Human Rights," *Human Rights Quarterly*, XXI, 4, November 1999, 980–1008.
7. One of the impressions that remains most vivid from my travels abroad is of an exhibit of the weights that had been attached to children in order to make their labor more arduous and painful as a punishment for slacking off in their production. This was in a former mill near Manchester that had been turned into a museum.
8. For a provoking treatment of the shift from a society based on unequal status to one based on equal "individuals" legitimized by the concept of the "contract," and the impact of that shift on women, see Carole Pateman, *The Sexual Contract* (Stanford: Stanford University Press, 1988). Nancy Fraser's work on dependency, need, and recognition is similarly laden with important implications for human rights. See her essays in *Unruly Practices* (New York: Routledge, 1989) and *Justice Interruptus* (New York: Routledge, 1997).
9. Alexis de Tocqueville, *Democracy in America*, trans. Henry Reeve, Vol. I., Ch. XVIII (New York: Colonial Press, 1900), 361–87.

10. For details on this, see the 2001–2002 "Torn from the Land" Associated Press series at http://wire.ap.org/Appackages/torn/.

11. See Pateman, *Sexual Contract,* 78–82. "Solidarity" and "all people" would have carried a more universalistic mutual recognition of rights than "fraternity" and "all men." But that was neither the theory nor the practice of the eighteenth-century male-dominated movement toward human rights, as Mary Wollestonecraft pointed out at the time in her *A Vindication of the Rights of Woman.*

12. G. W. F. Hegel, *Phenomenology of the Mind,* trans. J. B. Baillie (London: Allen and Unwin, 1966), 228–40.

13. Lewis B. Hinchman, "The Origins of Human Rights: A Hegelian Perspective," *The Western Political Quarterly* XXXVII, March 1984, 21–2.

14. Ibid., 25.

15. Axel Honneth, *The Struggle for Recognition: the Moral Grammar of Social Conflicts,* trans. Joel Anderson (Cambridge, MA: MIT Press, 1996), 118.

16. Ibid., 120, taken from Joel Feinberg, *Rights, Justice, and the Bounds of Liberty* (Princeton, NJ: Princeton University Press, 1980), 151.

17. Ibid.

18. See the discussion of Donnelly in the previous chapter and his *Universal Human Rights in Theory and Practice* (Ithaca, NY: Cornell University Press, 1989), Chapter 8.

19. Ibid., 149–50.

20. It is driven as much by the fear that the value of solidarity is always in a zero-sum relationship with the value of freedom. An interesting perspective on this is provided by Philippe van Parijs, who makes an argument that freedom and solidarity are not at all antithetical and that libertarians must accommodate what he calls a "solidaristic patriotism." See van Parijs's *Real Freedom for All* (Oxford: Clarendon Press, 1995).

21. I say "almost," because we could think of the refusal to respect due process of law or the use of torture to extract a confession in specific instances as the violation of the rights of only the specific person or of the entire membership of the body politic, which has an interest in and a right to a rights-respecting judicial and police system. But I will not press this argument here.

22. Martha Nussbaum, *Women and Human Development: The Capabilities Approach* (Cambridge: Cambridge University Press, 2000), 13.

23. Amartya Sen, *Development as Freedom* (New York: Alfred Knopf, 2000), 63–5.

24. Henry J. Steiner and Philip Alston, *International Human Rights in Context* (Oxford: Clarendon Press, 1996), 261.

25. The Labour prime minister Tony Blair announced that the British government was ending its opting out of the Social Chapter in June of 1997. But it was not until May 1, 1999 that it was formally extended to include the United Kingdom. I am grateful to Member of European Parliament

Glyn Ford and to Penny Richardson, staffperson in his European Office, for clarifying this for me.

26. Berlin, *Four Essays*. We saw in the last chapter that Henry Shue calls into question the analytical viability of even separating negative from positive liberty. For Hayek's views, see especially *The Mirage of Social Justice*, volume II of *Law, Legislation, and Liberty* (Chicago: University of Chicago Press, 1976). For Friedman's views, see Milton Friedman and Rose Friedman, *Free to Choose* (New York: Harcourt, Brace, Jovanovich, 1980).

27. Steiner and Alston, 268.

28. Arundhati Roy reports that the India Country Study contends that as many as fifty-six million rural and village people could have been displaced by the building of dams so that corporations such as Enron can try to reap their profits. Arundhati Roy, *Power Politics* (Cambridge, MA: South End Press), 54–67.

29. Jordan K. Ngubane, *Conflict of Minds* (New York: Books in Focus, 1979), 98–100.

CHAPTER 4   THE HOLDERS AND VIOLATORS OF
HUMAN RIGHTS

1. Jack Donnelly, *Universal Human Rights in Theory and Practice* (Ithaca, NY: Cornell University Press, 1989), 144–5.

2. See Asmarom Legesse, "Human Rights in African Political Culture," in Kenneth W. Thompson, ed., *The Moral Imperatives of Human Rights: A World Survey* (Washington, DC: University Press of America, 1980), 123–38; and Issa G. Shivji, *The Concept of Human Rights in Africa* (London: Codesria Book Series, 1989).

3. *New York Times*, November 19, 1995, 17. I say *usually* overturned because there is an increasing tendency on the part of courts in the United States to refuse to hear appeals based on new evidence once a conviction has been made. This is especially true where it is least acceptable, in capital cases.

4. I want to be clear that I am not using it here in the same universalistic or ontological sense that Jean-Paul Sartre does in *Being and Nothingness*. There, the "look" permeates human relationships, regardless of structural contexts. Here, it is perceived by people within the structure of socially constructed racial differentiation. For greater elaboration on Sartre's use of the concept, see Jean-Paul Sartre, *Being and Nothingness*, trans. Hazel Barnes (New York: Philosophical Library, 1956), 414–15. For a specific illustration of how it enters into race relations, see A. Belden Fields and Walter Feinberg, *Education and Democratic Theory: Finding a Place for Community Participation in Public School Reform* (Albany: State University of New York Press, 2001), 85–6.

5. Karl Marx, *The German Ideology*, in Robert C. Tucker, ed., *The Marx-Engels Reader*, 2nd edition (New York: W.W. Norton, 1978), 151 and 156–9.

6. Christine de Pizan, *The Book of the City of Women*, trans. Earl Jeffrey Richard (New York: Persea Books, 1982).

7. Olympe de Gouges, "The Declaration of the Rights of Woman," in Harriet Branson Applewhite et al., eds., *Women in Revolutionary Paris: Selected Documents With Notes and Commentary* (Urbana: University of Illinois Press, 1979), 87–95.

8. Indeed, a prominent scholar at my university who was to become a dean argued that the institution ought not to be concerned with the near absence of women in engineering because women were not naturally suited for such a profession. This was a few years after Aristotle, in the 1970s.

9. Quoted in Dee Brown, *Bury My Heart At Wounded Knee: An Indian History of the American West* (New York: Bantam Books, 1971), 116.

10. Mireille Rosello makes the point that the sit-in by sub-Saharan African immigrants without papers (*les sans-papiers*) in the Eglise St. Bernard in 1996, an action that gained them considerable public support, has changed the French stereotype of immigrants from Arab to more differentiated and from unsympathetic to more sympathetic. Mireille Rosello, "Visual Narratives and Illegal Immigration in France: (Trans)national Encodings of Exclusion," presentation in the colloquium series of the Unit for Criticism and Interpretive Theory at the University of Illinois, Urbana, April 28, 1997.

11. After having finished the first draft of this section, I was talking with a Vietnamese woman in Paris's Orly airport. We had arrived from Chicago on the same plane and both of us had carts with suitcases on them. Since I had helped her with her baggage at the carousel, and I exited that section of the airport with her, and continued to talk with her for about forty-five minutes, a reasonable assumption would have been that we were traveling together. All of a sudden French customs agents swooped down on us. They obliged her to take her bags and follow them into a customs room, but just left me standing alone with mine. Race was no accident here, any more than it is on Parisian sidewalks where I see so many Arabs stopped very close to me but I am never stopped myself. I am white, and being white is often one's best laissez-passer.

12. Sheldon Wolin, "Democracy, Difference, and Re-Cognition," *Political Theory*, XXI, 3, August 1993, 480.

13. William F. Felice, *Taking Suffering Seriously: The Importance of Collective Human Rights* (Albany: State University of New York Press, 1996), 122.

14. See Will Kymlicka, *Liberalism, Community, and Culture* (Oxford: Clarendon Press, 1989), and *Multicultural Citizenship* (Oxford: Clarendon Press, 1995).

15. Michael Sandel, *Liberalism and the Limits of Justice* (Cambridge: Cambridge University Press, 1982).

16. Some of the very best work on the issue of group versus individual rights is being done by Canadians. Aside from that of Kymlicka and Taylor, Michael McDonald's essay, "Should Communities Have Rights: Reflections on Liberal Individualism" in Abdullah Ahmed An-Na'im's edited volume

Human Rights in Cross-Cultural Perspective (Philadelphia: University of Pennsylvania Press, 1992), 133–61, is an excellent work by a Canadian communitarian theorist who is more comfortable with the concept of rights than is Taylor.

17. Kymlicka, *Multicultural Citizenship*, 84.
18. Charles Taylor, "The Politics of Recognition," in Amy Gutmann, ed., *Multiculturalism* (Princeton, NJ: Princeton University Press, 1994), 61.
19. Ibid., 68.
20. Ibid., 72–3.
21. Felice, *Taking Suffering Seriously*, 46.
22. Ibid., 48.
23. Ernest Gellner, *Nations and Nationalism* (Oxford: Basil Blackwell, 1983), 44–5.
24. Allen Buchanan, *Secession* (Boulder, CO: Westview Press, 1996), 152.
25. David Copp, "Democracy, Secession, and International Law: Comments on Buchanan," paper presented at a conference on The Ethics of Nationalism at the University of Illinois at Urbana-Champaign, April 22–4, 1994, 2. See also his broader essay "Democracy and Communal Self-Determination," in Robert McKim and Jeff McMahan, eds., *The Morality of Nationalism* (New York: Oxford University Press, 1997), 277–300.
26. Donnelly, *Universal Human Rights*, 145.
27. Iris Young, *Justice and the Politics of Difference* (Princeton, NJ: Princeton University Press, 1990), 174.
28. Donnelly, *Universal Human Rights*, 146.
29. Adolf Hitler, *Mein Kampf*, trans. Ralph Manheim (Boston: Houghton Mifflin, 1971), 402.
30. See Friedrich Nietzsche, *On the Genealogy of Morals*, trans. Walter Kaufmann (New York: Vintage, 1967), especially the Second Essay. Note especially his discussion of how German civilization could not have achieved the disciplined stage it had attained without the infliction of cruelty and suffering. Cruelty and suffering are a part of struggle, Nietzsche tells us, and he goes on: "A legal order thought of as sovereign and universal, and not as a means in the struggle between power-complexes but as a means of *preventing* all struggle in general—perhaps after the communistic cliché of Duhring, that every will must consider every other will its equal—would be a principle *hostile to life*, an agent of the dissolution and destruction of man, a sign of weariness, a secret path to nothingness" (76). So much for the presumption of human rights.
31. John Stuart Mill, *On Liberty*, Chapter III, in *Utilitarianism, Liberty, and Representative Government* (New York: E.P. Dutton, 1951), 152.
32. Henry Shue, "Contesting State Sovereignty: the Dawn of Principle," paper presented at a conference on The Ethics of Nationalism at the University of Illinois in Urbana-Champaign, April 22–4, 1994.
33. This is not the only case in which compulsion of young women in traditional societies poses human rights issues. In Papua, New Guinea, money,

animals, and a young woman constitute the price of making amends when a member of one clan kills a leader of another clan. One such woman-to-be-exchanged, Miriam Wilngal, refused to be turned over because she wanted to go to high school and become a typist. She was defended by a relative, Dr. John Muke, a Cambridge-trained professor of archeology at the University of Papua New Guinea, who stated his own feelings about his tribal tradition thus: " 'I analyze it and I practice it. I challenge it but only part of it. There are certain changes that we have not choice but to accept, like women's rights and notions of equality. But there are certain things that we have to hold onto.' " Seth Mydans, "When the Bartered Bride Opts out of the Bargain," *New York Times,* May 6, 1997, A4.

CHAPTER 5   TOWARD A POLITICAL ECONOMY OF
HUMAN RIGHTS

1. As of October 5, 2001, 145 states had signed and ratified the 1966 International Covenant on Economic, Social and Cultural Rights. Signing but not ratifying were the United States, Belize, Lao People's Democratic Republic, Liberia, Sao Tome and Principe, South Africa, and Turkmenistan. Data from United Nations, *Treaty Series,* Vol. 993, p. 3.

2. While the ILO was created by the Versailles Peace Treaty in 1919, it is now the oldest specialized agency of the United Nations. See Elizabeth McKeon, *Worker Rights in the Global Economy* (New York: The United Nations Association of the United States and The Business Council for the United Nations, 1999), 20–4.

3. Reported on CNN News, July 1, 1997. In March 2002, the World Health Organization (WHO) and the United Nations Children Fund reported that almost eleven million children die each year from preventable causes—malnutrition and disease that result from their impoverished conditions. *New York Times,* March 14, 2002, A13. For more data on hunger, malnutrition, and other human development indicators, see the yearly *Human Development Report* put out by the United Nations and published through Oxford University Press.

4. John Rawls, *A Theory of Justice* (Cambridge, MA: Harvard University Press, 1971).

5. *New York Times,* April 21, 1992, A1. The data for 1989 is the latest as of this writing on the disparity in wealth holding for families by five wealth-holding segments. But there are statistical indications that the disparity has gotten even worse since 1989. First, "the percentage of wealth held by the top 1.0 percent and the top 0.5 percent of the population [individuals here rather than families] did not change significantly [from 1989–1995]." Barry Johnson, "Personal Wealth, 1995," *SOI Bulletin* Federal Reserve Bank, Winter 1999/2000, 70. While the richest 5 percent of U.S. families earned 14.8 percent of total U.S. income in

1974, they earned 20.7 percent by 1998. Edward N. Wolff, "The Rich Get Richer," *Champaign-Urbana News-Gazette,* February 18, 2001, B1. This came out of the hide of the lower quintiles, which at the very bottom have negative wealth (higher debts than assets). In only two other countries are long-term time-series data available on household wealth inequality, the United Kingdom and Sweden. In the United Kingdom, there has been a downward trend in the wealth held by the top 1 percent since 1970, with a leveling off in 1980 that continued, with a slight upward and a slight downward blip, until 1989. The top 1 percent of British wealth holders own about 18 percent of the wealth. In Sweden, there has been a similar downward trend until about 1978 and then a slight upward trend to where the top 1 percent own slightly more than 20 percent of the total wealth. The U.S. top 1 percent owned a fraction over 20 percent of the wealth in 1979, but jumped to 39 percent in 1989. Edward N. Wolff, *Top Heavy: A Study of the Increasing Inequality of Wealth in America* (New York: The Twentieth Century Fund Press, 1995), 21–3.

6. *New York Times,* May 8, 1992, A1.

7. The U.S. Bureau of Labor Statistics put the percentage of working poor at 5.5 percent in 1990 and 5.1 percent in 1999 (BLS, Bulletin 2418 and Report 947). The actual percentage is much higher, some analysis putting it between 18 and 20 percent, because the formula used, which dates from the 1960s, assumes that a family need allocate no more than 30 percent of its earnings for housing. But in 1997, at least 5.4 million working families at the low end of the wage scale were paying over 50 percent of their income for housing or living in substandard (e.g., vehicles, homeless shelters, or run-down motels or hotels) conditions. AP, "Working Poor Paying Big Price for Housing," *Champaign-Urbana* (Illinois) *News-Gazette,* March 28, 2000, A4.

8. Michael Harrington, *The Other America* (New York: Macmillan, 1962).

9. McKeon, *Worker Rights,* 3.

10. *New York Times* March 18, 2002, A3.

11. "The moderns, then, after they have abolished slavery, have three prejudices to contend against, which are less easy to attack and far less easy to conquer than the mere fact of servitude: the prejudice of the master, the prejudice of the race, and the prejudice of color. Those who hope that the Europeans will ever be amalgamated with the Negroes appear to me to delude themselves.... slavery recedes, but the prejudice to which it has given birth is immovable. Whoever has inhabited the United States must have perceived that in those parts of the Union in which the Negroes are no longer slaves they have in no wise drawn nearer to the whites. On the contrary, the prejudice of race appears to be stronger in the states that have abolished slavery than in those where it still exists; and nowhere is it so intolerant as in those states where servitude has never been known. Thus it is in the United States that the prejudice which repels the Negroes seems to increase in proportion as they are emancipated, and equality is sanctioned by the manners while it is effaced from the laws of the country." Alexis de Tocqueville, *Democracy in America,* Vol. 1, trans. Henry Reeve

(New York: Vintage Classics, 1990), 358–60. Even the arch conservative theorist of political economy, Frederick von Hayek, no friend of economic or social human rights and an opponent of the very concept of "social justice," admits the gravity and the unfairness of the situation of African Americans in the United States, when he reflects on where to go to avoid the bombing of London in 1940. He reflected that while his established social position would benefit him more in Europe with its strong social distinctions, his children who had not attained social position would have more possibilities open to them in the United States: "I felt that the very absence in the USA of the sharp social distinctions which would favor me in the Old World should make me decide for them in favor of the former. (I should perhaps add that this was based on the tacit assumption that my children would there be placed with a white and not with a coloured family.)" Friedrich von Hayek, *The Mirage of Social Justice*, Vol 2. of *Law, Legislation, and Liberty* (Chicago: University of Chicago Press, 1976), 189.

12. Adetoun O. Ilumoka, "African Women's Economic, Social, And Cultural Rights-Toward a Relevant Theory and Practice," in Rebecca Cook, ed., *Human Rights of Women* (Philadelphia: University of Pennsylvania Press, 1994), 311.

13. McKeon, *Worker Rights*, and the numerous publications of the National Labor Committee in Support of Worker and Human Rights (http://www.nlcnet.org).

14. For an excellent article on Enron's international reach and damage, see John Nichols, "Enron's Global Crusade," *The Nation,* March 4 2002, 11–14.

15. Raymond Williams, *Towards 2000* (London: Verso, 1983), 262, quoted in Sam Gindin, "Socialism 'With Sober Senses': Developing Workers' Capacities," in Leo Panitch and Colin Leys, eds., *Socialist Register 1998,* 80. Another aspect of this totalitarianism is the inability of most people to even be able to think about an alternative way of ordering things. On this "There Is No Alternative," or TINA, see Daniel Singer's *Whose Millennium? Theirs or Ours?* (New York: Monthly Review Press, 1999).

16. Gianfranco Poggi, *The State: Its Nature, Development, and Prospects* (Stanford: Stanford University Press, 1990), 179.

17. I stress "within" because Philippe van Parijs argues for a system of "real freedom" based on these three values. The key element of his recommendation is a "highest unconditional [that is, people are not required to work to get it] income for all consistent with security and self-ownership." However, "self ownership" is not understood as ownership over the means of production and conditions under which one works, or at least not necessarily so. His proposal thus remains at the redistributive level. The major freedom is that of exit from work altogether, rather than the freedom of workers to collectively determine the conditions of their labor. See his *Real Freedom for All: What (if Anything) Can Justify Capitalism?* (Oxford: Clarendon Press, 1995), 33.

18. On these cooperatives, see Edward S. Greenberg, *Workplace Democracy: The Political Effects of Participation* (Ithaca, NY: Cornell University Press, 1986).

19. See Keith Bradley and Alan Gelb, *Cooperation at Work: The Mondragon Experience* (London: Heinemann, 1985); and William Foote Whyte, *Making Mondragon: the Growth and Dynamics of the Worker Cooperative Complex* (Ithaca, NY: Institute of Labor Relations Press, 1988).

20. That antipathy was carried into Germany by Eduard Bernstein who was heavily influenced by the Fabians. See his *Evolutionary Socialism*, trans. Edith C. Harvey (New York: Schocken, 1961), 109–35.

21. Peter Jay, "The Workers' Co-operative Economy," in Alasdair Clayre, ed., *The Political Economy of Co-operation and Participation* (Oxford: Oxford University Press, 1980), 40.

22. Robert A. Dahl, *A Preface to Economic Democracy* (Berkeley: University of California Press, 1985).

23. John Rawls, *A Theory of Justice* (Oxford: Oxford University Press, 1972).

24. Van Parijs, *Real Freedom.*

25. Peter Jay's discussion presupposes that all enterprises of over one hundred people be, by law, cooperative. Jay, "The Workers' Co-operative Economy," 9.

26. See also the same argument in Charles Lindblom, "Democracy and the Economy," in his *Democracy and the Market System* (Oslo: Norwegian University Press, 1988), 115–35.

27. See Charles A. Lindblom, *Politics and Markets* (New York: Basic Books, 1977). The concentration of wealth and its political power is even greater now than it was when Lindblom wrote his book about this up-to-then unmentionable subject among establishment political scientists.

28. A number of non-U.S. and multinational studies have shown an empirical positive relationship between participation at the workplace and participation outside. However, Greenberg's study of the plywood worker/owners in the U.S. northwest did not show this. Greenberg ascribes this to the larger U.S. culture (for example, versus the Israeli culture). It also is the case that these cooperatives, like a number of others, did not come into being out of design but, rather, out of the failure of individually or corporately owned enterprises, with the workers being given the option of losing their jobs or trying to make a go of it themselves. See Greenberg, *Workplace Democracy,* 118–20 and Ch. 8.

Chapter 6   The Modern State and Human Rights

1. One of the most interesting and incisive discussions of the treatment accorded to the Native Americans is Ward Churchill's "Bringing the Law Home: Application of the Genocide Convention in the United States," in his *Indians Are Us: Culture and Genocide in Native North America* (Monroe, ME: Common Courage Press, 1994), 11–46. Despite the title, Churchill does discuss the treatment of Indians in the Caribbean as well as in the United States, viii–ix.

2. *Europa World Yearbook* (Old Woking, U.K.: The Gresham Press, 1999), viii–ix.

3. See, for example, Kirkpatrick Sale, *Human Scale* (New York: Coward, McCann, and Geoghegan, 1980); and Robert A. Dahl and Edward R. Tufte, *Size and Democracy* (Stanford: Stanford University Press, 1973).

4. An interesting example of this is the book of the British writer Paul Hirst, *Associative Democracy* (London: Polity Press, 1994).

5. Two research historians at the United States Holocaust Museum in Washington are attempting to determine exactly what happened to each of the passengers. See the *New York Times,* March 31, 1999, A21.

6. A particularly good book on this from a human rights perspective is Douglas Porpora's *How Holocausts Happen: The United States in Central America* (Philadelphia: Temple University Press, 1990).

7. For an attempt to understand the dehumanization and cruelties of the twentieth century philosophically, see Jonathan Glover, *Humanity: A Moral History of the Twentieth Century* (New Haven, CT: Yale University Press, 1999).

8. Jean-Paul Sartre, *Anti-Semite and Jew* (New York: Grove Press, 1960).

9. This is particularly true in the case of asserted national security. Examples are the banning of the publication of former intelligence officer Peter Wright's book, *Spycatcher,* which had already been published in Australia, the threat to prosecute newspapers that printed portions of it, and the false criminal charges, imprisonments, and police executions associated with the attempt to control the Irish Republican Army. This kind of governmental behavior helped stimulate a movement for a written bill of rights in the 1980s.

10. Thomas Jefferson, "Notes on Virginia" in Philip A. Foner, ed., *Basic Writings of Thomas Jefferson* (Garden City, NY: Halcyon House, 1950), 51–181.

11. Frederick Douglass, *My Bondage and My Freedom* (Urbana: University of Illinois Press, 1987), 101.

12. Ibid., 99.

13. Quoted in Dee Brown, *Bury My Heart at Wounded Knee: An Indian History of the American West* (New York: Bantam Books, 1971), 236.

14. Pierre Clastres, *Society against the State: The Leader as Servant and the Humane Uses of Power among the Indians of the Americas,* trans. Robert Hurley (New York: Urizen Books, 1977), 130–1.

15. Jack Weatherford, *How the Indians of the Americas Transformed the World* (New York: Fawcett Columbine, 1988), 124.

16. Ibid., 125.

17. V. I. Lenin, *Collected Works,* Vol. 6, *January 1902–August 1903* (Moscow: Foreign Languages Publishing House, 1961), 29–30.

18. Constitution of the USSR, December 5, 1936, as amended to 1965, Chapter X, "Fundamental Rights and Duties of Citizens," in Amos J. Penslee, *Constitutions of Nations,* Vol. III *Europe* (The Hague: Martinus Nijoff, 1968), 1005.

19. Constitution of the Union of Soviet Socialist Republics, adopted on October 7, 1977 and amended on December 1, 1988, in Vadim Meish, *The Soviet Union,* 4th edition (Englewood Cliffs, NJ: Prentice-Hall, 1990), 368.

20. Ibid.

21. Max Weber, *Economy and Society,* Vol. I (Berkeley: University of California Press, 1978), 56.

22. Josephine Butler, "The Police Question" and "Chartist Meetings and Police," reprinted in Berenice A. Carroll and Hilda L. Smith, eds., *Women's Political and Social Thought: An Anthology* (Bloomington: Indiana University Press, 2001), 222.

23. I should say that this was not the kind of view of the police that I had when I was growing up in Chicago. The police in our district were notoriously corrupt. When we went on vacation, the last people we wanted to know that were the police officers, who had organized a robbery ring operating out of the station. There also was a rather constant shaking-down of motorists by police officers fabricating offenses, especially against younger motorists. Many Chicagoans drove around with a $5 bill stuck in their billfolds right next to their drivers' licenses. Guilty or innocent, there was much less pain in giving up the $5 than in being hassled by the police officer or in going to court. One way of avoiding or lessening traffic stops was to contribute to the Patrolmen's Benevolent Association that got you a sticker to put on your car. My father did that. His reward was that he could always park illegally. In fact, given a choice between a legal and an illegal spot, it seemed to me that he showed a distinct preference for the latter. After all, he and his business associates paid for it.

24. Harold Lasswell, *Politics: Who Gets What, When, and How* (New York: Peter Smith, 1950).

25. See Alan Wolfe, *The Seamy Side of Democracy* (New York: McKay, 1973). For rigorous historical presentation of this aspect of the U.S. state, see Robert Justin Goldstein, *Political Repression in Modern America* (Cambridge MA: Schenkman, 1977; reprint, Urbana: University of Illinois Press, 2000).

26. Michel Foucualt, *Discipline and Punish: The Birth of the Prison,* trans. Alan Sheridan (New York: Vintage, 1979), 3.

27. Ibid., 298.

28. Ibid., 308.

29. Marx rejected the concept of rights as it was understood in a capitalist society, but he attempted to offer an emancipatory vision that would do the work that he thought rights could not do within the parameters of capitalism. Foucault offers no emancipatory vision at all and seemed intent on demonstrating to those who engaged in anything other than spontaneous eruption that they were doomed to replicate the carceral power relationships. Under these conditions, what good is a concept of rights?

30. For my criticism of some of this thinking when it is centered around the concept of "social movements," see my "In Defense of Political Economic and Systemic Thought," in Larry Grossberg and Carey Nelson, eds., *Marxism and the Interpretation of Culture* (Urbana: University of Illinois Press, 1988), 141–56.

31. Joy James, *Resisting State Violence* (Minneapolis: University of Minnesota Press, 1996), 24–5.

Chapter 7   Perpetual War and Human Rights in the United States

1. Amnesty International, *United States of America: Rights for All* (New York, 1998), 51 (hereafter cited as AI, *Rights for All*).
2. Ibid., 23; *New York Times* November 19, 1995, 17.
3. Deborah Sontag and Dan Barry, "Using Settlements to Gauge Police Abuse," *New York Times,* September 17, 1997, A1, 10. See also Sarah Terry, "Experts Try to Pin Down Extent of Police Misconduct," *New York Times,* November 19, 1995, A19.
4. Dan Barry and Deborah Sontag, "New York Dismisses Police, but Few for Brutality," *New York Times,* October 6, 1997, A15.
5. Paul Chevigny, *Edge of the Knife: Police Violence in the Americas* (New York: The New Press, 1995), 101.
6. Amnesty International, *USA: Police Brutality in Los Angeles, California, United States of America* (London, 1992), 47 (hereafter cited as AI, Police Brutality).
7. Ibid., 61. The most sweeping study of racial bias in law enforcement, jury selection, trial conduct, and punishment is Randall Kennedy's *Race, Crime, and the Law* (New York: Pantheon Books, 1997).
8. Chevigny, *Edge of the Knife*, 48, 51, 102, 110.
9. Amnesty International writes: "One of the main barriers to both disciplinary and criminal action is the 'code of silence.' There are often no independent witnesses, and officers frequently fail to report misconduct, or file false or incomplete reports to cover up abuses" (*Rights for All*, 43). Those officers who do the right thing by breaking the code of conduct can lose their jobs and closest friends and live in fear of physical retaliation. See Alan Feuer's "Outcasts at the Blue Wall: Virtue is Cold Comfort for Police Who Inform on Peers," *New York Times,* December 30, 1998, B1. Also see Chevigny, *Edge of the Knife,* 51, 80, and 92 on the "code of silence."
10. AI, *Rights for All,* 22; *New York Times,* February 27, 1998, A1, 19. After this event, New York City Mayor Giuliani set up a task force to review police-community relations. In March 1998, he rejected most of its recommendations, contending that the task force had failed to take into account the police's role in combating crime. The federal government entered the case charging the officers with beating prior to arrest, then false arrest, followed by torture in the station, all constituting federal civil rights violations. The state courts then dropped the charges. In December 1999, the officer who did the actual torturing was convicted and sentenced by the federal judge to thirty years in prison with the possibility of parole.
11. Chevigny, *Edge of the Knife,* 80 and 139. For a report on a Harvard conference devoted largely to police lying and perjury, see the *New York Times,* November 19, 1995, A19.

12. AI, *Rights for All*, 43.

13. *New York Times*, September 21, 2000, A14.

14. Ibid.

15. *New York Times*, November 19, 1995, A17.

16. "Police Pay Out for Assaults on Black People," *Searchlight*, October 1997, 9.

17. A major reason that the case received so much attention was that it was presented as a play, "The Color of Justice" by Richard Norton-Taylor, on the London stage. It received kudos from the drama critics. *New York Times*, February 22, 1999, A3.

18. Quoted in the *Champaign-Urbana (Illinois) News-Gazette*, February 21, 1999, B8. Also see the *New York Times*, February 22, 1999, 3.

19. Reported on BBC News, July 3, 1997.

20 On racial profiling and traffic stops, see the *New York Times*, April 9, 1999, A21, and April 14, 1999, A24.

21. Louis Kushnick, *Race, Class and Struggle: Essays on Racism and Inequality in Britain, the U.S. and Western Europe* (London: Rivers Oram Press, 1998), 117.

22. In a city just next to the one in which I live, Champaign, Illinois, a SWAT team member grabbed an eighty-one-year-old African American grandmother by the throat and threw her to the ground, causing her both physical and psychological harm. A few weeks before that, the police conducted a practice raid into an apartment in an abandoned housing project in the almost exclusively African American part of town. The police invited the local T.V. stations to film and show the episode as black uniformed and jack-booted SWAT team members stormed the apartment.

23. *New York Times*, March 1, 1999, A1, 16.

24. In 1999, only 43.4 percent of New York's population were white, but 67.4 percent of its police officers were white, making it one of the three most racially distorted forces among large cities in the U.S. Ninety-four percent of the 449 captains were white. *New York Times*, March 8, 1999, A14.

25. Data from The Death Penalty Information Center, *The Federal Death Penalty System: A Statistial Survey (1988–2000)*, p. 3 (http://www. deathpenaltyinfo.org/fedrpt.html).

26. *New York Times*, September-12, 2000, 18.

27. Death Penalty Information Center, *Race of Defendents Executed Since 1976*, 2002, p. 1. The four states with the highest number of executions are Texas, Virginia, Florida, and Missouri, in that order. *New York Times*, January 29, 1999, A10.

28. AI, *Rights for All*, 109.

29. Quoted in ibid., 111.

30. Death Penalty Information Center, *Race*, p. 1.

31. Jeffrey H. Reiman, *The Rich Get Richer and the Poor Get Prison: Ideology, Class, and Criminal Justice*, 2nd edition (New York: John Wiley and Sons, 1984), 92.

32. Stephen Gettinger, *Sentenced to Die: The People, the Crimes, and the Controversy* (New York: Macmillan, 1979), 261, quoted in ibid., 93.

33. Stephen B. Bright, "Counsel for the Poor: The Death Sentence Not for the Worst Crime but for the Worst Lawyer," in Hugo Bedau, ed., *The Death Penalty in America: Current Controversies* (New York: Oxford University Press, 1997, 275–318.

34. *New York Times,* December 20, 2000, A17.

35. *New York Times,* January 5, 1999, A14.

36. AI, *Rights for All,* 100.

37. Ibid., 114.

38. Data offered by Paul Hoffman, chairman of Amnesty International, to the Associated Press. Reported in the Champaign-Urbana (Illinois) *News-Gazette,* December 19, 2000, 7.

39. Reinman, *The Rich Get Richer,* 90.

40. Ibid., 99–100.

41. Joan Petersilia, *Racial Disparities in the Criminal Justice System* (Santa Monica, CA: Rand, 1983), vii.

42. Ibid., 74–5.

43. David L. Evans, "Lost Behind Prison Bars," *Newsweek,* September 7, 1998, 20.

44. Reported on CNN News, January 30, 1997.

45. Randall Kennedy, *Race, Crime, and Law* (New York: Pantheon Books, 1997), 169.

46. Ibid., 195.

47. Rehnquist's logic was that any person from any group was subject to racially discriminatory strikes and thus, whites, too, were burdened by the same laws. Ibid., 207–8.

48. In March 1999, a Puerto Rican nationalist friend of the writer's was convicted in federal court by a jury from which all Latinos and Latinas in the pool were eliminated by the prosecutor's peremptory challenges.

49. Kennedy, *Race, Crime, and Law,* 208–9.

50. Vivien Stern, *A Sin Against the Future: Imprisonment in the World* (Boston: Northeastern University, 1998), 11.

51. Human Rights Watch, *Prison Conditions in the United States* (New York, 1991), 71 (cited hereafter as HRW, *Prison Conditions*).

52. Stern, *A Sin Against the Future,* 39.

53. Cited in HRW, *Prison Conditions,* 75–6.

54. Louis Kushnick, senior lecturer in American Studies at the University of Manchester and vice chair of the Institute of Race Relations in London, England, in a conversation with the author. In December 1999, Dr. Stuart Grassian, a Harvard psychiatrist who specializes in the effects of solidarity confinement on prisoners, filed a report that a prisoner held by the federal government in solidarity confinement and repeatedly stripped searched and surveilled, had degenerated psychologically so

badly that he might not even be fit enough to participate in his own defense. *New York Times,* December 15, 1999, 25.

55. For a treatment of the state's repression of the American Indian Movement, as well as of the Black Panther Party, see Ward Churchill and Jim Vander Wall, *Agents of Repression: the FBI's Secret Wars Against the Black Panther Party and the American Indian Movement* (Boston: South End Press, 1990).

56. For specific names of other political prisoners held at Marion, see HRW, *Prison Conditions,* 77.

57. Rick Bragg, "Prison Chief Encouraged Brutality, Witnesses Report," *New York Times,* July 1, 1997, A12.

58. Ibid.

59. Ibid.

60. AI, *Police Brutality,* 55–72; HRW, *Prison Conditions,* 52–3.

61. Mark Hamm et al., *The Myth of Humane Imprisonment: A Critical Analysis of Severe Discipline in Maximum Security Prisons, 1945–90,* Prison Discipline Study (Sacramento, CA, 1991) cited in HRW, *Prison Conditions,* 52. An earlier text, edited by Robert J. Minton Jr., *Inside: Prison American Style* (New York: Random House, 1971), details brutal prison conditions and their psychological and psychical effects, including two dozen suicides at California's Soledad Prison (133–6). In 1966, a U.S. District Court judge found that prisoners in the "hole" at Soledad were deprived of lighting, ventilation, even temperature, containment and disposal of human waste, water and soap, toothbrushes and toothpaste, and clothing (131–2).

62. National Public Radio interviews with both prisoners and prison authorities, March 4, 1999.

63. Peter T. Kilborn, "Stun Belts Offer Prisons Chainless Chain Gangs," *New York Times,* March 11, 1997, 11.

64. Ibid.

65. Bill Bergstrom, "Crime Does Not Pay, but in Florida, Criminals Do," Associated Press article in Champaign-Urbana (Illinois) *News-Gazette,* August 25, 1996, B1.

66. Quoted in the *New York Times,* February 1, 1999, A23.

67. Ibid.

68. Quoted in the *New York Times,* February 18, 1999, A25.

69. In the *New York Times* of September 20, 1996, on page A10 there appears a picture of two women chained together with a third woman of whom only the legs are showing. The two women whose faces are visible are African American and Latina. The sheriff who assembled what according to the *Times* is the first female chain gang, is quoted as saying: "I don't believe in discrimination in my jail system." Note the expression "my" system, which is indicative of the almost total control these people have over inmates.

70. Deborah Sontag and Dan Barry, "Using Settlements to Gauge Police Abuse," *New York Times,* September 17, 1997, A1, 19.

71. Barry R. McCaffrey, "Cocaine: Will Congress Act?" *Crisis* (magazine of the National Association for the Advancement of Colored People

[NAACP]), September 1998, 18. The Clinton administration recommended, unsuccessfully, that the differential be reduced but not eliminated. The administration defended some differential on the basis that it is potentially more addictive than powder.

72. Ibid.

73. Stern, *A Sin Against the Future,* 31–2.

74. Ibid., 61.

75. Ibid., 62.

76. Alfred W. McCoy, *The Politics of Heroin: CIA Complicity in the Global Drug Trade* (Brooklyn, NY: Lawrence Hill Books, 1991), 131–60. This book contains an important bibliography of scholarly material, reports of a number of concerned governments, and reports of international agencies.

77. Ibid., 162–78.

78. On the human rights violations of the Contras, see Amnesty International, *Nicaragua: The Human Rights Record,* 1986, 32–6; Americas Watch, *Compliance with the Human Rights Provisions of the Central American Peace Plan August 1987–August 1988,* 8; Dieter Eich and Carlos Rincon, *Contras* (Hamburg: Konkret Literatur Verlag, 1984); Reed Brody, *Contra Terror in Nicaragua: Report of a Fact-Finding Mission September 1984 –January 1985* (Boston: South End Press, 1985); Christopher Dickey, *With the Contras* (New York: Simon and Schuster, 1985); and the testimonial to Contra atrocities and terrorism by former Contra leader Edgar Chamorro in his letter to the *New York Times,* January 9, 1986. For a view of the U.S. government's human rights record in the larger Central American region, see my "Menschenrechtsverletzungen in Zentralamerika und die Rolle der USA" ("The U.S. Role in Human Rights Violations in Central America"), in Komitee für Grundrechte und Demokratie, *Jahrbuch '88/89* (Berlin, 1990), copies available in English from the author.

79. Important scholarly sources are McCoy, *The Politics of Heroin;* Peter Dale Scott and Jonathan Marshall, *Cocaine Politics: Drugs, Armies, and the CIA* (Berkeley and Los Angeles: University of California Press, 1991); and Peter Dale Scott, "Honduras, the Contra Support Networks, and Cocaine: How the U.S. Government Has Augmented America's Drug Crisis," in Alfred W. McCoy and Alan A. Block, eds., *War on Drugs: Studies in the Failure of U.S. Narcotics Policy* (Boulder, CO: Westview Press, 1992).

An early and more journalistic account is available in Leslie Cockburn, *Out of Control: The Story of the Reagan Administration's Secret War in Nicaragua, the Illegal Arms Pipeline, and the Contra Drug Connection* (New York: Atlantic Monthly Press, 1987). Later journalistic accounts include Alexander Cockburn and Jeffrey St. Clair, *Whiteout: The CIA, Drugs, and the Press* (London: Verso, 1998); and Gary Webb, *Dark Alliance: The CIA, the Contras, and the Crack Cocaine Explosion* (New York: Seven Stories Press, 1998).

A crucial document of the U.S. Senate is the report of the Senate Committee on Foreign Relations, Subcommittee on Narcotics,

Terrorism, and International Operations, December 1988 (100th Congress, 2nd session), *Drugs, Law Enforcement, and Foreign Policy.* This is usually referred to as the Kerry Committee Report, or the Kerry Hearings, after the subcommittee chair Senator John Kerry. The contentions made in the 1987 Coburn book about the relationship between drugs and the Contra war efforts were substantially confirmed by the December 1988 Senate subcommittee report. The scholarly work confirms but goes beyond the findings of the subcommittee report.

The first version of McCoy's book, which only dealt with Asia and was published in 1972, received four reviews, according to the 1972 edition of the *Book Review Digest.* Three were very strongly positive. One was overall negative, contending that the "allegations could rarely be proved in a court of law" (a test that few social scientists would wish to be judged by), but concluded, "Yet ... a reader may very well feel that there is something to the author's story. Even of only a few accusations are true, that could make the worst of the Harding Administration's scandals look rather quaint." Thus, three of the four reviewers had very high praise for McCoy's work, and the fourth, while critical, thought that if only some of the material were true there was a very grave problem. The following year the book was reviewed in the journal *Commonweal* and in the more formally academic journal *Pacific Affairs,* in which the reviewer, while critical of some aspects of the book, wrote that "it makes a positive contribution to the fields of Southeast Asian scholarship. The book is an absolute necessity for any serious mainland Southeast Asian scholar" (Vol. 46, No. 2, 344). An even more interesting comment was made by the *New York Times* writer specializing on drugs in the pages of the *New York Times Book Review:* "As a former CIA agent told Seymour Hirsh ... , McCoy's assertions are '10 percent tendentious and 90 percent of the most valuable contribution I can think of.... some leading intelligence officers inside the Government's program think his research is great.'" The *Times* writer adds, "Well they might. For McCoy has done his homework... he gives us a rich set of footnotes" (September 3, 1972, A1).

Despite the above CIA agent's admiration for McCoy's work, the CIA itself tried to prevent its publication and demanded that the publisher, Harper and Row, turn the manuscript over to them for inspection before it was published. Over McCoy's objections, because the book had already undergone the normal academic review process, Harper and Row complied. The CIA then attacked the accuracy of the manuscript. Their objections were rejected by the publisher and the book was printed as it was submitted to the CIA. The exchange of correspondence between the CIA, McCoy, and Harper and Row is can be found in the *New York Review of Books,* September 21, 1972, 26–35. There is little reason to believe that McCoy's work suddenly degenerated when he added the section on the relationship between the Contra war effort and the cocaine trade in the 1991 edition. And the Scott and Marshall book, published by the University of California Press, certainly went through an academic review process.

In addition to the quality of the research done by others on this topic, I bring to the reading and evaluation of this body of scholarship and documentation well over ten years of reading, writing, and active involvement over U.S. policy in Central America. I would prefer that a lot that I learned during the 1980s and early 1990s had not been true. What was done in Central America itself was bad enough. The domestic effects of such actions in the name of "national security" compound the horror. But one cannot wish away the actions of one's government when carefully researched evidence tells one otherwise.

80. Report of the U.S. Senate Subcommittee on Terrorism, Narcotics, and International Operations (often referred to as the Kerry Committee), page 36, note 26.

81. Eva Bertram et al., *Drug War Politics: The Price of Denial* (Berkeley: University of California Press, 1996), 112.

82. Asamblea Legislativa, *Segundo Informe de la Comision sobre el Narcotrafico* (San Jose, CA: Editorial Universidad Estatal a Distancia, 1989).

83. *New York Times*, October 21, 1996, A1, 10.

84. *New York Times*, February 24, 1999, A12. It appears that they did not ask the sample what they knew about other systems.

85. Chevigny, *Edge of the Knife*, 64.

86. *New York Times*, April 15, 1999, A1. For a more extensive treatment of such prisons, see Eric Schlosser, "The Prison-Industrial Complex," *The Atlantic Monthly*, Vol. 202, No. 6, December 1998, 51–77.

87. Local communities also have developed quite an interest in the production of criminality. In my own state of Illinois, between 1978 and 1997, sixteen "correctional" facilities were built in different cities and towns that competed desperately for the jobs they would bring. $576 million was spent to house 16,125 more inmates. More than $231 million was allocated as of July 1979 to fund still more construction. The Associated Press, "Illinois Prisons Opened Since 19789," *Champaign-Urbana News-Gazette*, July 20, 1997, B7. This is in a state that is near the bottom, forty-eighth out of fifty, in its per-pupil funding for education.

APPENDIX A

1. Staley's own promotional material; Lisa Mirable, ed., *The International Directory of Company Histories*, Vol. II (Chicago: St. James Press, 1990), 580.

2. Strohl's remarks were printed in *Deadly Corn: Workers Speak Out on Health, Safety, and Environmental Problems at the A. E. Staley Manufacturing Company*, issued by AIW Local 837. Copies can be obtained by writing to them at 2882 North Dineen St., Decatur, IL 62526.

3. Ibid.

4. It is ironic that in 1878, Henry Tate, prior to his company's merger with the Lyle operation, opened up his second refinery on the Thames in

London and worked his 250 employees twelve hours per day. At that time the work week was sixty hours. But it is interesting that the *International Directory of Company Histories* found it unusual enough to publish that Mr. Tate would work his employees so long each day. The same mentality would come back to Decatur, this time imposed by his successor transnational, well over a century later.

5. Interview of July 10, 1997.

6. Stephen Franklin, *Three Strikes* (New York: The Guilford Press, 2001), 181.

APPENDIX B

1. After the unconstitutional, rights-violating behavior of the FBI under the COINTEL program was made public, restraining safeguards were placed on the agency. President George W. Bush has taken those off in his "war" on terrorism. But even when the restraints were supposedly in place, the FBI was violating civil and human rights. On June 11, 2002, a federal jury in Oakland, California found that FBI agents, in collusion with the Oakland police, had framed two environmental activists in the late nineteen eighties and early nineteen nineties. The framed plaintiffs, Judi Bari and Darryl Cherney (the latter deceased by the time of the legal vindication) were awarded $4.4 million in damages for violation of their First and Fourth Amendment rights.

INDEX